2004 Supplement

to

FEDERAL CRIMINAL LAW AND ITS ENFORCEMENT

Third Edition

By

Norman Abrams

Interim Dean and Professor of Law
University of California, Los Angeles

Sara Sun Beale

Charles L.B. Lowndes Professor
Duke University School of Law

AMERICAN CASEBOOK SERIES®

Mat #40229077

American Casebook Series and West Group are trademarks
registered in the U.S. Patent and Trademark Office.

© 2004 West, a Thomson business
   610 Opperman Drive
   P.O. Box 64526
   St. Paul, MN 55164–0526
   1–800–328–9352

Printed in the United States of America

ISBN 0–314–15196–6

*TEXT IS PRINTED ON 10% POST
CONSUMER RECYCLED PAPER*

Table of Contents

CHAPTER 2

FEDERAL, STATE AND LOCAL
CRIMINAL ENFORCEMENT RESOURCES

Page 13. **Federal criminal caseload.**

The Sentencing Commission's Annual Report shows the breakdown of cases for the most recent year for which data is available, and also provides a graphic comparison of the changes in major categories of cases. The chart that follows depicts cases filed in fiscal 2001 (October 30, 2000 to September 30, 2001). When the Commission publishes subsequent statistics, they will be available on the Commission's internet site, http://www.ussc.gov.

Compare the new graphs to those in the main text on pages 14 and 15. Has there been much change? Note that it takes some time for change in government policies to manifest themselves in these figures. There is a lag between changes in investigative priorities and the filing of criminal cases, and a further lag in publication of statistics. For a discussion of some of the changes in enforcement priorities that are not yet reflected in these statistics, see Chapter 4, *infra*.

1

Figure A

DISTRIBUTION OF OFFENDERS IN EACH PRIMARY OFFENSE CATEGORY[1]
Fiscal Year 2001

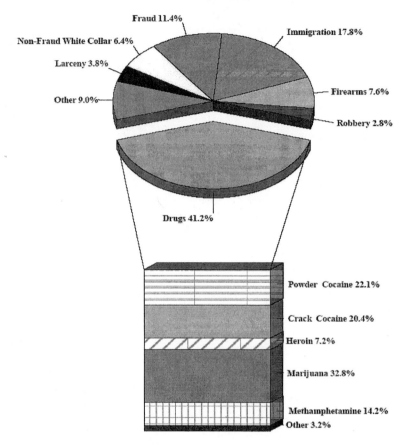

[1]Of the 59,897 guideline cases, 206 were excluded due to missing primary offense category. An additional 867 cases were excluded due to missing drug type. The Drug category includes the following offense types: Trafficking, Use of a Communication Facility, and Simple Possession. The Non-Fraud White Collar category includes the following offense types: Embezzlement, Forgery/Counterfeiting, Bribery, Money Laundering, and Tax. Descriptions of variables used in this figure are provided in Appendix A.

SOURCE: U.S. Sentencing Commission, 2001 Datafile, USSCFY01.

11

2

Figure B

NUMBER OF GUIDELINE OFFENDERS IN SELECTED OFFENSE TYPES[1]
Fiscal Year 1997 - Fiscal Year 2001

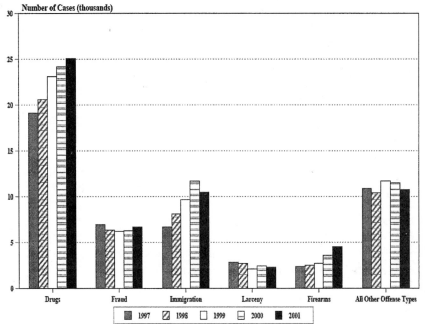

Number of Cases (thousands)

[1]Drug offenses in this bar chart include: trafficking, use of a communication facility, and simple possession. Descriptions of variables used in this figure are provided in Appendix A.

SOURCE: U.S. Sentencing Commission, 1997-2001 Datafiles, USSCFY97-USSCFY01.

CHAPTER 3

THE SCOPE OF
THE FEDERAL CRIMINAL LAWS

Page 53.   **Insert before the Notes.**

The Supreme Court returned to the issues in the *Lopez* opinion in the case that follows.

UNITED STATES v. MORRISON, 529 U.S. 598 (2000)

[Petitioner filed suit under the civil provisions of the Violence Against Women Act (VAWA), 42 U.S.C. § 13981, alleging that she was raped by the defendants while all were students at Virginia Polytechnic Institute. The Supreme Court upheld the dismissal of the complaint on the ground that Congress lacked the authority under the Commerce Clause (or § 5 of the Fourteenth Amendment) to enact the legislation. Writing for the majority, Chief Justice Rehnquist described the Court's analysis in *Lopez* and then turned to the case at hand.]

* * *

With these principles underlying our Commerce Clause jurisprudence as reference points, the proper resolution of the present cases is clear. Gender-motivated crimes of violence are not, in any sense of the phrase, economic activity. While we need not adopt a categorical rule against aggregating the effects of any noneconomic activity in order to decide these cases, thus far in our Nation's history our cases have upheld Commerce Clause regulation of intrastate activity only where that activity is economic in nature.

Like the Gun-Free School Zones Act at issue in *Lopez*, § 13981 contains no jurisdictional element establishing that the federal cause of action is in pursuance of Congress' power to regulate interstate commerce. Although *Lopez* makes clear that such a jurisdictional element would lend support to the argument that § 13981 is sufficiently tied to interstate commerce, Congress elected to cast § 13981's remedy over a wider, and more purely intrastate, body of violent crime.[5]

----

[5]Title 42 U.S.C. § 13981 is not the sole provision of the Violence Against Women Act of 1994 to provide a federal remedy for gender-motivated crime. Section 40221(a) of the Act creates a federal criminal remedy to punish "interstate crimes of abuse including crimes committed against spouses or intimate partners during interstate travel and crimes committed by spouses or intimate partners who cross State lines to continue the abuse." That criminal provision has been codified at 18 U.S.C. § 2261(a)(1), which states:

"A person who travels across a State line or enters or leaves Indian country

In contrast with the lack of congressional findings that we faced in *Lopez*, § 13981 is supported by numerous findings regarding the serious impact that gender-motivated violence has on victims and their families. But the existence of congressional findings is not sufficient, by itself, to sustain the constitutionality of Commerce Clause legislation. As we stated in *Lopez*, " '[S]imply because Congress may conclude that a particular activity substantially affects interstate commerce does not necessarily make it so.' " Rather, " '[w]hether particular operations affect interstate commerce sufficiently to come under the constitutional power of Congress to regulate them is ultimately a judicial rather than a legislative question, and can be settled finally only by this Court.' "

In these cases, Congress' findings are substantially weakened by the fact that they rely so heavily on a method of reasoning that we have already rejected as unworkable if we are to maintain the Constitution's enumeration of powers. Congress found that gender-motivated violence affects interstate commerce

> "by deterring potential victims from traveling interstate, from engaging in employment in interstate business, and from transacting with business, and in places involved in interstate commerce; ... by diminishing national productivity, increasing medical and other costs, and decreasing the supply of and the demand for interstate products."

Given these findings and petitioners' arguments, the concern that we expressed in *Lopez* that Congress might use the Commerce Clause to completely obliterate the Constitution's distinction between national and local authority seems well founded. The reasoning that petitioners advance seeks to follow the but-for causal chain from the initial occurrence of violent crime (the suppression of which has always been the prime object of the States' police power) to every attenuated effect upon interstate commerce. If accepted, petitioners' reasoning would allow Congress to regulate any crime as long as the nationwide, aggregated impact of that crime has substantial effects on employment, production, transit, or consumption. Indeed, if Congress may regulate gender-motivated violence, it would be able to regulate murder or any other type of violence since gender-motivated violence, as a subset of all violent crime, is certain to have lesser economic impacts than the larger class of which it is a part.

> with the intent to injure, harass, or intimidate that person's spouse or intimate partner, and who, in the course of or as a result of such travel, intentionally commits a crime of violence and thereby causes bodily injury to such spouse or intimate partner, shall be punished as provided in subsection (b)."

The Courts of Appeals have uniformly upheld this criminal sanction as an appropriate exercise of Congress' Commerce Clause authority, reasoning that "[t]he provision properly falls within the first of *Lopez*'s categories as it regulates the use of channels of interstate commerce-- i.e., the use of the interstate transportation routes through which persons and goods move."

Petitioners' reasoning, moreover, will not limit Congress to regulating violence but may, as we suggested in *Lopez*, be applied equally as well to family law and other areas of traditional state regulation since the aggregate effect of marriage, divorce, and childrearing on the national economy is undoubtedly significant. Congress may have recognized this specter when it expressly precluded § 13981 from being used in the family law context. Under our written Constitution, however, the limitation of congressional authority is not solely a matter of legislative grace.[7]

---

[7]Justice Souter's dissent theory that *Gibbons v. Ogden*, 9 Wheat. 1 (1824), *Garcia v. San Antonio Metropolitan Transit Authority*, 469 U.S. 528, (1985), and the Seventeenth Amendment provide the answer to these cases, is remarkable because it undermines this central principle of our constitutional system. As we have repeatedly noted, the Framers crafted the federal system of government so that the people's rights would be secured by the division of power. Departing from their parliamentary past, the Framers adopted a written Constitution that further divided authority at the federal level so that the Constitution's provisions would not be defined solely by the political branches nor the scope of legislative power limited only by public opinion and the legislature's self-restraint.

No doubt the political branches have a role in interpreting and applying the Constitution, but ever since *Marbury* this Court has remained the ultimate expositor of the constitutional text. * * *

Contrary to Justice Souter's suggestion, *Gibbons* did not exempt the commerce power from this cardinal rule of constitutional law. His assertion that, from *Gibbons* on, public opinion has been the only restraint on the congressional exercise of the commerce power is true only insofar as it contends that political accountability is and has been the only limit on Congress' exercise of the commerce power within that power's outer bounds. As the language surrounding that relied upon by Justice Souter makes clear, *Gibbons* did not remove from this Court the authority to define that boundary. *See Gibbons, supra*, at 194-195 ("It is not intended to say that these words comprehend that commerce, which is completely internal, which is carried on between man and man in a State, or between different parts of the same State, and which does not extend to or affect other States.... Comprehensive as the word 'among' is, it may very properly be restricted to that commerce which concerns more States than one. The phrase is not one which would probably have been selected to indicate the completely interior traffic of a State, because it is not an apt phrase for that purpose; and the enumeration of the particular classes of commerce to which the power was to be extended, would not have been made, had the intention been to extend the power to every description. The enumeration presupposes something not enumerated; and that something, if we regard the language or the subject of the sentence, must be the exclusively internal commerce of a State").

Justice SOUTER, with whom Justice STEVENS, Justice GINSBURG, and Justice BREYER join, dissenting.

* * *

One obvious difference from United States v. Lopez, 514 U.S. 549 (1995), is the mountain of data assembled by Congress, here showing the effects of violence against women on interstate commerce. Passage of the Act in 1994 was preceded by four years of hearings, which included testimony from physicians and law professors; from survivors of rape and domestic violence; and from representatives of state law enforcement and private business. The record includes reports on gender bias from task forces in 21 States, and we have the benefit of specific factual findings in the eight separate Reports issued by Congress and its committees over the long course leading to enactment.

With respect to domestic violence, Congress received evidence for the following findings:

"Three out of four American women will be victims of violent crimes sometime during their life."

"Violence is the leading cause of injuries to women ages 15 to 44...."

"[A]s many as 50 percent of homeless women and children are fleeing domestic violence."

"Since 1974, the assault rate against women has outstripped the rate for men by at least twice for some age groups and far more for others."

"[B]attering 'is the single largest cause of injury to women in the United States.' "

"An estimated 4 million American women are battered each year by their husbands or partners."

"Over 1 million women in the United States seek medical assistance each year for injuries sustained [from] their husbands or other partners."

"Between 2,000 and 4,000 women die every year from [domestic] abuse."

"[A]rrest rates may be as low as 1 for every 100 domestic assaults."

"Partial estimates show that violent crime against women costs this country at least 3 billion--not million, but billion--dollars a year."

"[E]stimates suggest that we spend $5 to $10 billion a year on health care, criminal justice, and other social costs of domestic violence."

7

Based on the data thus partially summarized, Congress found that

"crimes of violence motivated by gender have a substantial adverse effect on interstate commerce, by deterring potential victims from traveling interstate, from engaging in employment in interstate business, and from transacting with business, and in places involved, in interstate commerce ... [,] by diminishing national productivity, increasing medical and other costs, and decreasing the supply of and the demand for interstate products...."

Congress thereby explicitly stated the predicate for the exercise of its Commerce Clause power. Is its conclusion irrational in view of the data amassed? True, the methodology of particular studies may be challenged, and some of the figures arrived at may be disputed. But the sufficiency of the evidence before Congress to provide a rational basis for the finding cannot seriously be questioned.

Indeed, the legislative record here is far more voluminous than the record compiled by Congress and found sufficient in two prior cases upholding Title II of the Civil Rights Act of 1964 against Commerce Clause challenges. In *Heart of Atlanta Motel, Inc. v. United States*, 379 U.S. 241 (1964), and *Katzenbach v. McClung*, 379 U.S. 294 (1964), the Court referred to evidence showing the consequences of racial discrimination by motels and restaurants on interstate commerce. Congress had relied on compelling anecdotal reports that individual instances of segregation cost thousands to millions of dollars. Congress also had evidence that the average black family spent substantially less than the average white family in the same income range on public accommodations, and that discrimination accounted for much of the difference.

While Congress did not, to my knowledge, calculate aggregate dollar values for the nationwide effects of racial discrimination in 1964, in 1994 it did rely on evidence of the harms caused by domestic violence and sexual assault, citing annual costs of $3 billion in 1990, and $5 to $10 billion in 1993. Equally important, though, gender-based violence in the 1990's was shown to operate in a manner similar to racial discrimination in the 1960's in reducing the mobility of employees and their production and consumption of goods shipped in interstate commerce. Like racial discrimination, "[g]ender-based violence bars its most likely targets--women--from full partic[ipation] in the national economy."

If the analogy to the Civil Rights Act of 1964 is not plain enough, one can always look back a bit further. In *Wickard*, we upheld the application of the Agricultural Adjustment Act to the planting and consumption of homegrown wheat. The effect on interstate commerce in that case followed from the possibility that wheat grown at home for personal consumption could either be drawn into the market by rising prices, or relieve its grower of any need to purchase wheat in the market. The Commerce Clause predicate was simply the effect of the production of wheat for home consumption on supply and demand in interstate commerce. Supply and demand for goods in interstate commerce will also be affected by the deaths of 2,000 to 4,000 women annually at the hands of domestic abusers, and by the reduction in the work force by the 100,000 or more rape victims who lose their jobs each year or are forced to quit. Violence against women may be found to affect interstate commerce and affect it substantially.

II

The Act would have passed muster at any time between *Wickard* in 1942 and *Lopez* in 1995, a period in which the law enjoyed a stable understanding that congressional power under the Commerce Clause, complemented by the authority of the Necessary and Proper Clause, Art. I. § 8 cl. 18, extended to all activity that, when aggregated, has a substantial effect on interstate commerce. * * *

The fact that the Act does not pass muster before the Court today is therefore proof, to a degree that *Lopez* was not, that the Court's nominal adherence to the substantial effects test is merely that. Although a new jurisprudence has not emerged with any distinctness, it is clear that some congressional conclusions about obviously substantial, cumulative effects on commerce are being assigned lesser values than the once-stable doctrine would assign them. These devaluations are accomplished not by any express repudiation of the substantial effects test or its application through the aggregation of individual conduct, but by supplanting rational basis scrutiny with a new criterion of review.

Thus the elusive heart of the majority's analysis in these cases is its statement that Congress's findings of fact are "weakened" by the presence of a disfavored "method of reasoning." This seems to suggest that the "substantial effects" analysis is not a factual enquiry, for Congress in the first instance with subsequent judicial review looking only to the rationality of the congressional conclusion, but one of a rather different sort, dependent upon a uniquely judicial competence.

This new characterization of substantial effects has no support in our cases (the self-fulfilling prophecies of *Lopez* aside), least of all those the majority cites. Perhaps this explains why the majority is not content to rest on its cited precedent but claims a textual justification for moving toward its new system of congressional deference subject to selective discounts. Thus it purports to rely on the sensible and traditional understanding that the listing in the Constitution of some powers implies the exclusion of others unmentioned. *See Gibbons v. Ogden*, 9 Wheat. 1, 195, 6 L.Ed. 23 (1824); The Federalist No. 45, p. 313 (J. Cooke ed. 1961) (J. Madison). The majority stresses that Art. I, § 8, enumerates the powers of Congress, including the commerce power, an enumeration implying the exclusion of powers not enumerated. It follows, for the majority, not only that there must be some limits to "commerce," but that some particular subjects arguably within the commerce power can be identified in advance as excluded, on the basis of characteristics other than their commercial effects. Such exclusions come into sight when the activity regulated is not itself commercial or when the States have traditionally addressed

9

it in the exercise of the general police power, conferred under the state constitutions but never extended to Congress under the Constitution of the Nation.

The premise that the enumeration of powers implies that other powers are withheld is sound; the conclusion that some particular categories of subject matter are therefore presumptively beyond the reach of the commerce power is, however, a non sequitur. From the fact that Art. I, § 8, cl. 3 grants an authority limited to regulating commerce, it follows only that Congress may claim no authority under that section to address any subject that does not affect commerce. It does not at all follow that an activity affecting commerce nonetheless falls outside the commerce power, depending on the specific character of the activity, or the authority of a State to regulate it along with Congress. My disagreement with the majority is not, however, confined to logic, for history has shown that categorical exclusions have proven as unworkable in practice as they are unsupportable in theory.

A

Obviously, it would not be inconsistent with the text of the Commerce Clause itself to declare "noncommercial" primary activity beyond or presumptively beyond the scope of the commerce power. That variant of categorical approach is not, however, the sole textually permissible way of defining the scope of the Commerce Clause, and any such neat limitation would at least be suspect in the light of the final sentence of Article I, § 8, authorizing Congress to make "all Laws ... necessary and proper" to give effect to its enumerated powers such as commerce. Accordingly, for significant periods of our history, the Court has defined the commerce power as plenary, unsusceptible to categorical exclusions, and this was the view expressed throughout the latter part of the 20th century in the substantial effects test. These two conceptions of the commerce power, plenary and categorically limited, are in fact old rivals, and today's revival of their competition summons up familiar history, a brief reprise of which may be helpful in posing what I take to be the key question going to the legitimacy of the majority's decision to breathe new life into the approach of categorical limitation.

Chief Justice Marshall's seminal opinion in *Gibbons v. Ogden*, construed the commerce power from the start with "a breadth never yet exceeded," *Wickard v. Filburn*, 317 U.S., at 120. In particular, it is worth noting, the Court in *Wickard* did not regard its holding as exceeding the scope of Chief Justice Marshall's view of interstate commerce; *Wickard* applied an aggregate effects test to ostensibly domestic, noncommercial farming consistently with Chief Justice Marshall's indication that the commerce power may be understood by its exclusion of subjects, among others, "which do not affect other States," *Gibbons*, 9 Wheat., at 195. This plenary view of the power has either prevailed or been acknowledged by this Court at every stage of our jurisprudence. And it was this understanding, free of categorical qualifications, that prevailed in the period after 1937 through *Lopez*, as summed up by Justice Harlan: " 'Of course, the mere fact that Congress has said when particular activity shall be deemed to affect commerce does not preclude further examination by this Court. But where we find that the legislators ... have a

10

rational basis for finding a chosen regulatory scheme necessary to the protection of commerce, our investigation is at an end.' "

Justice Harlan spoke with the benefit of hindsight, for he had seen the result of rejecting the plenary view * * *. In the half century following the modern activation of the commerce power with passage of the Interstate Commerce Act in 1887, this Court from time to time created categorical enclaves beyond congressional reach by declaring such activities as "mining," "production," "manufacturing," and union membership to be outside the definition of "commerce" and by limiting application of the effects test to "direct" rather than "indirect" commercial consequences.

Since adherence to these formalistically contrived confines of commerce power in large measure provoked the judicial crisis of 1937, one might reasonably have doubted that Members of this Court would ever again toy with a return to the days before *NLRB v. Jones & Laughlin Steel Corp.*, 301 U.S. 1 (1937), which brought the earlier and nearly disastrous experiment to an end. And yet today's decision can only be seen as a step toward recapturing the prior mistakes. Its revival of a distinction between commercial and noncommercial conduct is at odds with *Wickard*, which repudiated that analysis, and the enquiry into commercial purpose, first intimated by the *Lopez* concurrence, is cousin to the intent-based analysis employed in *Hammer*, but rejected for Commerce Clause purposes in *Heart of Atlanta*, and *Darby*.

Why is the majority tempted to reject the lesson so painfully learned in 1937? An answer emerges from contrasting *Wickard* with one of the predecessor cases it superseded. It was obvious in *Wickard* that growing wheat for consumption right on the farm was not "commerce" in the common vocabulary,[13] but that did not matter constitutionally so long as the aggregated activity of domestic wheat growing affected commerce substantially. Just a few years before *Wickard*, however, it had certainly been no less obvious that "mining" practices could substantially affect commerce, even though *Carter Coal Co.*, had held mining regulation beyond the national commerce power. When we try to fathom the difference between the two cases, it is clear that they did not go in different directions because the *Carter Coal* Court could not understand a causal connection that the *Wickard* Court could grasp;

---

[13] Contrary to the Court's suggestion, *Wickard* applied the substantial effects test to domestic agricultural production for domestic consumption, an activity that cannot fairly be described as commercial, despite its commercial consequences in affecting or being affected by the demand for agricultural products in the commercial market. The *Wickard* Court admitted that Filburn's activity "may not be regarded as commerce" but insisted that "it may still, whatever its nature, be reached by Congress if it exerts a substantial economic effect on interstate commerce...." The characterization of home wheat production as "commerce" or not is, however, ultimately beside the point. For if substantial effects on commerce are proper subjects of concern under the Commerce Clause, what difference should it make whether the causes of those effects are themselves commercial? * * *

the difference, rather, turned on the fact that the Court in *Carter Coal* had a reason for trying to maintain its categorical, formalistic distinction, while that reason had been abandoned by the time *Wickard* was decided. The reason was laissez-faire economics, the point of which was to keep government interference to a minimum. The Court in *Carter Coal* was still trying to create a laissez-faire world out of the 20th-century economy, and formalistic commercial distinctions were thought to be useful instruments in achieving that object. The Court in *Wickard* knew it could not do any such thing and in the aftermath of the New Deal had long since stopped attempting the impossible. Without the animating economic theory, there was no point in contriving formalisms in a war with Chief Justice Marshall's conception of the commerce power.

If we now ask why the formalistic economic/noneconomic distinction might matter today, after its rejection in *Wickard*, the answer is not that the majority fails to see causal connections in an integrated economic world. The answer is that in the minds of the majority there is a new animating theory that makes categorical formalism seem useful again. Just as the old formalism had value in the service of an economic conception, the new one is useful in serving a conception of federalism. It is the instrument by which assertions of national power are to be limited in favor of preserving a supposedly discernible, proper sphere of state autonomy to legislate or refrain from legislating as the individual States see fit. The legitimacy of the Court's current emphasis on the noncommercial nature of regulated activity, then, does not turn on any logic serving the text of the Commerce Clause or on the realism of the majority's view of the national economy. The essential issue is rather the strength of the majority's claim to have a constitutional warrant for its current conception of a federal relationship enforceable by this Court through limits on otherwise plenary commerce power. This conception is the subject of the majority's second categorical discount applied today to the facts bearing on the substantial effects test.

B

The Court finds it relevant that the statute addresses conduct traditionally subject to state prohibition under domestic criminal law, a fact said to have some heightened significance when the violent conduct in question is not itself aimed directly at interstate commerce or its instrumentalities. Again, history seems to be recycling, for the theory of traditional state concern as grounding a limiting principle has been rejected previously, and more than once. * * * The effort to carve out inviolable state spheres within the spectrum of activities substantially affecting commerce was, of course, just as irreconcilable with *Gibbons*'s explanation of the national commerce power as being as "absolut[e] as it would be in a single government."

The objection to reviving traditional state spheres of action as a consideration in commerce analysis, however, not only rests on the portent of incoherence, but is compounded by a further defect just as fundamental. The defect, in essence, is the majority's rejection of the Founders' considered judgment that politics, not judicial review, should mediate between state and national interests as the strength and legislative jurisdiction of the National Government inevitably increased through the expected growth of the national economy. Whereas today's majority takes a leaf from the book of the old judicial economists in saying that the Court should somehow draw the line to keep the federal relationship in a proper balance, Madison, Wilson, and Marshall understood the Constitution very differently.

Although Madison had emphasized the conception of a National Government of discrete powers (a conception that a number of the ratifying conventions thought was too indeterminate to protect civil liberties), Madison himself must have sensed the potential scope of some of the powers granted (such as the authority to regulate commerce), for he took care in The Federalist No. 46 to hedge his argument for limited power by explaining the importance of national politics in protecting the States' interests. The National Government "will partake sufficiently of the spirit [of the States], to be disinclined to invade the rights of the individual States, or the prerogatives of their governments." James Wilson likewise noted that "it was a favorite object in the Convention" to secure the sovereignty of the States, and that it had been achieved through the structure of the Federal Government. The Framers of the Bill of Rights, in turn, may well have sensed that Madison and Wilson were right about politics as the determinant of the federal balance within the broad limits of a power like commerce, for they formulated the Tenth Amendment without any provision comparable to the specific guarantees proposed for individual liberties. In any case, this Court recognized the political component of federalism in the seminal *Gibbons* opinion. After declaring the plenary character of congressional power within the sphere of activity affecting commerce, the Chief Justice spoke for the Court in explaining that there was only one restraint on its valid exercise:

> "The wisdom and the discretion of Congress, their identity with the people, and the influence which their constituents possess at elections, are, in this, as in many other instances, as that, for example, of declaring war, the sole restraints on which they have relied, to secure them from its abuse. They are the restraints on which the people must often rely solely, in all representative governments."

Politics as the moderator of the congressional employment of the commerce power was the theme many years later in *Wickard*, for after the Court acknowledged the breadth of the *Gibbons* formulation it invoked Chief Justice Marshall yet again in adding that "[h]e made emphatic the embracing and penetrating nature of this power by warning that effective restraints on its exercise must proceed from political rather than judicial processes." *Wickard*, 317 U.S., at 120. Hence, "conflicts of economic interest ... are wisely left under our system to resolution by Congress under its more flexible and responsible legislative process. Such conflicts rarely lend themselves to judicial determination. And with the wisdom, workability, or fairness, of the plan of regulation we have nothing to do."

As with "conflicts of economic interest," so with supposed conflicts of sovereign political interests implicated by the Commerce Clause: the Constitution remits them to politics. The point can be put no more clearly than the Court put it the last time it repudiated the notion that some state activities categorically defied the commerce power as understood in accordance with generally accepted concepts. After confirming Madison's and Wilson's views with a recitation of the sources of state influence in the structure of the National Constitution, *Garcia*, 469 U.S., at 550-552, the Court disposed of the possibility of identifying "principled constitutional limitations on the scope of Congress' Commerce Clause powers over the States merely by relying on a priori definitions of state sovereignty." It concluded that

> "the Framers chose to rely on a federal system in which special restraints on federal power over the States inhered principally in the workings of the National Government itself, rather than in discrete limitations on the objects of federal authority. State sovereign interests, then, are more properly protected by procedural safeguards inherent in the structure of the federal system than by judicially created limitations on federal power."

The *Garcia* Court's rejection of "judicially created limitations" in favor of the intended reliance on national politics was all the more powerful owing to the Court's explicit recognition that in the centuries since the framing the relative powers of the two sovereign systems have markedly changed. Nationwide economic integration is the norm, the national political power has been augmented by its vast revenues, and the power of the States has been drawn down by the Seventeenth Amendment, eliminating selection of senators by state legislature in favor of direct election.

The *Garcia* majority recognized that economic growth and the burgeoning of federal revenue have not amended the Constitution, which contains no circuit breaker to preclude the political consequences of these developments. Nor is there any justification for attempts to nullify the natural political impact of the particular amendment that was adopted. The significance for state political power of ending state legislative selection of senators was no secret in 1913, and the amendment was approved despite public comment on that very issue.***

* * *

III

All of this convinces me that today's ebb of the commerce power rests on error, and at the same time leads me to doubt that the majority's view will prove to be enduring law. There is yet one more reason for doubt. Although we sense the presence of *Carter Coal*, *Schechter*, and *Usery* once again, the majority embraces them only at arm's-length. Where such decisions once stood for rules, today's opinion points to considerations by which substantial effects are discounted. Cases standing for the sufficiency of substantial effects are not overruled; cases overruled since 1937 are not quite revived. The Court's [approach is reminiscent of the]

14

unsteady state of obscenity law between *Redrup v. New York*, 386 U.S. 767 (1967) (per curiam), and *Miller v. California*, 413 U.S. 15 (1973), a period in which the failure to provide a workable definition left this Court to review each case ad hoc.

As our predecessors learned then, the practice of such ad hoc review cannot preserve the distinction between the judicial and the legislative, and this Court, in any event, lacks the institutional capacity to maintain such a regime for very long. This one will end when the majority realizes that the conception of the commerce power for which it entertains hopes would inevitably fail the test expressed in Justice Holmes's statement that "[t]he first call of a theory of law is that it should fit the facts." The facts that cannot be ignored today are the facts of integrated national commerce and a political relationship between States and Nation much affected by their respective treasuries and constitutional modifications adopted by the people. The federalism of some earlier time is no more adequate to account for those facts today than the theory of laissez-faire was able to govern the national economy 70 years ago.

Justice BREYER, with whom Justice STEVENS joins, and with whom Justice SOUTER and Justice GINSBURG join as to Part I-A, dissenting.

* * *

The majority holds that the federal commerce power does not extend to such "noneconomic" activities as "noneconomic, violent criminal conduct" that significantly affects interstate commerce only if we "aggregate" the interstate "effect[s]" of individual instances. Justice Souter explains why history, precedent, and legal logic militate against the majority's approach. I agree and join his opinion. I add that the majority's holding illustrates the difficulty of finding a workable judicial Commerce Clause touchstone--a set of comprehensible interpretive rules that courts might use to impose some meaningful limit, but not too great a limit, upon the scope of the legislative authority that the Commerce Clause delegates to Congress.

A

Consider the problems. The "economic/noneconomic" distinction is not easy to apply. Does the local street corner mugger engage in "economic" activity or "noneconomic" activity when he mugs for money? Would evidence that desire for economic domination underlies many brutal crimes against women save the present statute?

The line becomes yet harder to draw given the need for exceptions. The Court itself would permit Congress to aggregate, hence regulate, "noneconomic" activity taking place at economic establishments. And it would permit Congress to regulate where that regulation is "an essential part of a larger regulation of economic activity, in which the regulatory scheme could be undercut unless the intrastate activity were regulated." Given the former exception, can Congress simply rewrite the present law and limit its application to restaurants, hotels, perhaps universities, and other places of public accommodation? Given the latter exception, can

Congress save the present law by including it, or much of it, in a broader "Safe Transport" or "Workplace Safety" act?

More important, why should we give critical constitutional importance to the economic, or noneconomic, nature of an interstate-commerce-affecting cause? If chemical emanations through indirect environmental change cause identical, severe commercial harm outside a State, why should it matter whether local factories or home fireplaces release them? The Constitution itself refers only to Congress' power to "regulate Commerce ... among the several States," and to make laws "necessary and proper" to implement that power. Art. I, § 8, cls. 3, 18. The language says nothing about either the local nature, or the economic nature, of an interstate-commerce- affecting cause.

This Court has long held that only the interstate commercial effects, not the local nature of the cause, are constitutionally relevant. *See NLRB v. Jones & Laughlin Steel Corp.*, 301 U.S. 1, 38-39 (1937) (focusing upon interstate effects); *Wickard v. Filburn*, 317 U.S. 111, 125, (1942) (aggregating interstate effects of wheat grown for home consumption); *Heart of Atlanta Motel*, ("'[I]f it is interstate commerce that feels the pinch, it does not matter how local the operation which applies the squeeze' ")). Nothing in the Constitution's language, or that of earlier cases prior to *Lopez*, explains why the Court should ignore one highly relevant characteristic of an interstate-commerce-affecting cause (how "local" it is), while placing critical constitutional weight upon a different, less obviously relevant, feature (how "economic" it is).

Most important, the Court's complex rules seem unlikely to help secure the very object that they seek, namely, the protection of "areas of traditional state regulation" from federal intrusion. The Court's rules, even if broadly interpreted, are underinclusive. The local pickpocket is no less a traditional subject of state regulation than is the local gender-motivated assault. Regardless, the Court reaffirms, as it should, Congress' well-established and frequently exercised power to enact laws that satisfy a commerce-related jurisdictional prerequisite--for example, that some item relevant to the federally regulated activity has at some time crossed a state line.

And in a world where most everyday products or their component parts cross interstate boundaries, Congress will frequently find it possible to redraft a statute using language that ties the regulation to the interstate movement of some relevant object, thereby regulating local criminal activity or, for that matter, family affairs. *See, e.g.*, Child Support Recovery Act of 1992, 18 U.S.C. § 228. Although this possibility does not give the Federal Government the power to regulate everything, it means that any substantive limitation will apply randomly in terms of the interests the majority seeks to protect. How much would be gained, for example, were Congress to reenact the present law in the form of "An Act Forbidding Violence Against Women Perpetrated at Public Accommodations or by Those Who Have Moved in, or through the Use of Items that Have Moved in, Interstate Commerce"? Complex Commerce Clause rules creating fine distinctions that achieve only random results do little to further the important federalist interests that called them into being. That is why modern (pre-*Lopez*) case law rejected them.

The majority, aware of these difficulties, is nonetheless concerned with what it sees as an important contrary consideration. To determine the lawfulness of statutes simply by asking whether Congress could reasonably have found that aggregated local instances significantly affect interstate commerce will allow Congress to regulate almost anything. Virtually all local activity, when instances are aggregated, can have "substantial effects on employment, production, transit, or consumption." Hence Congress could "regulate any crime," and perhaps "marriage, divorce, and childrearing" as well, obliterating the "Constitution's distinction between national and local authority."

This consideration, however, while serious, does not reflect a jurisprudential defect, so much as it reflects a practical reality. We live in a Nation knit together by two centuries of scientific, technological, commercial, and environmental change. Those changes, taken together, mean that virtually every kind of activity, no matter how local, genuinely can affect commerce, or its conditions, outside the State--at least when considered in the aggregate. *Heart of Atlanta Motel*, 379 U.S., at 251. And that fact makes it close to impossible for courts to develop meaningful subject-matter categories that would exclude some kinds of local activities from ordinary Commerce Clause "aggregation" rules without, at the same time, depriving Congress of the power to regulate activities that have a genuine and important effect upon interstate commerce.

Since judges cannot change the world, the "defect" means that, within the bounds of the rational, Congress, not the courts, must remain primarily responsible for striking the appropriate state/federal balance. Congress is institutionally motivated to do so. Its Members represent state and local district interests. They consider the views of state and local officials when they legislate, and they have even developed formal procedures to ensure that such consideration takes place. Moreover, Congress often can better reflect state concerns for autonomy in the details of sophisticated statutory schemes than can the judiciary, which cannot easily gather the relevant facts and which must apply more general legal rules and categories. Not surprisingly, the bulk of American law is still state law, and overwhelmingly so.

B

I would also note that Congress, when it enacted the statute, followed procedures that help to protect the federalism values at stake. It provided adequate notice to the States of its intent to legislate in an "are[a] of traditional state regulation." And in response, attorneys general in the overwhelming majority of States (38) supported congressional legislation, telling Congress that "[o]ur experience as Attorneys General strengthens our belief that the problem of violence against women is a national one, requiring federal attention, federal leadership, and federal funds."

Moreover, as Justice Souter has pointed out, Congress compiled a "mountain of data" explicitly documenting the interstate commercial effects of gender- motivated crimes of violence. After considering alternatives, it focused the federal law upon documented deficiencies in state legal systems. And it tailored the law to prevent its use in certain areas of traditional state concern, such as divorce, alimony, or child custody. 42 U.S.C. § 13981(e)(4). Consequently, the law before us seems to represent an instance, not of state/federal conflict, but of state/federal efforts to cooperate in order to help solve a mutually acknowledged national problem.

I call attention to the legislative process leading up to enactment of this statute because, as the majority recognizes, it far surpasses that which led to the enactment of the statute we considered in *Lopez*. And even were I to accept *Lopez* as an accurate statement of the law, which I do not, that distinction provides a possible basis for upholding the law here. This Court on occasion has pointed to the importance of procedural limitations in keeping the power of Congress in check.

Commentators also have suggested that the thoroughness of legislative procedures--e.g., whether Congress took a "hard look"--might sometimes make a determinative difference in a Commerce Clause case, say when Congress legislates in an area of traditional state regulation. Of course, any judicial insistence that Congress follow particular procedures might itself intrude upon congressional prerogatives and embody difficult definitional problems. But the intrusion, problems, and consequences all would seem less serious than those embodied in the majority's approach.

I continue to agree with Justice SOUTER that the Court's traditional "rational basis" approach is sufficient. But I recognize that the law in this area is unstable and that time and experience may demonstrate both the unworkability of the majority's rules and the superiority of Congress' own procedural approach--in which case the law may evolve towards a rule that, in certain difficult Commerce Clause cases, takes account of the thoroughness with which Congress has considered the federalism issue.

For these reasons, as well as those set forth by Justice SOUTER, this statute falls well within Congress's Commerce Clause authority, and I dissent from the Court's contrary conclusion.

* * *

18

Page 56   **Insert in note d.**

The Supreme Court avoided the constitutional issue in the *Jones* case, discussed in note d. A unanimous Court held that the arson statute applies only to property that is actively "used" in interstate commerce, and hence the statute does not reach the arson of an owner-occupied private residence. *Jones v. United States*, 529 U.S. 848 (2000).

Page 60   **Consider in connection with note c.**

The Supreme Court did not reach the constitutional issue in *Jones*. *See* the discussion of note d, p. 56, *supra*.

CHAPTER 4

TECHNIQUES FOR LIMITING
FEDERAL CRIMINAL AUTHORITY

**Page 103.   ADMINISTRATIVE   TARGETING   OF   AREAS   OF
PROSECUTION AND CASES TO PROSECUTE**

The Department of Justice Strategic Plan for 2001-06 is available online at
http://www.usdoj.gov/jmd/mps/strategic2001-2006/index.htm . Chapter 2 lists the
Department's first goal as protecting America against the threat of terrorism by
prevention, investigation, and prosecution of those who commit or intend to commit
terrorist acts. The Department's second stated goal is enforcing federal criminal
laws, with the following objectives:

● reducing the threat, incidence and prevalence of violent crime, especially
as it stems from illegal use of guns or from organized criminal enterprises

● reducing the threat, trafficking, and related acts of violence of illegal
drugs by identifying, disrupting, and dismantling drug trafficking organizations

● combating espionage against the United States by strengthening
counterintelligence capabilities

● combating white collar crime, especially cybercrime

● combating crimes against children and other vulnerable victims of
violence and exploitation.

The plan also contains a discussion of the strategies to accomplish each of these
objectives.

In the wake of the terrorist attacks on September 11, 2001, the FBI's focus
has shifted from crime investigation to terrorism prevention. As a result of the
agency overhaul, as many as 674 agents were shifted from crime investigation to
counterterrorism, and overall over 2000 of the FBI's 8881 domestic agents are now
working on counterterrorism. Gary Fields and John R. Wilke, *The Ex Files: FBI's
New Focus Places Big Burden On Local Police*, THE WALL STREET JOURNAL, June
30, 2003 at A1. This has had a natural effect on the development of other kinds of
federal cases, particularly drug offenses. From 2000 to 2002 new drug cases fell
from 1825 per fiscal year to 944, and the indication is that new drug cases are
falling even further. Id. The FBI has also raised the threshold for bank robberies
and shifted out of investigating many violent and white-collar crimes. *Id.* In
Washington, D.C. where over 100 agents were shifted to counterterrorism, the

number of agents working on white-collar and violent crime was cut in half. *Id*
The FBI has also opened more foreign offices as part of its new mandate. It is difficult to measure the success of the shift toward counterterrorism operations, yet one clear result is that the FBI's law enforcement mission has declined. For instance, while there has been a spike in the FBI's referral of terror-related cases to prosecutors, the overall number of referrals to prosecutors has gone down. Chitra Ragavan, et al., *Special Report: Inside the FBI; Mueller's Mandate*, U.S. NEWS & WORLD REPORT, May 26, 2003. Further, even with the spike in referrals, terrorism only represents 3.7 % of overall caseload. *Id.* This change in referrals will naturally have an effect on the prosecution of federal crimes, though of course federal prosecutors receive referrals from many sources other than the FBI, including a wide array of federal agencies as well as state enforcement officials.

CHAPTER 5

MAIL FRAUD

Page 127. 18 U.S.C. §§ 1341 and 1343 were both amended by the Sarbanes-Oxley Act of 2002 to state that the basic penalty is 20 years imprisonment (rather than 5).

Page 147   **Insert at the end of note 1.**

A recent economic study provides some support for the argument that federal prosecutors systematically employ their charging discretion in a manner that enhances their own career prospects. *See* Edward L. Glaser, et al., *What Do Prosecutors Maximize? An Analysis of the Federalization of Drug Crimes*, 2 AM. L. & ECON. REV. 259 (2000). Studying federal and state inmates convicted of drug offenses, the authors found that the federal prisoners had higher education and income, were more often white, were more likely to be represented by retained counsel, and were less likely to have prior offenses than their state counterparts. The authors suggest that this pattern may indicate that federal prosecutors choose cases with wealthier more prestigious defendants represented by more prestigious counsel.

Page 149.   **Insert at the end of note 2.**

In *United States v. Handakas*, 286 F.3d 92 (2d Cir.), *cert. denied*, 537 U.S. 894 (2002), the court of appeals held that the honest services provision of the mail fraud statute was void for vagueness as applied to the defendant in question. The defendant was a contractor whose conviction was based on the claim that he deprived the New York City School Construction Authority (SCA) of his honest services by failing to pay his employees the prevailing wage required by state law. A divided panel held the honest services provision to be constitutionally inadequate both for its failure to provide a clear indication on its face of what conduct is forbidden, and its failure to provide adequate standards to enforcement authorities, thereby creating the opportunity for the misuse of government power. The majority noted that the government had, in essence, relied on the defendant's breach of his contract as the basis for its claim that he had deprived the SCA of his honest services. The court found this interpretation unprecedented and far too sweeping:

> If the "honest services" clause can be used to punish a failure to honor the SCA's insistence on the payment of prevailing rate of wages, it could make a criminal out of anyone who breaches any contractual representation: that

tuna was netted dolphin-free; that stationery is made of recycled paper; that sneakers or T-shirts are not made by child workers; that grapes are picked by union labor--in sum so called consumer protection law and far more.

Even someone familiar with the cases construing the mail fraud statute would, the court concluded, "lack any comprehensible notice that federal law has criminalized breaches of contract." The court declined to define the key terms and coverage of the statute. It also noted that the "absence of discernible standards in the "honest services" doctrine implicates principles of federalism." In effect, federal authorities had exercised prosecutorial discretion to sharpen the penalty for state laws that these authorities believed had been insufficiently policed or punished by the state. The dissent argued that it was improper to reach the constitutional issue, which had not been raised in the district court, and also found that the defendant's conduct fell within established honest service parameters since he not only breached his contract, but also violated duties imposed by state law.

Page 151.   Insert at the end of note 4.

In *United States v. Murphy*, 323 F.3d 102 (3d Cir. 2003), the court explicitly rejected *Margiotta*'s holding that a local party official could be prosecuted under the mail and wire fraud statute for depriving the state and its citizens of his own honest services. The court agreed with many of the concerns Judge Winter expressed in his dissenting opinion in *Margiotta*. Holding that it was improper to allow the jury to conjure a duty of honest services to the public "out of a fog of assumptions," a divided panel of the court of appeals also endorsed the need for a "state law limiting principle for honest services fraud." The court did not reach the question whether a state-law created duty is required to sustain an honest services conviction, because it found no basis in state law for the recognition of a fiduciary relationship of any nature. In so doing, the court recognized that the defendant's conduct may have violated the state bribery law (as the jury had found in reaching its verdict on the Travel Act count), but it concluded that the bribery law did not to create a fiduciary relationship between the county political chair and the public.

Pages 165-74.

Delete the *Toulabi* and *Salvatore* cases, as well as note 1 on page 174, and substitute the following.

United States v. Cleveland, 531 U.S. 12, 121 S.Ct. 365 (2000)

Justice GINSBURG delivered the opinion of the Court.

This case presents the question whether the federal mail fraud statute, 18 U.S.C. § 1341, reaches false statements made in an application for a state license. Section 1341 proscribes use of the mails in furtherance of "any scheme or artifice to defraud, or for obtaining money or property by means of false or fraudulent pretenses, representations, or promises." Petitioner Carl W. Cleveland and others were prosecuted under this federal measure for making false statements in applying to the Louisiana State Police for permission to operate video poker machines. We conclude that permits or licenses of this order do not qualify as "property" within § 1341's compass. It does not suffice, we clarify, that the object of the fraud may become property in the recipient's hands; for purposes of the mail fraud statute, the thing obtained must be property in the hands of the victim. State and municipal licenses in general, and Louisiana's video poker licenses in particular, we hold, do not rank as "property," for purposes of § 1341, in the hands of the official licensor.

I

Louisiana law allows certain businesses to operate video poker machines. La.Rev.Stat. Ann. §§ 27:301 to 27:324 (West Supp.2000). The State itself, however, does not run such machinery. The law requires prospective owners of video poker machines to apply for a license from the State. § 27:306. The licenses are not transferable, § 27:311(G), and must be renewed annually, La. Admin. Code, tit. 42, § 2405(B)(3) (2000). To qualify for a license, an applicant must meet suitability requirements designed to ensure that licensees have good character and fiscal integrity.

In 1992, Fred Goodson and his family formed a limited partnership, Truck Stop Gaming, Ltd. (TSG), in order to participate in the video poker business at their truck stop in Slidell, Louisiana. Cleveland, a New Orleans lawyer, assisted Goodson in preparing TSG's application for a video poker license. The application required TSG to identify its partners and to submit personal financial statements for all partners. It also required TSG to affirm that the listed partners were the sole beneficial owners of the business and that no partner held an interest in the partnership merely as an agent or nominee, or intended to transfer the interest in the future.

TSG's application identified Goodson's adult children, Alex and Maria, as the sole beneficial owners of the partnership. It also showed that Goodson and Cleveland's law firm had loaned Alex and Maria all initial capital for the partnership and that Goodson was TSG's general manager. In May 1992, the State approved the application and issued a license. TSG successfully renewed the license in 1993, 1994, and 1995 pursuant to La. Admin. Code, tit. 42, § 2405(B)(3) (2000). Each renewal application identified no ownership interests other than those of Alex and Maria.

In 1996, the FBI discovered evidence that Cleveland and Goodson had participated in a scheme to bribe state legislators to vote in a manner favorable to the video poker industry. The Government charged Cleveland and Goodson with multiple counts of money laundering under 18 U.S.C. § 1957, as well as racketeering and conspiracy under § 1962. Among the predicate acts supporting these charges were four counts of mail fraud under § 1341.[14] The indictment alleged that Cleveland and Goodson had violated § 1341 by fraudulently concealing that they were the true owners of TSG in the initial license application and three renewal applications mailed to the State. They concealed their ownership interests, according to the Government, because they had tax and financial problems that could have undermined their suitability to receive a video poker license.

Before trial, Cleveland moved to dismiss the mail fraud counts on the ground that the alleged fraud did not deprive the State of "property" under § 1341. The District Court denied the motion, concluding that "licenses constitute property even before they are issued." A jury found Cleveland guilty on two counts of mail fraud (based on the 1994 and 1995 license renewals) and on money laundering, racketeering, and conspiracy counts predicated on the mail fraud. The District Court sentenced Cleveland to 121 months in prison.

On appeal, Cleveland again argued that Louisiana had no property interest in video poker licenses, relying on several Court of Appeals decisions holding that the government does not relinquish "property" for purposes of § 1341 when it issues a permit or license. The Court of Appeals for the Fifth Circuit nevertheless affirmed Cleveland's conviction and sentence, *United States v. Bankston*, 182 F.3d 296, 309 (1999), considering itself bound by its holding in *United States v. Salvatore*, 110 F.3d 1131, 1138 (1997), that Louisiana video poker licenses constitute "property" in the hands of the State. Two other Circuits have concluded that the issuing authority has a property interest in unissued licenses under § 1341. *United States v. Bucuvalas*, 970 F.2d 937, 945 (C.A.1 1992) (entertainment and liquor license); *United States v. Martinez*, 905 F.2d 709, 715 (C.A.3 1990) (medical license).

We granted certiorari to resolve the conflict among the Courts of Appeals, and now reverse the Fifth Circuit's judgment.

II

In *McNally v. United States*, 483 U.S. 350, 360 (1987), this Court held that the federal mail fraud statute is "limited in scope to the protection of property

---

[14]Title 18 U.S.C. § 1341 provides in relevant part: "Whoever, having devised or intending to devise any scheme or artifice to defraud, or for obtaining money or property by means of false or fraudulent pretenses, representations, or promises, ... for the purpose of executing such scheme or artifice or attempting so to do, [uses the mails or causes them to be used], shall be fined under this title or imprisoned not more than five years, or both." The Racketeer Influenced and Corrupt Organizations Act (RICO) prohibits participation and conspiracy to participate in a pattern of "racketeering activity," 18 U.S.C. §§ 1962(c), (d), and defines "racketeering activity" to include "any act which is indictable under ... section 1341," § 1961(1). The money laundering statute prohibits various activities designed to conceal or promote "specified unlawful activity," § 1956, and defines "specified unlawful activity" to include (with an exception not relevant here) "any act or activity constituting an offense listed in section 1961(1) of this title," § 1956(c)(7)(A).

rights." *McNally* reversed the mail fraud convictions of two individuals charged with participating in "a self-dealing patronage scheme" that defrauded Kentucky citizens of "the right to have the Commonwealth's affairs conducted honestly." Id., at 352, 107 S.Ct. 2875. At the time *McNally* was decided, federal prosecutors had been using § 1341 to attack various forms of corruption that deprived victims of "intangible rights" unrelated to money or property. Reviewing the history of § 1341, we concluded that "the original impetus behind the mail fraud statute was to protect the people from schemes to deprive them of their money or property."

As first enacted in 1872, § 1341 proscribed use of the mails to further " 'any scheme or artifice to defraud.' " In 1896, this Court held in *Durland v. United States*, 161 U.S. 306, 313, that the statute covered fraud not only by "representations as to the past or present," but also by "suggestions and promises as to the future." In 1909, Congress amended § 1341 to add after "any scheme or artifice to defraud" the phrase "or for obtaining money or property by means of false or fraudulent pretenses, representations, or promises." We explained in *McNally* that the 1909 amendment "codified the holding of *Durland*," and "simply made it unmistakable that the statute reached false promises and misrepresentations as to the future as well as other frauds involving money or property." Rejecting the argument that "the money-or-property requirement of the latter phrase does not limit schemes to defraud to those aimed at causing deprivation of money or property," we concluded that the 1909 amendment signaled no intent by Congress to "depar[t] from [the] common understanding" that "the words 'to defraud' commonly refer 'to wronging one in his property rights.' "

Soon after *McNally*, in *Carpenter v. United States*, 484 U.S. 19, 25 (1987), we again stated that § 1341 protects property rights only. *Carpenter* upheld convictions under § 1341 and the federal wire fraud statute, 18 U.S.C. § 1343, of defendants who had defrauded the Wall Street Journal of confidential business information. Citing decisions of this Court as well as a corporate law treatise, we observed that "[c]onfidential business information has long been recognized as property."

The following year, Congress amended the law specifically to cover one of the "intangible rights" that lower courts had protected under § 1341 prior to *McNally*: "the intangible right of honest services." Anti-Drug Abuse Act of 1988, § 7603(a), 18 U.S.C. § 1346. Significantly, Congress covered only the intangible right of honest services even though federal courts, relying on *McNally*, had dismissed, for want of monetary loss to any victim, prosecutions under § 1341 for diverse forms of public corruption, including licensing fraud.[3]

---

[3]For example, in *United States v. Murphy*, 836 F.2d 248, 254 (C.A.6 1988), the court overturned the mail fraud conviction of a state official charged with using false information to help a charitable organization obtain a state bingo license. Acknowledging "the *McNally* limitations" on § 1341, the court said that the issue "distills to a consideration of whether Tennessee's 'right to control or object' with respect to the issuance of a bingo permit to a charitable organization constitutes

III

In this case, there is no assertion that Louisiana's video poker licensing scheme implicates the intangible right of honest services. The question presented is whether, for purposes of the federal mail fraud statute, a government regulator parts with "property" when it issues a license. For the reasons we now set out, we hold that § 1341 does not reach fraud in obtaining a state or municipal license of the kind here involved, for such a license is not "property" in the government regulator's hands. Again, as we said in *McNally*, "[i]f Congress desires to go further, it must speak more clearly than it has."

To begin with, we think it beyond genuine dispute that whatever interests Louisiana might be said to have in its video poker licenses, the State's core concern is regulatory. Louisiana recognizes the importance of "public confidence and trust that gaming activities ... are conducted honestly and are free from criminal and corruptive elements." La.Rev.Stat. Ann. § 27:306(A)(1) (West Supp.2000). The video poker licensing statute accordingly asserts the State's "legitimate interest in providing strict regulation of all persons, practices, associations, and activities related to the operation of ... establishments licensed to offer video draw poker devices." Ibid. The statute assigns the Office of State Police, a part of the Department of Public Safety and Corrections, the responsibility to promulgate rules and regulations concerning the licensing process. § 27:308(A). It also authorizes the State Police to deny, condition, suspend, or revoke licenses, to levy fines of up to $1,000 per violation of any rule, and to inspect all premises where video poker devices are offered for play. §§ 27:308(B), (E)(1). In addition, the statute defines criminal penalties for unauthorized use of video poker devices, and prescribes detailed suitability requirements for licensees.

In short, the statute establishes a typical regulatory program. It licenses, subject to certain conditions, engagement in pursuits that private actors may not undertake without official authorization. In this regard, it resembles other licensing schemes long characterized by this Court as exercises of state police powers.

Acknowledging Louisiana's regulatory interests, the Government offers two reasons why the State also has a property interest in its video poker licenses. First, the State receives a substantial sum of money in exchange for each license and continues to receive payments from the licensee as long as the license remains in effect. Second, the State has significant control over the issuance, renewal, suspension, and revocation of licenses.

Without doubt, Louisiana has a substantial economic stake in the video poker industry. The State collects an upfront "processing fee" for each new license application ($10,000 for truck stops), a separate "processing fee" for each renewal

---

'property.' " It then held that "the certificate of registration or the bingo license may well be 'property' once issued, insofar as the charitable organization is concerned, but certainly an unissued certificate of registration is not property of the State of Tennessee and once issued, it is not the property of the State of Tennessee."

application ($1,000 for truck stops), an "annual fee" from each device owner ($2,000), an additional "device operation" fee ($1,000 for truck stops), and, most importantly, a fixed percentage of net revenue from each video poker device (32.5% for truck stops). It is hardly evident, however, why these tolls should make video poker licenses "property" in the hands of the State. The State receives the lion's share of its expected revenue not while the licenses remain in its own hands, but only after they have been issued to licensees. Licenses pre-issuance do not generate an ongoing stream of revenue. At most, they entitle the State to collect a processing fee from applicants for new licenses. Were an entitlement of this order sufficient to establish a state property right, one could scarcely avoid the conclusion that States have property rights in any license or permit requiring an upfront fee, including drivers' licenses, medical licenses, and fishing and hunting licenses. Such licenses, as the Government itself concedes, are "purely regulatory."

Tellingly, as to the character of Louisiana's stake in its video poker licenses, the Government nowhere alleges that Cleveland defrauded the State of any money to which the State was entitled by law. Indeed, there is no dispute that TSG paid the State of Louisiana its proper share of revenue, which totaled more than $1.2 million, between 1993 and 1995. If Cleveland defrauded the State of "property," the nature of that property cannot be economic.

Addressing this concern, the Government argues that Cleveland frustrated the State's right to control the issuance, renewal, and revocation of video poker licenses under La.Rev.Stat. Ann. §§ 27:306, 27:308 (West Supp.2000). The Fifth Circuit has characterized the protected interest as " Louisiana's right to choose the persons to whom it issues video poker licenses." But far from composing an interest that "has long been recognized as property," *Carpenter*, these intangible rights of allocation, exclusion, and control amount to no more and no less than Louisiana's sovereign power to regulate. Notably, the Government overlooks the fact that these rights include the distinctively sovereign authority to impose criminal penalties for violations of the licensing scheme, including making false statements in a license application. Even when tied to an expected stream of revenue, the State's right of control does not create a property interest any more than a law licensing liquor sales in a State that levies a sales tax on liquor. Such regulations are paradigmatic exercises of the States' traditional police powers.

The Government compares the State's interest in video poker licenses to a patent holder's interest in a patent that she has not yet licensed. Although it is true that both involve the right to exclude, we think the congruence ends there. Louisiana does not conduct gaming operations itself, it does not hold video poker licenses to reserve that prerogative, and it does not "sell" video poker licenses in the ordinary commercial sense. Furthermore, while a patent holder may sell her patent, see 35 U.S.C. § 261 ("patents shall have the attributes of personal property"), the State may not sell its licensing authority. Instead of a patent holder's interest in an unlicensed patent, the better analogy is to the Federal Government's interest in an unissued patent. That interest, like the State's interest in licensing video poker operations, surely implicates the Government's role as sovereign, not as property holder.

The Government also compares the State's licensing power to a franchisor's right to select its franchisees. On this view, Louisiana's video poker licensing scheme represents the State's venture into the video poker business. Although the State could have chosen to run the business itself, the Government says, it decided to franchise private entities to carry out the operations instead. However, a franchisor's right to select its franchisees typically derives from its ownership of a trademark, brand name, business strategy, or other product that it may trade or sell in the open market. Louisiana's authority to select video poker licensees rests on no similar asset. It rests instead upon the State's sovereign right to exclude applicants deemed unsuitable to run video poker operations. A right to exclude in that governing capacity is not one appropriately labeled "property." Moreover, unlike an entrepreneur or business partner who shares both losses and gains arising from a business venture, Louisiana cannot be said to have put its labor or capital at risk through its fee-laden licensing scheme. In short, the State did not decide to venture into the video poker business; it decided typically to permit, regulate, and tax private operators of the games.

We reject the Government's theories of property rights not simply because they stray from traditional concepts of property. We resist the Government's reading of § 1341 as well because it invites us to approve a sweeping expansion of federal criminal jurisdiction in the absence of a clear statement by Congress. Equating issuance of licenses or permits with deprivation of property would subject to federal mail fraud prosecution a wide range of conduct traditionally regulated by state and local authorities. We note in this regard that Louisiana's video poker statute typically and unambiguously imposes criminal penalties for making false statements on license applications. As we reiterated last Term, " 'unless Congress conveys its purpose clearly, it will not be deemed to have significantly changed the federal-state balance' in the prosecution of crimes." *Jones v. United States*, 529 U.S. 848, 858 (2000) (quoting *United States v. Bass*, 404 U.S. 336, 349 (1971)).

Moreover, to the extent that the word "property" is ambiguous as placed in § 1341, we have instructed that "ambiguity concerning the ambit of criminal statutes should be resolved in favor of lenity." *Rewis v. United States*, 401 U.S. 808, 812 (1971). This interpretive guide is especially appropriate in construing § 1341 because, as this case demonstrates, mail fraud is a predicate offense under RICO, 18 U.S.C. § 1961(1), and the money laundering statute, § 1956(c)(7)(A). In deciding what is "property" under § 1341, we think "it is appropriate, before we choose the harsher alternative, to require that Congress should have spoken in language that is clear and definite."

Finally, in an argument not raised below but urged as an alternate ground for affirmance, the Government contends that § 1341, as amended in 1909, defines two independent offenses: (1) "any scheme or artifice to defraud" and (2) "any scheme or artifice ... for obtaining money or property by means of false or fraudulent pretenses, representations, or promises." Because a video poker license is property in the hands of the licensee, the Government says, Cleveland "obtain[ed] ... property" and thereby committed the second offense even if the license is not property in the hands of the State.

Although we do not here question that video poker licensees may have property interests in their licenses,[4] we nevertheless disagree with the Government's reading of § 1341. In *McNally*, we recognized that "[b]ecause the two phrases identifying the proscribed schemes appear in the disjunctive, it is arguable that they are to be construed independently." But we rejected that construction of the statute, instead concluding that the second phrase simply modifies the first by "ma[king] it unmistakable that the statute reached false promises and misrepresentations as to the future as well as other frauds involving money or property." Indeed, directly contradicting the Government's view, we said that "the mail fraud statute ... had its origin in the desire to protect individual property rights, and any benefit which the Government derives from the statute must be limited to the Government's interests as property holder." We reaffirm our reading of § 1341 in *McNally*. Were the Government correct that the second phrase of § 1341 defines a separate offense, the statute would appear to arm federal prosecutors with power to police false statements in an enormous range of submissions to state and local authorities. For reasons already stated, we decline to attribute to § 1341 a purpose so encompassing where Congress has not made such a design clear.

IV

We conclude that § 1341 requires the object of the fraud to be "property" in the victim's hands and that a Louisiana video poker license in the State's hands is not "property" under § 1341. Absent clear statement by Congress, we will not read the mail fraud statute to place under federal superintendence a vast array of conduct traditionally policed by the States. Our holding means that Cleveland's § 1341 conviction must be vacated. Accordingly, the judgment of the United States Court of Appeals for the Fifth Circuit is reversed, and the case is remanded for further proceedings consistent with this opinion.

Notes

1. Note that the issue in *Cleveland* was the nature of the government's interest in the licenses that it issues. What if the case involves an effort to defraud a licensee? For many purposes licenses or permits in the hands of grantees are treated as their property. Is there any reason that they should not be treated as property for purposes of the mail and wire fraud statutes?

---

[4]Notwithstanding the State's declaration that "[a]ny license issued or renewed ... is not property or a protected interest under the constitutions of either the United States or the state of Louisiana," "[t]he question whether a state-law right constitutes 'property' or 'rights to property' is a matter of federal law," *Drye v. United States*, 528 U.S. 49, (1999). In some contexts, we have held that individuals have constitutionally protected property interests in state-issued licenses essential to pursuing an occupation or livelihood. *See, e.g., Bell v. Burson*, 402 U.S. 535, 539 (1971) (driver's license).

CHAPTER 6

THE HOBBS ACT

Page 202.   **Insert at end of note 4.**

Although the Attorney General eventually permitted the defendants to be transferred to Virginia authorities to be prosecuted for capital murder, the snipers who terrorized the Washington area in 2002 were originally arrested on Hobbs Act charges based upon an extortion note found at the scene of one of the killings that demanded $10 million dollars. The Attorney General ordered that the defendants be released into the custody of Virginia state authorities, where both defendants could receive the death penalty. Federal law does not permit the imposition of the death penalty on juveniles.

The federal complaint against John Muhammad is available at http://news.findlaw.com/wp/docs/sniper/usmhmmd102902fcmp.pdf .

Page 229.   **Insert at the end of note 1.**

The Fifth Circuit continues to be the main judicial arena for debate about the proper application of the commerce clause to the Hobbs Act (and by extension, to other federal criminal legislation). In *United States v. McFarland*, 311 F.3d 376 (5th Cir. 2002), the court again granted en banc review to consider this issue, and, as in *Hickman,* the 16 judges deadlocked, 8 to 8. The facts of the case before the court show how important this issue can be in practical terms. The defendant, who brandished a pistol, robbed four retail convenience stores in Texas during a one month period; he obtained a total estimated to be between $1,700 and $2,000. He was prosecuted for four counts of Hobbs Act robbery, and four federal felony gun counts in connection with the robberies. He was sentenced to a total of 1,170 months (more than 97 years): four concurrent terms of 210 months for the Hobbs Act violations, plus 60 months on the first gun count, and 300 months on each of the remaining gun counts. Since federal law has no provision for parole, even with the maximum credit for good behavior ("good time") McFarland will have to serve at least 85% of this term. Under state law, in contrast, the minimum sentence would have been 5 years, and even if McFarland had been sentenced to a longer term he would have been eligible for parole after serving half his sentence or 30 years, whichever was less. The record contained no indication why McFarland was selected for federal prosecution.

The judges who voted to affirm did not file an opinion in the en banc case, and only a brief per curiam opinion was filed by the original panel. *See* 264 F.3d 557. The panel opinion adopted the aggregation principle. Since the jurisdictional provision of the Hobbs Act requires proof of an effect on interstate commerce in each case, the panel concluded that "[i]t follows with the inexorable logic of the multiplication table that the cumulative result of many Hobbs Act violations is a substantial effect upon interstate commerce." In contrast, the dissenters in the en banc case filed three opinions that take up nearly 50 pages in the Federal Reporter, and expand upon the themes discussed in Judge Higgenbotham's dissenting opinion in *Hickman*.

At this writing, Senate Democrats are filibustering the nomination of conservative Texas Supreme Court Justice Priscilla Owen to the Fifth Circuit. If Owen or another conservative is confirmed to the Fifth Circuit, it seems likely that the court will have the necessary ninth vote to hold that the Hobbs Act exceeds the scope of congressional power under the Commerce Clause. Supreme Court review would almost certainly follow.

Page 229   Read in conjunction with note 1.

The Supreme Court avoided the constitutional issue in the *Jones* case, discussed in note 1. A unanimous Court held that the arson statute applies only to property actively "used" in interstate commerce, and hence the statute does not reach the arson of an owner-occupied private residence. *Jones v. United States*, 529 U.S. 848 (2000).

Page 232.   Insert at the end of the page, in note 3.

In *Scheidler v. National Organization for Women, Inc.*, 123 S.Ct. 1057 (2003), the Supreme Court took up the issue raised in *Arena* in a Chicago case also involving violent protests at abortion clinics. An earlier decision by the Supreme Court in *Scheidler* (p. 457 main text) held that RICO is not limited to cases in which there is an economic motivation, and the case was remanded. After a seven week civil trial, the jury found defendants responsible for a pattern of racketeering activity including 21 violations of the Hobbs Act, 25 violations of the state extortion law, 25 instances of attempts or conspiracy to violate federal or state extortion laws, 23 violations of the Travel Act, and 23 attempts to violate the Travel Act. The jury awarded approximately $31,000 in actual damages, which was trebled pursuant to 18 U.S.C. § 1964(c). The district court also issued a permanent nationwide injunction barring defendants from obstructing access to the clinics, trespassing on clinic property, damaging clinic property, or using violence or threats against the clinics, employees or patients.

The Hobbs Act defines extortion as "the obtaining of property from another, with his consent, induced by wrongful use of actual or threatened force, violence, or fear...." Writing for eight members of the Court, the Chief Justice concluded that the defendants's conduct did not fall within this definition because they did not "obtain" property from the plaintiffs. The Court emphasized both the language of the act and its legislative history. Both of the two sources upon which Congress based the Hobbs Act – the New York Penal Code and the Field Code – defined extortion as obtaining property from another, and this entailed both deprivation and acquisition of property. Although the defendants interfered with, disrupted, and in some cases completely deprived the plaintiffs of their ability to exercise their property rights, they did not acquire the property. They "neither pursued nor received 'something of value from' respondents that they could exercise, transfer, or sell." Defining the defendants' conduct as extortion would eliminate the requirement that property must be obtained, and also erase the distinction between extortion and the distinct crime of coercion. Under the New York Penal Code coercion was a separate and lesser offense when Congress drafted the Hobbs Act. The distinction between extortion and coercion was "clearly drawn in New York law," and Anti-Racketeering Act of 1934 (based on New York law) included both extortion and coercion. But when Congress replaced the Anti-Racketeering Act with the Hobbs Act, it included extortion but not coercion.

The Court recognized the apparent tension between its statements in prior Hobbs Act cases, and explained how they should be reconciled. In *Culbert* (page 83 main text) the Court stated that Congress intended to use all of its constitutional power in the Hobbs Act, but other Hobbs Act cases apply the rule of lenity. The Court noted that the statement in *Culbert* referred to Congress's intention to employ the full scope of its power under the commerce clause. Here, however, there was no claim that the conduct in question did not affect interstate commerce, and the rule of lenity was appropriate to determine which of two rational readings of the statute to adopt. Accordingly the Court concluded that "If the distinction between extortion and coercion, which we find controls these cases, is to be abandoned, such a significant expansion of the law's coverage must come from Congress, and not from the courts."

Justice Ginsburg concurred in an opinion joined by Justice Breyer. She emphasized that the principal effect of the Court's decision would be in other cases pursued under RICO. In light of the severe criminal penalties and hefty civil liability available under RICO, she stated her view that the Court was "rightly reluctant" to extend RICO's domain further by endorsing the lower courts' expansive definition of extortion. In a footnote she noted the possibility that the plaintiffs' interpretation would have made the Hobbs Act – and thus RICO – applicable to the civil rights sit ins.

Justice Stevens dissented, arguing that the majority appeared to limit extortion under the Hobbs Act to the acquisition of tangible property, despite decades of lower court decisions to the contrary. He quoted at length from *United States v. Tropiano*, 418 F.3d 1069 (2nd Cir. 1969), which held that threats of physical violence aimed at deterring the owners of a competing trash removal company from soliciting customers in certain areas violated the Hobbs Act. The *Tropiano* court concluded that the right to solicit customers was a property right under the Hobbs Act. This analysis has been widely followed by the lower federal courts, and Stevens argued that uniform construction of the Act should remain the law unless Congress decides to amend the statute. That is especially true, he reasoned, since both the Supreme Court and lower courts have recognized that Congress intended the Hobbs Act to be given a broad construction. Justice Stevens predicted that the principal beneficiaries of the Court's decision would be the professional criminals who were the original target of the Hobbs Act and the legislation it superceded. In a footnote, he noted that Congress had overturned the Supreme Court's narrow reading of the mail fraud statute despite a similar unbroken pattern of lower court decisions (see main text pages 131-35), and he commented that "Congress remains free to correct the Court's error in these cases as well."

CHAPTER 7

OFFICIAL BRIBERY AND GRATUITIES

Page 246.   **Insert at the end of note 3.**

What exactly does the term "corruptly" in § 201(b)(1) mean? That issue was raised in *United States v. Alfisi*, 308 F.3d 144 (2d. Cir. 2002). The defendant, an employee for a produce wholesaler, had been convicted of bribery for payments he made to a USDA produce inspector. At trial, Alfisi's primary defense was that he had been extorted by the inspector and was paying him merely to perform his duty legally. On appeal, he attacked a jury charge which defined the term "corruptly" as entailing the "specific intent to influence [the inspector's] official acts of performing inspections and certifying the condition and grade of fruits and vegetables." Alfisi argued that the instruction was erroneous because it allowed the jury to convict him for bribery even if the quid pro quo sought from the inspector was simply the faithful execution of his duties.

After mentioning in a footnote that the "proper response to coercion" is "to go to the authorities, not to make the payoff," the court rejected Alfisi's argument. First, the court defined the "corrupt intent" required as the intention "to procure a quid pro quo agreement–'to influence an official act,'" and concluded that "[i]t cannot be seriously argued that Alfisi's payments did not fall within that broad language, even if he was paying [the inspector] solely to make accurate inspections." Second, the court determined that "sound legislative purpose" favored reading the statute broadly, as the danger of an underinclusive interpretation was much greater than that of an overinclusive one.

The dissent argued that the majority's definition of "corruptly" was too broad:

Our cases * * * provide that a payment made in the course of a shakedown * * * is not a bribe. A person who makes a payment pursuant to such extortion intends not to cultivate such corruption, but only to avoid the tendrils of a corruption already sprouted. Such a person does not act "corruptly" within the meaning of the statute because he does not seek the lawlessness that the bribery statute seeks to prevent.

Further, the dissent argued that the definition of "corruptly" used by the district court and the majority, "the specific intent to influence . . . official acts," if inserted in place of the term "corruptly" in § 203 (b)(1), would render the term superfluous:

The district court effectively instructed the jury that Alfisi committed bribery if he "directly or indirectly, *with the specific intent to influence official acts* [the court's definition of "corruptly"], [gave], offered, or promised something of value to [a] public official with the *intent to influence any official act.*" (emphasis added; ellipses omitted).

Which construction of the statute seems more plausible? Which is better policy? The government charged Alfisi under § 203 (b)(1)(A), which requires proof that the defendant had intent to "influence any official act." Note that § 203 (b)(1)(C) criminalizes the making of corrupt payments with the intent "to induce * * * [a public official] to do or omit to do any act in violation of the lawful duty of such official or person." Neither the majority nor the dissent discussed § 203 (b)(1)(C). How is that provision, an alternative to § 203 (b)(1)(A), relevant to the construction of § 203 (b)(1)(A)?

Page 257   Insert at the end of note 1.

The Department of Justice apparently does not endorse the broadest possible reading of § 666. The DEPARTMENT OF JUSTICE CRIMINAL RESOURCE MANUAL notes that the "very broad language of the statute" .... seemingly permits the prosecution of any state agent, regardless of whether his or her specific agency received the necessary Federal assistance, as long as the state received the required Federal assistance," and notes that "[t]his broad reading, while statutorily permissible, would Federalize many state offenses in which the Federal interest is slight or nonexistent." To ensure that only "significant" Federal interests are protected and to follow Congressional intent, the MANUAL "strongly suggest[s]" that government attorneys adopt a narrower reading of § 666 requiring "that the agent must have illegally obtained cash or property from the agency that received the necessary Federal assistance." *See* DEPARTMENT OF JUSTICE, CRIMINAL RESOURCE MANUAL at 1001, *available at* http://www.usdoj.gov/usao/eousa/foia_reading_room/usam/title9/crm01001.htm (last visited Nov. 2, 2003).

Page 259.   Insert at the end of note 3.

The Supreme Court has granted certiorari in a case raising the related questions discussed in notes 2 and 3. In *United States v. Sabri*, 326 F.3d 937 (8th Cir. 2003), a divided panel of the Eight Circuit held that (1) other than the threshold showing that the agency in question received more than $10,000 in federal funds in one year, § 666 requires no nexus between the criminal activity and the federal funds, and (2) the statute is nonetheless a legitimate exercise of Congress's authority under the necessary and proper clause.

The majority rejected the argument that § 666 is a condition placed on the receipt of federal funds, since it neither imposes an affirmative duty on the recipient of federal funds nor proscribes conduct on the part of the recipient. Instead, it regulates the conduct of third parties who are not the recipients of the federal benefits. Instead, the court sustained the statute as a law necessary and proper to the execution of the congressional spending power. Reasoning that § 666 is "designed to protect the integrity of the vast sums of federal monies disbursed through federal programs," the majority concluded that "Congress has made a determination that the most effective way to protect the integrity of federal funds is to police the agencies administering those funds." Money is fungible, and a more limited scheme would be rendered toothless because of the difficulty of tracing funds. Moreover, maladministration in one part of an agency can affect the allocation of funds throughout the organization. If the statute were not to be sustained, the court noted that protection of federal funds would be left to enforcement by state and local officials, who may be the ones posing the threat to the funds. The court also noted that the jurisdictional provision of the statute ensured that the federal prosecutions could be brought only where there was a substantial federal interest at stake.

These arguments did not persuade Judge Bye, who dissented. He noted that the majority's analysis ignored half of the necessary and proper clause. Even assuming that § 666 is "necessary" in a constitutional sense, that does not establish that it is also "proper," as that term was construed in *Alden v. Maine*, 527 U.S. 706 (1999), and *Printz v. United States*, 521 U.S. 898 (1997). A law is proper, Judge Bye wrote, only if it "hews to constitutional principles of limited federal government and state sovereignty. Federal laws that usurp the traditional domain of state authority are therefor not proper." Since nearly every state, county, tribe, and city receives in excess of $10,000 each year, Judge Bye found a all too real a risk "that federal anticorruption efforts will swamp state and local efforts to combat bribery." Characterizing the real-world effects of the majority's decision as "startling," the dissent noted it would be a federal crime for an auto mechanic to persuade a public high school principal to hire him to teach the shop class by offering the principal free car repair. This violated the underlying principle of Lopez and Morrison, which requires that the courts preserve the distinction between the national and the truly local.

The Supreme Court granted certiorari in *Sabri v. United States*, No. 03-44, October 14, 2003.

Page 260   Insert in note 5.

In *Fischer v. United States*, 529 U.S. 667 (2000), the Supreme Court held that a health care provider who received Medicare payments received "benefits" and thus was subject to prosecution under the § 666. The Court did not announce any broad principles for the interpretation of the program bribery statute, though it did provide some guidance for future cases.

The Court declined to adopt the broadest possible interpretation of the statute, which would reach any receipt of federal funds, saying this would give the statute a virtually limitless reach and upset the proper federal-state balance. It stated that in order to determine whether an organization is receiving "benefits" under § 666 the courts should "examine the program's structure, operation, and purpose," as well as the conditions under which the organization receives federal payments.

Applying this test, the Court concluded that "the Government has a legitimate and significant interest in prohibiting financial fraud or acts of bribery being perpetrated on Medicare providers," and that fraud "threatens the program's integrity." The Court concluded that medical providers as well as patients are beneficiaries of the Medicare program.

Justice Thomas dissented. He argued that medical providers engage in a market transaction and are compensated, and thus do not receive government benefits. Similarly, grocery stores that receive food stamps–though they are regulated by the government like health care providers–are not recipients of a government benefit. Thomas's opinion contains an interesting footnote (n.3) in which he comments on the constitutional significance of provisions to ensure that the exercise of the spending power is related to a federal interest.

CHAPTER 8

AN OVERVIEW OF FEDERAL CRIMES DEALING WITH POLITICAL CORRUPTION

Page 262.   **Insert at the beginning of the text.**

The prosecution of state and local corruption continues to be an important federal function. As Professor George Brown explains:

> Between 1981 and 2000, 1,704 state officials were indicted on corruption offenses, 1,462 were convicted, and 554 were awaiting trial at the end of 2000. The twenty-year totals for local officials were as follows: 4,968 were indicted, 4,233 were convicted, and 1,735 were awaiting trial as of the end of the year. These prosecutions are sometimes the result of extensive investigations using all the tools of high- tech law enforcement as well as more classic methods. "Operation Plunder Dome," involving corruption in Providence, Rhode Island, has already been mentioned. Another equally colorful title is "Operation Lost Trust." This investigation stemmed from a "narcotics sting operation against a prominent lobbyist and former state legislator" in South Carolina. The investigation centered on a bill that would have legalized gambling on horse and dog races. The former legislator cooperated with the FBI and posed as a lobbyist for an FBI dummy corporation, offering cash during meetings which were wired and videotaped. The operation led to the indictment of twenty-eight individuals, primarily on extortion and drug charges.

George D. Brown, *New Federalism's Unanswered Question: Who Should Prosecute State and Local Officials For Political Corruption*, 60 WASH. & LEE L. REV. 417, 421-22 (2003). Professor Brown's article contains an excellent summary of the statutory bases for prosecuting state and local corruption, and an insightful discussion of the tension between the government's role in policing the fairness of political and governmental processes at this level – which may advance goals such as protecting civil rights and the function of the electoral process – and the goals and themes of the new federalism.

Pages 264-66.   Delete point 3 and substitute:

3. The penalty structure of the statutes in question and the Sentencing Guidelines should be considered in evaluating the effect of these provisions.

Both Congress and the Sentencing Commission have substantially revised the provisions discussed in the main text. At the statutory level, Congress increased the basic penalty for mail and wire fraud from 5 years to 20 years. This brings those statutes into line with the Hobbs Act (maximum penalty 20 years) and into rough parity with the bribery provisions of § 201 (maximum penalty 15 years). The maximum penalty for a gratuity violation under § 201 is 5 years. Higher penalties are available under the mail and wire fraud statutes for cases involving financial institutions. These statutes merely set the maximum penalties. The penalties actually imposed are determined by the Sentencing Guidelines.

The Commission has reorganized, revised, and rationalized the provisions applicable to the Hobbs Act, the mail and wire fraud statutes, and the bribery and gratuities provisions. Under U.S.S.G. § 2C1.1, Hobbs Act extortion under color of official right is subject to the same sentence as bribery under 18 U.S.C. § 201. 2C1.1 provides for a base offense level of 10, and two possible upward adjustments – one based upon the amount of the bribe or extortion, and the other an 8 level upward departure applicable in cases involving a payment intended to influence an elected official or any official holding "a high level decision-making or sensitive position." Although wire and mail fraud now fall under a separate guideline, U.S.S.G. § 2C1.7, it adopts the same standards as § 2C1.1. Finally, gratutities cases under 18 U.S.C. § 201 now fall under U.S.S.G. § 2C1.2, which has a lower base offense level (7), but then allows for the same adjustments as the provisions governing bribery. Accordingly, sentencing considerations should no longer play a major role in determining which statute prosecutors will employ in charging political corruption cases. Or, to look at the matter from the defendant's perspective, the sentence imposed isn't likely to vary depending on which statute is charged. U.S.S.G. §§ 2C1.1, 2C1.2, and 2C1.7 are reprinted infra at 158-165.

CHAPTER 9

DRUG OFFENSE ENFORCEMENT

Page 284   **Insert at end of first paragraph.**

The lawsuit challenging the California law (discussed in the text and cited in footnote dd) eventually made it to the Supreme Court, which vindicated the federal government's position.   The Court held that the federal Controlled Substances Act does not recognize or create any implied medical necessity exception to the prohibitions on manufacture and distribution of marijuana, and accordingly the district court could not consider medical necessity when exercising its discretion to fashion injunctive relief. *United States v. Oakland Cannabis Buyers' Cooperative*, 532 U.S. 483 (2001). On the other hand, the government suffered a setback in another case, when the Supreme Court let stand a ruling of the Ninth Circuit that found a First Amendment bar to the government's efforts to sanction California physicians who recommend marijuana to their patients. In *Conant v. Walters*, 309 F.3d 629 (9th Cir. 2002), *cert. denied*, 72 U.S.L.W. 3092, 3263, 3266, (U.S. Oct. 14, 2003) (No. 03-40), the court of appeals upheld an injunction the prohibited the government from seeking to revoke a physician's license to prescribe controlled substances based solely on the physician's professional recommendation of the medical use of marijuana.

Page 286   **Insert at the end of the introduction.**

For an argument that the federal drug laws have worked and reduced drug usage when pursued actively, see Stephen D. Easton, *Everybody Knows It, But Is It True? A Challenge to the Conventional Wisdom that the War on Drugs Is Ineffective*, 14 FED. SENT. REP. 132 (2002).

There is evidence that many front-line participants in the federal criminal justice system now view the drug sentencing laws as unnecessarily harsh, and that they are quietly exercising their discretion in ways that have significantly reduced federal drug sentences. Frank Bowman and Michael Heise have presented data showing a downward trend in drug sentence length since 1992 that, in their view, cannot be entirely explained on non-discretionary grounds. They argue their data shows:

> (1) at virtually every point in the Guidelines sentencing process where prosecutors and judges can exercise discretionary authority to reduce drug sentences, they have done so; and (2) where we can measure trends, the trend since roughly 1992 has always been toward exercising discretion in favor of leniency with increasing frequency.

Frank O. Bowman & Michael Heise, *Quiet Rebellion II: An Empirical Analysis of*

Declining Federal Drug Sentences Including Data from the District Level, 87 IOWA L.REV. 477 (2002). How large has the decline been? Bowman and Heise found a decrease in the average sentence of nearly two years (or 22%) as measured by data from the Administrative Office of the U.S. Courts, and a decrease of 13 months (or 14%) as measured by the Sentencing Commission's data. Moving from national data to data at the district and circuit level, they found :

> a remarkable degree of variation in both sentence length and change in average sentence length. For example, in 1992, the average drug sentence within a district ranged from 22 months to 176 months, and forty-one of the ninety-four judicial districts actually had higher average drug sentences in 1999 than in 1992.

> * * * [N]either population density nor district size as expressed by the number of Assistant United States Attorneys employed by the district shows a statistically significant relationship to the increase or decrease of the average drug sentence within a district.

> * * * [I]ncreases in prosecutorial workload correlate consistently with decreases in drug sentence length, but oddly, increases in judicial workload demonstrate virtually no such relationship. events in the Mexican border districts exerted particular influence from 1996-1999.

Id. at 482-83. For a different view of the decline, see John Scalia, Jr., *The Impact of Changes in Federal Law and Policy on the Sentencing Of, and Time Served in Prison By, Drug Defendants Convicted in U.S. District Courts*, 14 FED. SENT. REP. 152 (2002). Scalia believes that the decline did not begin until 1995, and attributes it, at least in part, to different factors: the greater influence of sentences for marijuana defendants, the increase in the number of defendants receiving a downward departure for substantial assistance and other reasons, and the impact of the 'safety valve' that exempted certain defendants from otherwise applicable mandatory penalties and reduce the guideline range by two levels.

Page 298   Insert after note 3.

3(a). As noted above, Congress has relied heavily on mandatory minimum sentences in the drug laws. The effect of these mandatory minimum statutes has been ameliorated, to a degree, by the statutory "safety valve" provision, 18 U.S.C. § 3553(f). Section § 3553(f) provides that in cases brought under 21 U.S.C. §§ 841, 844, 846, and 21 U.S.C. §§960 and 963, the court shall impose a sentence pursuant to guidelines "without regard to any statutory minimum sentence" if the court makes the following findings at sentencing:

> (1) the defendant does not have more than 1 criminal history point, as determined under the sentencing guidelines;

(2) the defendant did not use violence or credible threats of violence or possess a firearm or other dangerous weapon (or induce another participant to do so) in connection with the offense;

(3) the offense did not result in death or serious bodily injury to any person;

(4) the defendant was not an organizer, leader, manager, or supervisor of others in the offense, as determined under the sentencing guidelines and was not engaged in a continuing criminal enterprise, as defined in section 408 of the Controlled Substances Act; and

(5) not later than the time of the sentencing hearing, the defendant has truthfully provided to the Government all information and evidence the defendant has concerning the offense or offenses that were part of the same course of conduct or of a common scheme or plan, but the fact that the defendant has no relevant or useful other information to provide or that the Government is already aware of the information shall not preclude a determination by the court that the defendant has complied with this requirement.

How broad (or narrow) is the safety valve provision? Note that a defendant must meet all five criteria to be eligible. In your view, does this provision correctly define the universe of defendants who should receive more lenient treatment? Of course that question assumes that having a safety valve is a good idea. Does the existence of such a safety valve undermine the deterrent effect, or the social meaning that Congress intended to produce when it enacted mandatory minimum statutes? Note that the guidelines also provide something that is referred to as a "safety valve provision," § 2D1.1(b)(6), which reduces the sentence otherwise applicable by 2 levels.

Page 298   **Substitute for note 5.**

5. What procedures must be followed when the government seeks to impose enhanced penalties under § 841(b)? Prior to the Supreme Court's decision in *Apprendi v. New Jersey*, 530 U.S. 466 (2000), it was generally held that drug type and quantity were not elements of the offense, but rather sentencing factors relevant to determining the penalty. For that reason, neither proof beyond a reasonable doubt nor a right to jury trial were regarded as applicable. In *Apprendi* the Supreme Court held that any fact that increases the penalty beyond the ordinary statutory maximum must be submitted to the jury and proved beyond a reasonable doubt. Subsequently, the Court ruled in *Harris v. United States*, 536 U.S. 545 (2002), that mandatory minimum sentences do not have to be submitted to the jury and proved beyond a reasonable doubt. These decisions are discussed at greater length at 115-133.

How then does *Apprendi* affect drug cases under § 841? The structure of § 841 is extremely complex, and it includes several statutory maxima. As one court explained:

> Section 841(b) delineates several different default statutory maximums based on drug quantity (and other factors not relevant here, such as drug type and whether or not seriously bodily injury resulted): 20 years if no drug quantity is specified, 40 years for five or more grams of cocaine base, and life for fifty or more grams of cocaine base. 21 U.S.C. § 841(b)(1)(A)-(C); *See also United States v. Martinez-Medina*, 279 F.3d 105, 121 (1st Cir.) (identifying default statutory maximum under § 841(b)(1)(A) as life); *Robinson*, 241 F.3d at 119 (identifying default statutory maximum as twenty years under § 841(b)(1)(C), where no quantity had been determined beyond a reasonable doubt); *United States v. Baltas*, 236 F.3d 27, 41 (1st Cir.2001) (same); *Smith*, 308 F.3d at 741 (finding a default statutory maximum of 20 years for more than fifty kilograms of marijuana under § 841(b)(1)(C)).

United States v. Goodine, 326 F.3d 26, 32 (1st Cir. 2003), *petition for cert. filed,* Oct. 16, 2003, No. 03-596. Under *Apprendi* the facts necessary to increase the sentence above the relevant default must be proven to the jury beyond a reasonable doubt.[*] *Apprendi* thus requires the courts to parse the statutory language to discover the default statutory penalties for each offense. This is sometimes rather challenging.

On the other hand, as long as drug quantity and type affect sentencing but do not raise the statutory maximum, they are not subject to the heightened procedures under *Apprendi*. Accordingly, for purposes of the guidelines calculations, and for purposes of determining the applicability of mandatory minimum sentences the judge can find the facts using the preponderance standard at sentencing as long as the sentence is below the statutory maximum authorized by the jury's factual findings.

Because there are such a very large number of pre-*Apprendi* cases in the pipeline, the lower courts have struggled mightily with the questions of how this decision applies to cases on appeal and on collateral attack (raising issues such as whether the decision applies collaterally, when it is plain error, harmless error, etc.). The ruling is less problematic for the future, because it is not difficult for the government to charge and prove drug quantity and type at trial, or to resolve this issue as part of a plea agreement.

Page 310   Insert at the end of note 2.

---

[*] Note, however, that some courts do not label these facts "elements," reasoning that Congress did not intend them to be elements, even if the Constitution requires some heightened procedures. *Cf. United States v. Villarce*, 323 F.3d 435, 439 (6th Cir. 2003) (drug type and quantity are not elements for purposes of mens rea analysis).

The debate about the 100:1 crack to cocaine ratio has still not been resolved. In 2002 the Sentencing Commission provided a report to Congress, entitled COCAINE AND FEDERAL SENTENCING POLICY, that set forth recommendations for statutory and guideline modifications to the federal sentencing structure for cocaine offenses. By providing a recommendation rather than promulgating its own proposed legislation and guidelines–which might suggest a lack of deference to Congress on the underlying policy issues--the Commission seems to have been attempting to avoid a confrontation and to cultivate a more productive relationship with Congress. Unfortunately, this proposal has not garnered support, and the events surrounding the PROTECT Act of 2003 indicate that the relationship between the Commission and Congress is severely frayed.

The Commission's 2002 press release summarized its recommendations as follows:

The Sentencing Commission recommends that Congress adopt a three-pronged approach for revising federal cocaine sentencing policy:

(1) increase the quantity of crack cocaine required that triggers an automatic mandatory minium sentence. Specifically, the five-year mandatory minimum threshold quantity for crack cocaine offenses should be adjusted from the current 5 grams trigger to at least 25 grams and the current ten-year threshold quantity from 50 grams to at least 250 grams (and repeal the mandatory minimum for simple possession of crack cocaine);

(2) direct the Sentencing Commission to provide appropriate sentencing enhancements to increase penalties should the drug crime involve: (a) a dangerous weapon (including a firearm); (b) bodily injury resulting from violence; (c) distribution to protected individuals and/or locations; (d) repeat felony drug trafficking offenders; and (e) importation of drugs by offenders who do not perform a mitigating role in the offense; and

(3) maintain the current statutory minimum threshold quantities for powder cocaine offenses at 500 grams triggering the five-year mandatory minimum penalty and 5,000 grams for the ten-year mandatory minimum penalty (understanding that the contemplated specific guideline sentencing enhancements would effectively increase penalties for the more dangerous and more culpable powder cocaine offenders).

The recommendations, if adopted, would narrow the difference between average sentences for crack cocaine and powder cocaine offenses from 44 months to approximately one year. Specifically, the Commission estimates that the average sentence for crack cocaine offenses would decrease from 118 months to 95 months, and the average sentence for powder cocaine offenses would increase from 74 months to 83 months. Importantly, the guideline sentencing range based solely on drug quantity for crack cocaine offenses still would be significantly longer (approximately two-to-four times longer) than powder cocaine offenses involving equivalent drug quantities.

* * *

In justifying its recommendations, the Commission made the following major findings about cocaine offender profiles examined between fiscal years 1995 and 2000:

• Contrary to the general objective of the 1986 legislation to target "serious" and "major" traffickers, two-thirds of federal crack cocaine offenders were street-level dealers. Only 5.9 percent of federal crack cocaine offenders performed trafficking functions most consistent with the functions described in the legislative history of the Anti-Drug Abuse Act of 1986 as warranting a five-year penalty, and 15.2 percent performed trafficking functions most consistent with the functions described as warranting a ten-year penalty;

• The current penalty structure was based on beliefs about the association of crack cocaine offenses with certain harmful conduct – particularly violence – that are no longer accurate. In 2000, for example, three quarters of federal crack cocaine offenders had no personal weapon involvement, and only 2.3 percent discharged a weapon. Therefore, to the extent that the 100-to-1 drug quantity ratio was designed in part to account for this harmful conduct, it sweeps too broadly by treating all crack cocaine offenders as if they committed those more harmful acts, even though most crack cocaine offenders, in fact, had not;

• The negative effects of prenatal crack cocaine exposure are identical to the negative effects of prenatal powder cocaine exposure and are significantly less severe than previously believed;

• The overwhelming majority of offenders subject to the heightened crack cocaine penalties are black, about 85 percent in 2000. This has contributed to a widely held perception that the current penalty structure promotes unwarranted disparity based on race. Although this assertion cannot be scientifically evaluated, the Commission finds even the perception of racial disparity problematic because it fosters disrespect for and lack of confidence in the criminal justice system. These conclusions led the Commission to unanimously conclude that the various congressional objectives can be achieved more effectively by decreasing the 100-to-1 drug quantity ratio.

Page 316-17.   Insert at the end of the first paragraph of note 6.

Most circuits have now concluded that § 860 creates a separate offense rather than simply an enhancement provision. *See, e.g., United States v. Gonzalez-Rodriguez*, 239 F.3d 948 (8th Cir. 2001) (collecting cases).

7. Conviction under a piggy back statute may also have another very significant impact: barring the application of the so-called "safety valve" provision. *See, e.g., United States v. Kakatin*, 214 F.3d 1049 (9th Cir. 2000) (holding conviction under § 860 is not eligible for sentence reduction under the safety valve provision of 18 U.S.C. § 3553(f). The statutory criteria for the safety valve are described in note 3(a), *supra* at 42-43.

Page 338   **Insert at the end of note 5.**

If the defendant participated in large scale drug transactions, that may be sufficient to support a CCE conviction, even if there is no evidence that the defendant owned a great deal of property or had a luxurious lifestyle. *See, e.g., United States v. Henderson*, 2003 WL 22347008 (10th Cir. 2003) (upholding conviction of defendant who participated in drug transactions worth $486,000, despite his claim that he reinvested all sums to purchase additional drugs, owned only one significant asset, a Cadillac Escalade valued at $21,000 and no other luxury items, had $27,000 of debt, and had court-appointed counsel for his trial.)

Page 370   **Insert at the end of the notes.**

Alvarez-Machain was acquitted of murder, and subsequently brought suit under the Alien Tort Claims Act (ATCA) and the Federal Tort Claims Act seeking damages against the United States, DEA agents, former Mexican policemen, and Mexican civilians, alleging that his arrest violated his civil rights. The district court entered summary judgment against the Mexican policemen, substituted the United States for the DEA agents, and dismissed the FTCA claims. On appeal, the court heard the case en banc and affirmed in part, reversed in part, and remanded. In addition to the majority opinion, various members of the court filed a concurring opinion and two dissenting opinions, which in total take up 61 pages of the Federal Reporter. In summary, the court held, inter alia, that the abductors could be held liable for kidnapping under ATCA; the damages would determined by federal common law, rather than Mexican law; the abductors' liability was limited to the period from unlawful abduction until the lawful arrest in U.S.; the claims were not barred by the foreign activities exception to FTCA, headquarters doctrine, orintentional tort exception; and DEA officers were liable for false arrest. *Alvarez-Machain v. United States*, 331 F.3d 604 (9th Cir. 2003) (en banc), *petition for cert. filed*, 72 U.S.L.W. 3248, October 1, 2003, No. 03-485.

CHAPTER 10

CURRENCY REPORTING OFFENSES
AND MONEY LAUNDERING

Pages 397-98. Read in conjunction with the final paragraph on page 397, which carries over to 398.

Amendments to the sentencing guidelines that became effective at the end of 2001 have significantly reduced the incentive to charge other criminal conduct as money laundering to inflate the applicable penalties. Although the amendments increase the penalties for defendants who laundered funds derived from particularly serious criminal conduct (such as drug trafficking, crimes of violence, and fraud offenses that generate relatively high loss amounts), they decreases penalties for defendants who laundered funds derived from less serious underlying criminal conduct, such as small frauds. The amendments tie the offense levels for money laundering more closely to the underlying conduct that was the source of the criminally derived funds. They separate money laundering offenders into two categories for purposes of determining the base offense level. The base offense level for "direct" money launderers (who launder funds derived from their own criminal conduct) is the level for the underlying offense. In the case of "indirect" or "third party" launderers, who launder funds derived from the conduct of third parties for whose conduct they are not responsible, the base offense level is 8, plus an increase based on the value of the laundered funds. Then other adjustments are made, such as a six-level enhancement for third party money launderers who knew or believed that any of the laundered funds were the proceeds of, or were intended to promote, certain more serious underlying criminal conduct (specifically, drug trafficking, crimes of violence, offenses involving firearms, explosives, national security, terrorism, and the sexual exploitation of a minor). Finally, the new guidelines provide for a relatively small enhancement above the base level of the underlying offense to provide additional punishment for the money laundering: a one-level increase if the defendant was convicted under 18 U.S.C. § 1957, and a two-level increase if the defendant was convicted under 18 U.S.C. § 1956. The difference reflects the fact that § 1956 has a longer maximum statutory penalty than § 1957. The amended guidelines are reprinted *infra* at 167-174.

Page 398.   Insert at the end of the introduction.

In 2003 the Department of Justice released a report analyzing its money laundering and currency reporting prosecutions from 1994 through 2001. The report, which is available online at http://www.ojp.usdoj.gov/bjs/pub/pdf/mlo01.pdf found that prosecutions increased approximately 200 percent over the period in question. The report distinguished between money laundering and currency recording and reporting offenses. The number of defendants charged with money laundering rose from 1994 to 1998, and has since dropped. Currency reporting charges also peaked in 1998, and then decreased slightly. Most of the detailed information presented concerned 2001. In that year, 84% of the total prosecutions in which these offenses were the most serious charge were for money laundering; 74.5% were brought under 18 U.S.C. § 1956, and 9.5% under § 1957. Currency reporting offenses made up the remaining 16% of the cases: 9.1% were failure to file cases brought under 31 U.S.C. § 5316, and 6.4% were structuring cases brought under 31 U.S.C. § 5324. Businesses comprised less than 2% of money-laundering defendants in 2001. The 22 business defendants included auto dealerships, grocery stores, banks, furniture stores, restaurants, physicians' offices, and beauty shops. Although 79% of defendants convicted of money laundering received a prison term, only 40% of those convicted of currency reporting were sentenced to prison. Information was also provided regarding cases in which money laundering charges were filed as a secondary offense: in 90% of these cases the most serious offense was drug-related. Cases in which money laundering was a secondary charge also peaked in 1998. Money laundering cases have been geographically concentrated; nearly half of all matters were referred in six areas designated as High Intensity Financial Crime Areas by the Departments of Treasury and Justice.

The report also provides information about the investigation of money laundering offenses. From 1997 to 2001 the number of Suspicious Activity Reports increased 206%. The rate of filing varied enormously be geographic area. California, New York, and Nevada had the highest rates. The New York metropolitan area alone generated 14,000 Suspicious Activity Reports in fiscal years 1998 and 1999, with a reported aggregate amount of more than $33 billion.

Mariano-Florentino Cuellar has provided a comprehensive critique of the effectiveness of the current money laundering enforcement scheme, including not only prosecutions but also the rules administered by regulators and the detection systems run primarily by investigators. He concludes that the regime has limited effectiveness, involving the disproportionate imposition of severe penalties on predicate offenders who are easily detected, a limited capacity to detect a range of chargeable domestic and international offenses, and global diffusion that leaves authorities with room for both discretion and lax enforcement. *See* Mariano-Florentino Cuellar, *The Tenuous Relationship Between the Fight Against Money Laundering and the Disruption of Criminal Finance*, 93 J. CRIM. L. & CRIMINOLOGY 311 (2003). Cuellar served as Senior Advisor to the Under Secretary of the Treasury (Enforcement) from 1997-99.

Pages 398-402.   Section 1956 has been amended in several respects. The most important changes were part of the USA Patriot Act. Note that the Act also created a new money laundering offense, bulk cash smuggling, 18 U.S.C. § 5332, which prohibits the concealment and transfer of more than $10,000 across the border with the intent to evade reporting requirements.

Three changes in § 1956 are particularly significant. Each is at least partially a response to the threat of international terrorism.

- The definition of "financial institution" in subsection (c)(6) has been amended to include "any foreign bank" as defined in the International Banking Act of 1978.

- New offenses have been added to the list of specified unlawful activities (SUA'S) under subsection (c)(7), including the provision of material support to terrorists, foreign corruption, and computer fraud and abuse offenses. There are now over 250 SUA's.

- Subsection (b), governing civil penalties, has been revised extensively. Subsection (b)(1) includes a new reference to § 1957, and (b)(2)-(4) are new provisions creating long arm jurisdiction over foreign persons and financial institutions, and effectuating that authority by permitting pretrial restraining orders and the appointment of a federal receiver. Subsection (b) now provides as follows:

(b) Penalties.--

(1) In general.--Whoever conducts or attempts to conduct a transaction described in subsection (a)(1) or (a)(3), or section 1957, or a transportation, transmission, or transfer described in subsection (a)(2), is liable to the United States for a civil penalty of not more than the greater of--

(A) the value of the property, funds, or monetary instruments involved in the transaction; or

(B) $10,000.

(2) Jurisdiction over foreign persons.--For purposes of adjudicating an action filed or enforcing a penalty ordered under this section, the district courts shall have jurisdiction over any foreign person, including any financial institution authorized under the laws of a foreign country, against whom the action is brought, if service of process upon the foreign person is made under the Federal Rules of Civil Procedure or the laws of the country in which the foreign person is found, and--

(A) the foreign person commits an offense under subsection (a) involving a financial transaction that occurs in whole or in part in the United States;

(B) the foreign person converts, to his or her own use, property in which the United States has an ownership interest by virtue of the entry of an order of forfeiture by a court of the United States; or

(C) the foreign person is a financial institution that maintains a bank account at a financial institution in the United States.

(3) Court authority over assets.--A court described in paragraph (2) may issue a pretrial restraining order or take any other action necessary to ensure that any bank account or other property held by the defendant in the United States is available to satisfy a judgment under this section.

(4) Federal receiver.--

(A) In general.--A court described in paragraph (2) may appoint a Federal Receiver, in accordance with subparagraph (B) of this paragraph, to collect, marshal, and take custody, control, and possession of all assets of the defendant, wherever located, to satisfy a civil judgment under this subsection, a forfeiture judgment under section 981 or 982, or a criminal sentence under section 1957 or subsection (a) of this section, including an order of restitution to any victim of a specified unlawful activity.

(B) Appointment and authority.--A Federal Receiver described in subparagraph (A)--

(i) may be appointed upon application of a Federal prosecutor or a Federal or State regulator, by the court having jurisdiction over the defendant in the case;

(ii) shall be an officer of the court, and the powers of the Federal Receiver shall include the powers set out in section 754 of title 28, United States Code; and

(iii) shall have standing equivalent to that of a Federal prosecutor for the purpose of submitting requests to obtain information regarding the assets of the defendant--

(I) from the Financial Crimes Enforcement Network of the Department of the Treasury; or

(II) from a foreign country pursuant to a mutual legal assistance treaty, multilateral agreement, or other arrangement for international law enforcement assistance, provided that such requests are in accordance with the policies and procedures of the Attorney General.

For a general summary of the provisions of the *USA Patriot Act, see Broad Anti-Terrorism Package Passed by Congress, Signed By President*, 70 CRIM. L. REP. 93,

94-95 (2001). As this summary explains, many of the provisions of the Act were directed at the banking industry. One significant provision that was dropped before enactment was a measure in the House bill that would have made it a criminal offense to misrepresent a customer's identification when conducting a finacial transaction with a financial institution or opening an account with such an institution. *Id.*

Page 420.   **Insert at the end of note (d).**

For additional discussions of the tracing issue, see United States v. Braxtonbrown-Smith, 278 F.3d 1348, 1352-55 (D.C. Cir. 2002) (rejecting requirement of full tracing and reviewing cases from all circuits); Joseph R. Miller, Note, *Federal Money Laundering Crimes–Should Direct Tracing of Funds Be Required?*, 90 KY. L.J. 441 (2002).

Page 431.   **Insert at the end of note 5.**

A controversial "gatekeeper" proposal has been made to require lawyers and accountants who participate in the financial system to put systems in place to detect and prevent money laundering. The proposal is an outgrowth of the work of the Financial Action Task Force on Anti-Money Laundering (FATF), a group established at the G-7 in 1989 to combat money laundering more effectively. Twenty nine countries are now members of FATF. In May 2002 the FATF issued a report (a "consulting paper") including a "gatekeeper initiative" extending to lawyers and accountants. The Departments of Justice and Treasury have been working with the FATF to develop a recommendation on the role that U.S. attorneys may be required to play. The key elements under discussion are whether attorneys will be required to file suspicious activity reports when they engage in financial transactions on behalf of their clients and become aware of illegal client activity, as well as requirements that attorneys know their clients, and enquire about the source of the client's funds associated with any financial transaction. An American Bar Association Task Force strongly opposes the requirement that lawyers report suspicious activity reports as well as the "no tipping" rule that would also prevent lawyers from notifying their client if they provide such a report. The Task Force contends that such requirements would be contrary to the ethical rules governing lawyers, would impair client compliance with the law, and could ultimately undermine the fundamental principles underlying the United States legal system. The American Bar Association's Task Force Report is available online at http://www1.oecd.org/fatf/pdf/REV_US-AmericanBarAssn.pdf. The FATF may accept a Swiss proposal to narrow its gatekeeper proposal to apply to lawyers, notaries and independent legal professionals only when they "prepare for or carry out" transactions for their client concerning particular activities including buying and selling of real estate, and managing of client money, securities bank, savings or securities accounts, and buying and selling business entities. It appears that the term "prepare for" will not include giving legal advice. *See* Bruce Zagaris, *FATF Gatekeepers Likely to Settle on a Modified Swiss Version of the Law*, 19 (No. 7) INT'L ENFORCEMENT L. REP. 249 (2003), *available on Westlaw at* 19 No.7 INTELREP 249.

CHAPTER 11

RICO–THE RACKETEER INFLUENCED AND CORRUPT ORGANIZATIONS STATUTE

Page 435.   **Add a fourth bullet.**

● Is the RICO statute potentially an effective weapon to use against terrorist organizations? [The USA PATRIOT Act, Pub. Law 107-56, enacted in the wake of the terrorist attacks of September 11 2001, amended section 1961 by adding specific terrorist offenses (see infra, the next note) to the existing long list of offenses in that section.]

Page 436.   **18 U.S.C. § 1961 has been amended. Add the following at the end of the paragraph after "financial gain," but before the semi-colon.**

", or (G) any act that is indictable under any provision listed in section 2332b(g)(5)(B)"

Page 449.   **Replace note 10 with the following:**

10. The First and Second Circuits have also rejected the *Bledsoe* court's ascertainable structure requirement. *See United States v. Patrick*, 248 F.3d 11 (1st Cir. 2001) ("While 'enterprise' and 'pattern of racketeering activity' are separate elements of a RICO offense, proof of these two elements need not be separate. . . . Since . . . [criminal enterprises] may not observe the niceties of legitimate organizational structures, we refuse to import an 'ascertainable structure' requirement into jury instructions."); *United States v. Coonan*, 938 F.2d 1553, 1559 (2d Cir. 1991) ("Common sense suggests that the existence of an association-in-fact is oftentimes more readily proven by what it does, rather than by an abstract analysis of structure."); *see also United States v. Mazzei*, 700 F.2d 85 (2d Cir. 1983).

Page 461.   **Change the word "Note" to "Notes". Before the words "In 1994," insert "1." Add after the first full paragraph.**

In 2003, after a jury verdict in favor of the plaintiffs in *NOW v. Scheidler* case, the matter returned to the United States Supreme Court. The Court held that the defendant protestors did not obtain property from the plaintiffs and therefore did not commit extortion under the Hobbs Act. The Court stated: "We further hold that our determination with respect to extortion under the Hobbs Act renders insufficient the other bases or predicate acts of racketeering supporting the jury's conclusion that petitioners violated RICO. Therefore, we reverse ....″ *Scheidler v. NOW*, 537 U.S. 393 (2003). For further discussion of the Court's treatment of the obtaining property issue under the Hobbs Act, see infra, p.

Page 461.   Revise B. to read: THE 'PERSON' WHO MAY BE CHARGED AS A RICO DEFENDANT: MORE ON DISTINGUISHING BETWEEN THE 'PERSON' AND THE 'ENTERPRISE'

Page 462.   Insert following Note 6.

Cedric Kushner Promotions Ltd. v. King
533 U.S. 158 (2001)

Justice Breyer delivered the opinion of the Court.

This case focuses upon a person who is the president and sole shareholder of a closely held corporation. The plaintiff claims that the president has conducted the corporation's affairs through the forbidden "pattern," though for present purposes it is conceded that, in doing so, he acted within the scope of his authority as the corporation's employee. In these circumstances, are there two entities, a "person" and a separate "enterprise"? Assuming, as we must given the posture of this case, that the allegations in the complaint are true, we conclude that the "person" and "enterprise" here are distinct and that the RICO provision applies.

Petitioner, Cedric Kushner Promotions, Ltd., is a corporation that promotes boxing matches. Petitioner sued Don King, the president and sole shareholder of Don King Productions, a corporation, claiming that King had conducted the boxing-related affairs of Don King Productions in part through a RICO "pattern," *i.e.,* through the alleged commission of at least two instances of fraud and other RICO predicate crimes. ... In the appellate court's view, § 1962(c) applies only where a plaintiff shows the existence of two separate entities, a "person" and a distinct "enterprise," the affairs of which that "person" improperly conducts. In this instance, "it is undisputed that King was an employee" of the corporation Don King Productions and also "acting within the scope of his authority." Under the Court of Appeals' analysis, King, in a legal sense, was part of, not separate from, the corporation. There was no "person," distinct from the "enterprise," who improperly conducted the "enterprise's affairs." ...

Other Circuits, applying § 1962(c) in roughly similar circumstances, have reached a contrary conclusion. We granted certiorari to resolve the conflict. We now agree with these Circuits and hold that the Second Circuit's interpretation of § 1962(c) is erroneous.

... The Act says that it applies to "person[s]" who are "employed by or associated with" the "enterprise." § 1962(c). In ordinary English one speaks of employing, being employed by, or associating with others, not oneself. ...In addition, the Act's purposes are consistent with that principle. Whether the Act seeks to prevent a person from victimizing, say, a small business, ... or to prevent a person from using a corporation for criminal purposes, the person and the victim, or the person and the tool, are different entities, not the same.

The [Government] reads § 1962(c) "to require some distinctness between the RICO defendant and the RICO enterprise." And it says that this requirement is "legally sound and workable." We agree with its assessment, particularly in light of the fact that 12 Courts of Appeals have interpreted the statute as embodying some such distinctness requirement without creating discernible mischief in the administration of RICO. ... Indeed, this Court previously has said that liability "depends on showing that the defendants conducted or participated in the conduct of the 'enterprise's affairs,' not just their *own* affairs." *Reves v. Ernst & Young,* 507 U.S. 170, 185, 113 S.Ct. 1163, 122 L.Ed.2d 525 (1993).

While accepting the "distinctness" principle, we nonetheless disagree with the appellate court's application of that principle to the present circumstances-- circumstances in which a corporate employee, "acting within the scope of his authority," allegedly conducts the corporation's affairs in a RICO-forbidden way. The corporate owner/employee, a natural person, is distinct from the corporation itself, a legally different entity with different rights and responsibilities due to its different legal status. And we can find nothing in the statute that requires more "separateness" than that. ...

Linguistically speaking, an employee who conducts the affairs of a corporation through illegal acts comes within the terms of a statute that forbids any "person" unlawfully to conduct an "enterprise," particularly when the statute explicitly defines "person" to include "any individual ... capable of holding a legal or beneficial interest in property," and defines "enterprise" to include a "corporation." 18 U.S.C. §§ 1961(3), (4). And, linguistically speaking, the employee and the corporation are different "persons," even where the employee is the corporation's sole owner. After all, incorporation's basic purpose is to create a distinct legal entity, with legal rights, obligations, powers, and privileges different from those of the natural individuals who created it, who own it, or whom it employs. ... We note that the Second Circuit relied on earlier Circuit precedent for its decision. But that precedent involved quite different circumstances which are not presented here. ...

Further, to apply the RICO statute in present circumstances is consistent with the statute's basic purposes as this Court has defined them. The Court has held that RICO both protects a legitimate "enterprise" from those who would use unlawful acts to victimize it, *United States v. Turkette,* 452 U.S. 576, 591, 101 S.Ct. 2524, 69 L.Ed.2d 246 (1981), and also protects the public from those who would unlawfully use an "enterprise" (whether legitimate or illegitimate) as a "vehicle" through which "unlawful ... activity is committed," *National Organization for Women, Inc., supra,* at 259, 114 S.Ct. 798. A corporate employee who conducts the corporation's affairs through an unlawful RICO "pattern ... of activity," § 1962(c), uses that corporation as a "vehicle" whether he is, or is not, its sole owner. Conversely, the appellate court's critical legal distinction--between employees acting within the scope of corporate authority and those acting outside that authority--is inconsistent with a basic statutory purpose. ... It would immunize from RICO liability many of those at whom this Court has said RICO directly aims-- *e.g.,* high-ranking individuals in an illegitimate criminal enterprise, who, seeking to further the purposes of that enterprise, act within the scope of their authority.

...

Finally, we have found nothing in the statute's history that significantly favors an alternative interpretation. That history not only refers frequently to the importance of undermining organized crime's influence upon legitimate businesses but also refers to the need to protect the public from those who would run "organization[s] in a manner detrimental to the public interest." S.Rep. No. 91-617, at 82. This latter purpose, as we have said, invites the legal principle we endorse, namely, that in present circumstances the statute requires no more than the formal legal distinction between "person" and "enterprise" (namely, incorporation) that is present here.

In reply, King argues that the lower court's rule is consistent with (1) the principle that a corporation acts only through its directors, officers, and agents, (2) the principle that a corporation should not be liable for the criminal acts of its employees where Congress so intends, Brief for Respondents 20-21, and (3) the Sherman Act principle limiting liability under 15 U.S.C. § 1 by excluding "from unlawful combinations or conspiracies the activities of a single firm," *Copperweld Corp. v. Independence Tube Corp., 467 U.S. 752, 769-770, n. 15, 104 S.Ct. 2731, 81 L.Ed.2d 628 (1984).* The alternative that we endorse, however, is no less consistent with these principles. It does not deny that a corporation acts through its employees; it says only that the corporation and its employees are not legally identical. It does not assert that ordinary *respondeat superior* principles make a corporation legally liable under RICO for the criminal acts of its employees; that is a matter of congressional intent not before us. See, *e.g., Gasoline Sales, Inc., 39 F.3d, at 73* (holding that corporation cannot be "vicariously liable" for § 1962(c) violations committed by its vice president). Neither is it inconsistent with antitrust law's intracorporate conspiracy doctrine; that doctrine turns on specific antitrust objectives. See *Copperweld Corp., supra, at 770-771, 104 S.Ct. 2731.* Rather, we hold simply that the need for two distinct entities is satisfied; hence, the RICO provision before us applies when a corporate employee unlawfully conducts the affairs of the corporation of which he is the sole owner--whether he conducts those affairs within the scope, or beyond the scope, of corporate authority.

...

Notes

1. What is the difference, if any, between Judge Posner's decision in *McCullough v. Suter*, supra, note 5, p. 462 and the decision in the *Cedric Kushner* case?

2. What is the difference, if any, between the *Cedric Kushner* decision and the decision in the *Fitzgerald* case, *infra.*

Page 465.   **Add the following as note 1 and renumber existing note 1 as 2:**

1. In the *Cedric Kushner* case, Justice Breyer also stated: "This case concerns a claim that a corporate employee is the "person" and the corporation is the "enterprise." It is natural to speak of a corporate employee as a "person employed by" the corporation. § 1962(c). The earlier Second Circuit precedent concerned a claim that a corporation was the "person" and the corporation, together with all its employees and agents, were the "enterprise." See *Riverwoods Chappaqua Corp. v. Marine Midland Bank, N. A.,* 30 F.3d 339, 344 (1994) (affirming dismissal of complaint). It is less natural to speak of a corporation as "employed by" or "associated with" this latter oddly constructed entity. ..."

Page 466. Add the following as notes 3 and 4 and renumber existing notes 2 and 3 as notes 5 and 6.

3. For a narrow interpretation of the *Fitzgerald* holding, see *Majchrowski v. Norwest Mortgage, Inc.*, 6 F. Supp. 2d 946 (N.D. Ill. 1998):

> The complaints in [*Fitzgerald*, and *Emery*] were not defective simply because the RICO person and enterprise were related corporate entities functioning in a hierarchical structure. Rather, they failed because either (1) the entities in the RICO enterprise did not have a role in facilitating or masking the RICO person's alleged fraud or (2) the RICO person had no role in the alleged fraud perpetrated by its agents. Consequently, the RICO persons in these cases were held to be conducting only their own affairs. As shown in *Fitzgerald* and *Emery*, the problem in general with parent-person and subsidiary-enterprise pleading is that subsidiaries conduct the affairs of their parent not vice versa. *Id.* at 956.

4. Not all courts have agreed with the *Majchrowski* reading of *Fitzgerald*. *See Bachman v. Bear, Stearns & Co.*, 178 F. 3d 930, 932 (7th Cir. 1999) ("A firm and its employees, or a parent and its subsidiaries, are not an enterprise separate from the firm itself. To add the corporations to . . . their employees . . . is thus to add nothing"); *Bodtker v. Forest City Trading Group*, 1999 WL 778583, at 9 (disagreeing explicitly with *Majchrowski*'s interpretation of *Fitzgerald* and *Emery*).

NOTE ON THE USE OF AIDING & ABETTING LIABILITY
IN CONNECTION WITH THE REVES DOCTRINE

Reves involved the question of whether an accounting firm that provided auditing information to a corporation could be held liable for a §1962(c) RICO violation as a "person...associated with ...[the] enterprise [that is, the corporation]...." The *Reves'* test was used to determine the liability of "person" under the language of § 1962(c); it thus addressed the liability of a principal in a RICO violation. Reves established that in order to violate the statute as a principal, one must participate in the operation or management of the enterprise.

Suppose, however, that a criminal prosecutor charges an accounting firm or a law firm (or any similar outside-of-the-enterprise operation that provides a service to the enterprise) not as a principal in a RICO violation but rather as an aider and abettor? If a RICO violation is a substantive criminal crime, one would assume that ordinary accomplice liability applies to it. An accomplice is one who, (using the Model Penal Code formulation) "with the purpose of promoting or facilitating the commission of the offense...aids...[an]other person in planning or committing it...." Even though Arthur Young, the auditing firm, did not participate in the operation or management of the enterprise, might the firm nevertheless be held criminally liable as an aider and abettor to the violation of the RICO statute by Jack White, the general manager, who would be, under this revised theory of the case, the RICO "person"? (There is, of course, a question as to what mens rea is required to be an accomplice in this setting. We return to that issue below.)

The plaintiff in *Reves* did not use an aiding and abetting theory in pursuing the action. Why not? The answer probably lies in a difference between civil and criminal RICO. Until now, we have generally assumed equivalence between civil and criminal RICO, although it has been suggested earlier (note 5, p. 474) that there may be different leeways of interpretation at work in the two arenas.

The aider and abettor theory under which Arthur Young might be held *criminally* liable for a violation of §1962(c) requires invocation of two provisions of Title 18 of the United States Code, §1962(c) (the RICO provision) and § 2. Section 2 provides "Whoever... aids, abets... commission [of an offense against the United States] is punishable as a principal."

Section 1964(c), Title 18, U.S.C., provides that any "person injured in his business or property by reason of a violation of section 1962... may sue therefore...." A *civil* RICO action is thus based on a violation of § 1962. If in order to find civil liability under RICO, one must also rely on § 2 of Title 18, is § 1964 (c) applicable? Stating the issue another way, do RICO civil suits relying on § 1962(c) extend to aiders and abettors? The issue in part is an issue of statutory interpretation. Do the words "by reason of a violation of section 1962" carry with them the implication that liability based on § 2 is included within the words "a violation of section 1962"? If the civil liability is based in § 1962(a), the issue may be different since 1962(a) mentions § 2.

The aiding and abetting-RICO case law involving aiding and abetting issues typically consists of civil suits, not criminal prosecutions.

Penn. Ass'n of Edwards Heirs v. Rightenhour
235 F.3d 839 (3d Cir. 2000)

FUENTES, Circuit Judge:

Appellant Pennsylvania Association of Edwards Heirs ("the Association") appeals from a grant of summary judgment dismissing its complaint, which alleged that Wachovia Bank of Georgia ("Wachovia Bank") aided and abetted in the commission of a RICO violation. In *Rolo v. City Investing Co. Liquidating Trust*, 155 F.3d 644 (3d Cir.1998), we extended the Supreme Court's reasoning in *Central Bank of Denver v. First Interstate Bank of Denver*, 511 U.S. 164, 114 S.Ct. 1439, 128 L.Ed.2d 119 (1994), to RICO, and held that, because RICO's statutory text does not provide for a private cause of action for aiding and abetting and 18 U.S.C. § 2 cannot be used to imply this private right, no such cause of action exists under RICO. Appellant argues that our holding in *Rolo* leaves open the possibility that a civil aiding and abetting RICO claim could be recognized as a common law civil remedy. We disagree, and hold that *Rolo's* holding extends as well to common law-based RICO civil aiding and abetting claims. Therefore, we will affirm.

I.

The Association is a non-profit corporation dedicated to pursuing a proper settlement of the ancient estate of a Welsh seaman, Robert Edwards, who allegedly owned a significant portion of lower Manhattan, including some areas in Wall Street, that never passed to his rightful heirs. This claim dates back to the initial Dutch and British settlers who formed a colony in lower Manhattan, well before the nation's founding. The Association raised funds through membership contributions by 3,200 prospective heirs, who each paid $450 to buy an equal share of the professed $24 billion estate. The Association raised a large portion of its membership contributions between 1983 and 1985 when former officers solicited alleged heirs.

By the spring of 1988, the Association discovered that some of its former officers had depleted all of the membership fees for unintended purposes. After electing new officers, the Association began an effort to trace and recoup the money. They discovered that the most significantly involved financial institution was the North Georgia Savings and Loan Association, a predecessor to Wachovia Bank, in which over $300,000 in membership fees had been deposited between 1984 and 1986. The Association contended that Wachovia Bank had aided and abetted the Association's former officers with misappropriating membership funds in violation of the Racketeer Influenced and Corrupt Organizations Act ("RICO"), 18 U.S.C. §§

1962(b), (c), and (d). Specifically, the Association claimed that Wachovia Bank had aided and abetted RICO predicate acts of mail and wire fraud in violation of 18 U.S.C. §§ 1341 and 1343, and further conspired to commit money laundering and the laundering of monetary instruments contrary to 18 U.S.C. §§ 1956 and 1957.

According to the Association, its vice-president at the time, a local Baptist preacher named Douglas Wayne Edwards, had a close and personal relationship with the financial institution's president. The Association alleged that Edwards and the Association's treasurer, David Paul Rightenour, wrongly applied for, and received, personal loans from Wachovia Bank's predecessor by using as collateral certificates of deposit belonging to the Association. Allegedly, when Edwards and Rightenour defaulted on the loans, Wachovia Bank's predecessor improperly cashed the certificates and used the proceeds to satisfy any outstanding loan debt. In addition, the Association claimed that $50,000 of a cashed certificate, the proceeds of which were at least partly paid over to Edwards, remained unaccounted. In sum, the Association alleged that Wachovia Bank allowed itself to be used as a conduit by aiding and abetting the fraudulent schemes of its former officers, resulting in the dissipation of nearly $1.5 million in membership contributions.

After having unsuccessfully applied for summary judgment on timeliness grounds, Wachovia Bank filed a second summary judgment motion arguing that the Association's claim against it was barred because no private cause of action exists under RICO for aiding and abetting. This argument was based on a case we decided during the course of the litigation, *Rolo v. City Investing Co. Liquidating Trust*, 155 F.3d 644 (3d Cir.1998), which extended the Supreme Court's reasoning in *Central Bank of Denver v. First Interstate Bank of Denver*, 511 U.S. 164, 114 S.Ct. 1439, 128 L.Ed.2d 119 (1994).

In *Central Bank*, 511 U.S. at 177, 191, 114 S.Ct. 1439, the Supreme Court had ruled that private aiding and abetting suits were not authorized by § 10(b) of the Securities Exchange Act of 1934, 15 U.S.C. § 78j. In *Rolo*, 155 F.3d at 656-57, we applied similar reasoning in the RICO context, ruling that a private plaintiff could not maintain a claim of aiding and abetting an alleged RICO violation. The Association responded by relying upon *Jaguar Cars, Inc. v. Royal Oaks Motor Car Co.*, 46 F.3d 258 (3d Cir.1995), which had been decided after *Central Bank*, but before *Rolo*, and dealt with a RICO aiding and abetting claim on the merits. The Association argued that a conflict exists in this circuit between *Jaguar Cars* and *Rolo*, which should be resolved by rejecting *Rolo*.

In an order entered March 22, 1999, the District Court concluded that *Rolo* was controlling and granted summary judgment in favor of Wachovia Bank. The Court further opined that, to the extent a conflict existed, we would have to resolve it.

...

III.

A.

Prior to *Central Bank*, private aiding and abetting claims relating to § 10(b) of the Securities Exchange Act were widely thought to be legitimate.

> In hundreds of judicial and administrative proceedings in every Circuit in the federal system, the courts and the SEC have concluded that aiders and abettors are subject to liability under § 10(b).... While we have reserved decision on the legitimacy of the theory in two cases that did not present it, all 11 Courts of Appeals to have considered the question have recognized a private cause of action against aiders and abettors under § 10(b)....*Central Bank*, 511 U.S. at 192, 114 S.Ct. 1439 (Stevens, J., dissenting).

However, the Supreme Court dramatically altered the landscape with its decision in *Central Bank*, wherein the majority ruled that, "[b]ecause the text of § 10(b) does not prohibit aiding and abetting, we hold that a private plaintiff may not maintain an aiding and abetting suit under § 10(b)." *Id.*

As the Supreme Court recognized, the judiciary had previously determined that private § 10(b) enforcement actions had been impliedly authorized from the statutory language. Beyond that, however, the Court emphasized that "[w]ith respect ... to ... the scope of conduct prohibited by § 10(b), the text of the statute controls our decision.... We have refused to allow [§ 10(b)] challenges to conduct not prohibited by the text of the statute." *Id.* at 173, 114 S.Ct. 1439. Thus, the Supreme Court directed that "the statutory text controls the definition of conduct covered by § 10(b)." *Id.* at 175, 114 S.Ct. 1439. Applying this paradigm, the Court wrote:

> Congress knew how to impose aiding and abetting liability when it chose to do so. If ... Congress intended to impose aiding and abetting liability, we presume it would have used the words "aid" and "abet" in the statutory text. But it did not.
>
> We reach the uncontroversial conclusion, accepted even by those courts recognizing a § 10(b) aiding and abetting cause of action, that the text of the 1934 Act does not itself reach those who aid and abet a § 10(b) violation. Unlike those courts, however, we think that conclusion resolves the case. It is inconsistent with settled methodology in § 10(b) cases to extend liability beyond the scope of conduct prohibited by the statutory text. To be sure, aiding and abetting a wrongdoer ought to be actionable in certain instances. The issue, however, is not whether imposing private civil liability on aiders and abettors is good policy but whether aiding and abetting is covered by the statute.
>
> .... The [§ 10(b)] proscription does not include giving aid to a person who commits a manipulative or deceptive act. We cannot amend the statute to create liability for acts that are not themselves manipulative or deceptive within the meaning of the statute. *Id.* at 177-78, 114 S.Ct. 1439.

In reaching this holding, the majority also addressed and discounted numerous arguments, including policy considerations, that would have supported a civil aiding and abetting claim relevant to § 10(b).

B.

Several years later, in *Rolo v. City Investing Co. Liquidating Trust*, we affirmed the dismissal of a private plaintiff's RICO aiding and abetting claim because we were "convinced that a private cause of action for aiding and abetting a RICO violation cannot survive the Supreme Court's decision in [*Central Bank*]." *Rolo*, 155 F.3d at 656. After briefly reviewing *Central Bank*'s reasoning, we concluded "that the same analysis controls our construction of the civil RICO provision." *Id.* at 657.

Like § 10(b), the text of [RICO] § 1962 itself contains no indication that Congress intended to impose private civil aiding and abetting liability under RICO....

... [D]espite the existence of cogent policy arguments in support of extending civil liability to aiders and abettors of RICO violations, under [*Central Bank*], we must "interpret and apply the law as Congress has written it, and not imply private causes of action merely to effectuate the purported purposes of the statute." Because the text of the RICO statute does not encompass a private cause of action for aiding and abetting a RICO violation, "in accordance with the policies articulated in *Central Bank of Denver*", we have no authority to imply one. On this basis, we will affirm the district court's dismissal of the RICO claims....

We find this reasoning as fully persuasive today as when we decided *Rolo*, and therefore, reject the Association's argument.

As the *Rolo* panel persuasively explained, no conflict really exists. In justifying its holding that, after *Central Bank*, aiding and abetting liability under RICO was no longer available, the *Rolo* court wrote:

> [W]e reach this result despite our discussion of aiding and abetting liability in *Jaguar Cars*, a case decided after [*Central Bank*]. See 46 F.3d at 270. *In Jaguar Cars, the opinion did not address the impact of [Central Bank] on earlier cases that had recognized a private cause of action for aiding and abetting under RICO.* The decision in *Jaguar Cars* focused on whether there had been sufficient evidence to find the defendant liable for aiding and abetting a RICO violation. *See* 46 F.3d at 270. The parties did not challenge the existence of a cause of action for aiding and abetting, and we did not raise the issue *sua sponte*. Although, under this Court's Internal Operating Procedures, we are bound by, and lack the authority to overrule, a published decision by a prior panel, *see* I.O.P. 9.1, *we conclude that the discussion of a private cause of action for aiding and abetting a RICO violation in Jaguar Cars does not control our analysis in this case. The decision in [Central Bank] was not called to the attention of the panel in Jaguar Cars, and the panel's opinion neither explicitly nor implicitly decided the impact of [Central Bank] on the continued availability of a private cause of action for aiding and abetting a RICO violation. Rolo,* 155 F.3d at 657 (emphasis added).

[A]cceptance of the Association's common law argument would fundamentally undermine the constrained approach to aiding and abetting liability that the Supreme Court set forth in _Central Bank_ and which we subsequently followed in _Rolo_. Moreover, the common law perspective is significantly undermined, if not totally discredited, by the Supreme Court's discussion in _Central Bank_ regarding the history of aiding and abetting liability.

> Aiding and abetting is an ancient criminal law doctrine. Though there is no federal common law of crimes, Congress in 1909 enacted what is now 18 U.S.C. § 2, a general aiding and abetting statute applicable to all federal criminal offenses. The statute decrees that those who provide knowing aid to persons committing federal crimes, with the intent to facilitate the crime, are themselves committing a crime.
>
> ....
>
> ... Congress has not enacted a general civil aiding and abetting statute-- either for suits by the Government (when the Government sues for civil penalties or injunctive relief) or for suits by private parties. Thus, when Congress enacts a statute under which a person may sue and recover damages from a private defendant for the defendant's violation of some statutory norm, _there is no general presumption that the plaintiff may also sue aiders and abettors._
>
> Congress instead has taken a statute-by-statute approach to civil aiding and abetting liability. _Central Bank_, 511 U.S. at 181-82, 114 S.Ct. 1439 (emphasis added and citations omitted).

The Supreme Court's language makes it abundantly clear that, in the absence of statutory authorization, there is no presumption in favor of recognizing a civil aiding and abetting claim. Therefore, we must reject the Association's argument that, under common law principles, a civil aiding and abetting claim must be recognized with respect to RICO.

With regard to the policy arguments, _Central Bank_ instructs that they are of no avail to the Association unless an unacceptably aberrant result would entail. ... The Association is unable to identify any such "bizarre" consequences of any merit. Thus, the controlling issue "is not whether imposing private civil liability on aiders and abettors is good policy but whether aiding and abetting is covered by the statute." _Central Bank_, 511 U.S. at 177, 114 S.Ct. 1439. In _Rolo_, we answered that inquiry in the negative with respect to the RICO statute. We accordingly adhere to our prior decision.

...

1. We had previously seen the *Jaguar Cars* case, discussed in *Edwards Heirs,* in note 2, p. 466 of the main text, where a different portion of the case is treated.

2. *Hayden v. Paul Weiss, Rifkind, Wharton & Garrison*, 955 F.Supp. 248 (S.D.N.Y. 1997) illustrates the interplay of the *Reves* doctrine with the aiding and abetting issue as well as related issues:

> In this case, plaintiffs concede, as they must, that their aiding and abetting claims under § 10(b) and Rule 10b-5 must be dismissed in light of the Supreme Court's holding in *Central Bank of Denver v. First Interstate Bank of Denver*.... Plaintiffs' primary RICO claims under 18 U.S.C. § 1962(c) must also be dismissed because plaintiffs have neither alleged nor presented facts permitting a rational inference that Price participated in the "operation or management" of a RICO enterprise....Indeed, it is well established that the provision of professional services by outsiders, such as accountants, to a racketeering enterprise, is insufficient to satisfy the participation requirement of RICO, since participation requires some part in directing the affairs of the enterprise itself. This remains true even if the accountants, such as Price, provided services which were essential to the success of the enterprise. ...
>
> Nor does RICO's proscription of participation "directly or indirectly" in a RICO enterprise give rise to private civil liability for aiding and abetting. The Court in *Central Bank* noted that § 10(b) and Rule 10b-5 employ the term "directly or indirectly" and expressly rejected the argument that this language creates a private right of action for aiding and abetting. *Central Bank*, 511 U.S. at 176. The Court reasoned that "aiding and abetting liability extends beyond persons who engage, even indirectly, in a proscribed activity; aiding and abetting liability reaches persons who do not engage in the proscribed activities *at all*, but who give a degree of aid to those who do." *Id*. (emphasis added). The Court adopted similar reasoning in *Reves*. *See Reves*, 507 U.S. at 179 (requiring affirmative directing of enterprise affairs before imposing RICO liability).
>
> Plaintiffs also argue that since civil liability under RICO turns on whether a criminal violation has occurred, that criminal concepts of aiding and abetting should be construed to be applicable to RICO even if they are not applicable to securities violations. However, this argument, if accepted, would undermine *Central Bank*, since its holding could be circumvented by the simple expedient of alleging a pattern of criminal securities law violations as predicate acts, and based upon that pattern seek to impose civil liability under RICO on the basis of aiding and abetting a RICO violation when, under *Central Bank*, that conduct could not be a basis for civil liability under the securities laws. In any event, since the arguments for inferring aiding and abetting liability under § 10(b) are stronger than in the

case of RICO because the common law doctrine of aiding and abetting is presumably more readily applied to a judicially implied cause of action under § 10(b) than a statutory right of action under RICO, the reasoning of *Central Bank* should have even more force when applied to RICO.

The *Hayden* case, *supra* note 2 also contained the following footnote discussion of another kind of interplay between *Reves* and aiding and abetting liability:

> Plaintiffs reliance upon *131 Main Street Associates v. Manko*, 897 F. Supp. 1507 (S.D.N.Y.1995) is also misplaced. In that case, the court held that aiding and abetting a violation of § 10(b) and Rule 10b-5 may constitute predicate acts for a primary RICO violation by those who manage the affairs of a RICO enterprise. The *Manko* court reasoned that even after *Reves,* a person who *operates or manages an enterprise*, but who merely aids or abets the commission of predicate acts, may still be liable for a RICO violation. Nothing in this case suggests that persons who do not participate in the operation or management of the enterprise are subject to civil liability merely because they aid or abet predicate acts.

Suppose civil RICO liability is based in § 1962 (d), that is, conspiring to violate one of the other subsections of 1962, let us say, § 1962(c). Is this a viable alternative to relying on aiding and abetting. Consider in this connection, *Salinas v. United States*, main text at p. 495 and particularly note 2, p. 499. Also consider the implications of *Salinas* and the material in note 2, p. 499 for the mens rea that an aider and abettor to a RICO violation must have in order to impose criminal liability.

For other recent decisions that have applied the effects of *Reves* and *Central Bank* on RICO aiding and abetting, see, e.g.: *Am. Automotive Accessories, Inc. v. Fishman*, 175 F.3d 534 (7th Cir. 1999); *Goldfine v. Sichenzia*, 118 F. Supp. 2d 392 (S.D.N.Y. 2000); *Jubelirer v. Mastercard Int'l, Inc.*, 68 F. Supp. 2d 1049 (W.D. Wis. 1999).

In response to *Central Bank*, Congress amended 15 U.S.C. § 78t. The statute, amended in 2000, reads as follows:

15 U.S.C. § 78t (2002)

Liability of controlling persons and persons who aid and abet violations.

(a) Joint and several liability; good faith defense

Every person who, directly or indirectly, controls any person liable under any provision of this chapter or of any rule or regulation thereunder shall also be liable jointly and severally with and to the same extent as such controlled person to any person to whom such controlled person is liable, unless the controlling person acted in good faith and did not directly or indirectly induce the act or acts constituting the violation or cause of action.

(b) Unlawful activity through or by means of any other person

It shall be unlawful for any person, directly or indirectly, to do any act or thing which it would be unlawful for such person to do under the provisions of this chapter or any rule or regulation thereunder through or by means of any other person.

* * *

(e) Prosecution of persons who aid and abet violations

* *[A]ny person that knowingly provides substantial assistance to another person in violation of a provision of this chapter, or of any rule or regulation issued under this chapter, shall be deemed to be in violation of such provision to the same extent as the person to whom such assistance is provided. * * *

What implications do you think this amendment has for the civil RICO aiding and abetting issue?

Page 486.   Add to note 2c.

The District of Columbia Circuit subsequently followed up the decision in *Edmondson* with *Western Assocs. Ltd. P'ship v. Mkt. Square Assocs.*, 235 F.3d 629, 636-37 (D.C. Cir. 2001), a decision that sheds further light on the notion of a single scheme and the length of time that is required for there to be a "pattern.":

Market Square is a mixed-use property in downtown Washington, D.C. that consists of office and retail space and residential condominium units. In 1985, Western, a District of Columbia limited partnership, formed Avenue Associates Limited Partnership ("Avenue Associates") to "develop, own, manage, and ultimately dispose of the Market Square Project." In 1987, Western invited Market Square Associates, a Washington, D.C. general partnership, to join Avenue Associates. Upon completion of the construction of the project, Western held a 30 percent limited partnership interest, and Market Square Associates owned a 67.5 percent limited partnership interest and a 2.5 percent general partnership interest.

In October 1997, Western filed suit in the United States District Court for the District of Columbia, alleging that beginning in 1988 and continuing for more than eight years thereafter, Market repeatedly violated partnership agreements, transmitted fraudulent accounting statements, and stole the value of Western's partnership interest. At the heart of the alleged fraud are alleged misrepresentations of expected costs and profits that Market made in budget projections for the Market Square project. According to the complaint, after Western was deceived into approving a fraudulent budget in 1989, Market covered up its misrepresentations by exaggerating the economic viability of the project in annual financial statements. ...

The following month, in November 1997, Western filed for an injunction to prevent Market from transferring some of its interests in the Market Square Project. Relying on Edmondson, the district court denied the request for an injunction, ruling that because Western had alleged a single scheme, a single discrete injury, and a single victim, Western had not demonstrated the requisite "pattern of racketeering activity" under § 1961(5) of the RICO Act, and thus, was unlikely to succeed on the merits.

Subsequently, Western filed an amended complaint, increasing the number of chemes and victims alleged. The amended complaint alleges that Market conspired to commit and engaged in four separate but related schemes to defraud Avenue Associates, Western, and the general and limited partners that make up Western. The four schemes consist of: (1) the Revised Budget-Approval Scheme; (2) the Cost-Shifting Scheme; (3) the Income Projection Scheme; and (4) the Going-Concern Scheme.

The four alleged schemes are briefly summarized as follows. (1) The Revised Budget-Approval Scheme was a plot to conceal cost overruns. According to the complaint, Market knew as early as April 1988 that the total cost of the project would exceed the original budget, and improperly approved and conspired to conceal cost increases. In August 1989, after 18 months, Market sent a revised budget to Western, knowing that the cost projections in this budget were also inaccurate. Western relied on the false representations in the revised budget and approved it in December 1989. (2) The Cost-Shifting Scheme addresses the priority of allocations and the continuing cost increases. The partnership's budgets called for costs to be divided into "guaranteed" and "non-guaranteed" categories, and prohibited guaranteed cost overruns from being repaid from partnership cash flow.

According to the complaint, Market circumvented these accounting restrictions by shifting guaranteed cost items into the non-guaranteed category, used improperly authorized optional loans to cover these cost increases, and repaid these loans out of partnership distributions. This fraudulent scheme was concealed by annual financial statements mailed to Western each year between 1990 and 1996. (3) The Income Projection Scheme arises from Market's attempt to conceal the impact of the budget overruns. According to the complaint, in 1992, in a series of financial documents, Market falsely represented the expected revenues from Market Square over the next 15 years, overstated the value the cost increases had added to the project, and deceived Western regarding the partnership's debt. …(4) The Going-Concern Scheme relates to a failure to provide honest annual accounting statements. The complaint alleges that from 1994 to 1996, Market sent Western financial statements that omitted a "going-concern clause," in an effort to conceal Avenue Associates' burdensome debt.
…

The district court granted Market's motion to dismiss ….

Edmondson identified six factors that a court should consider "in deciding whether a [RICO] pattern has been established." These factors are: "the number of unlawful acts, the length of time over which the acts were committed, the similarity of the acts, the number of victims, the number of perpetrators, and the character of the unlawful activity." Edmondson does not establish a rigid test, but rather presents a flexible guide for analyzing RICO allegations on a case by case basis. The court in Edmondson acknowledged that in some cases "some factors will weigh so strongly in one direction as to be dispositive." Id. The court also indicated that if a plaintiff alleges only a single scheme, a single injury, and few victims it is "virtually impossible for plaintiffs to state a RICO claim." Id.
Analyzing the allegations of the amended complaint through the six-factor lens of Edmondson inexorably leads to the conclusion that Western failed to state a legally cognizable claim under RICO. Edmondson provides a compelling analogy because Western has alleged only a single scheme, a single injury, and a single victim (or single set of victims). Thus, Western has failed to satisfy the continuity prong of RICO's "pattern of racketeering activity" requirement.

…Western's four-scheme division appears specious on its face. Comparing the amended complaint with the original complaint further demonstrates that Western's four purported schemes are merely a cosmetic disguise of a single scheme. The amended complaint simply subdivides Western's initial allegations.

It is true that depending on the specific circumstances a single scheme may suffice for purposes of RICO. The Supreme Court in H.J. Inc. rejected the idea that multiple schemes must be proved to establish a pattern of racketeering activity. See H.J. Inc., 492 U.S. at 240, 109 S.Ct. 2893. Our holding in Edmondson is not to the contrary. See Edmondson, 48 F.3d at 1265. The Supreme Court also emphasized that the concept of a racketeering "scheme" does not appear in the RICO statute, and indicated that it should be applied with caution because it is amorphous, highly elastic, and subject to "the level of generality at which criminal activity is viewed." H.J. Inc., 492 U.S. at 241 n. 3, 109 S.Ct. 2893. However, the number of schemes alleged remains a useful consideration. For example, the Supreme Court in H.J. Inc. stated that "proof that a RICO defendant has been involved in multiple criminal schemes would certainly be highly relevant to the inquiry into the continuity of the defendant's racketeering activity." Id. at 240, 109 S.Ct. 2893.

The instant case serves as an example of a vain attempt to make a RICO claim seem more viable by parsing one scheme into multiple schemes Western's subdivision of Market's alleged fraudulent activity is unavailing because the four schemes are so similar in nature and purpose (i.e., they involve contested bookkeeping entries), and they resulted in a single harm rather than separate injuries. For the term "scheme" to retain any utility, it cannot be so easily invoked that it allows such closely related accounting misrepresentations involving a single project to be considered distinct schemes. ...

Western's allegations of multiple victims are dubious for similar reasons. By alleging harm to each individual member of its partnership, Western has again artificially subdivided an aspect of its allegations in a transparent effort to make Market's alleged fraudulent conduct seem more expansive. For the purposes of RICO pattern analysis, this set of victims should be viewed as a single victim...To the extent that Western's partners were injured, they were injured indirectly, which does not make them individual victims under RICO.
Furthermore, the concept of a single set of victims is distinct from a class of victims who are all similarly and directly injured, and who should not be considered to be a single victim. For example, in H.J. Inc. the class of victims was thousands of customers who were each directly injured by a telephone company accused of charging unreasonable rates. Similarly, the single injury to Western was its diminished partnership interest, and Western does not appear to have alleged multiple injuries.

Consequently, Western can meet the RICO pattern requirement only if it is able to effectively distinguish Edmondson. Western's primary contention in that regard focuses on the length of time during which Market mailed and faxed alleged financial misrepresentations. The amended complaint alleges dozens of predicate acts extending continually over an eight-year period, in contrast with Edmondson, where the predicate acts extended only over three years, with most of the acts occurring in a one-month period. Western relies on the Supreme Court's statement that "continuity is centrally a temporal concept," H.J. Inc., 492 U.S. at 242, 109 S.Ct. 2893, in maintaining that the time difference between the two fact patterns is sufficient to establish a dispositive difference. According to Western, the district court misinterpreted Edmondson by not regarding the length of time over which the predicate acts occurred as the most important factor in its analysis.

This line of reasoning is unpersuasive for at least two reasons: it distorts both Supreme Court and D.C. Circuit precedent. ..Western misinterprets H.J. Inc. to the extent that it claims that time is such an important factor that an eight-year span must create a viable RICO action. As the district court explained, "[t]he mere longevity of a scheme or schemes does not necessarily mean that a 'pattern of racketeering activity' is present." H.J. Inc. requires that predicate acts be committed over a period longer than "a few weeks or months," but an eight-year time period, though highly relevant, is not dispositive. Even if temporal length was supposed to be the most heavily weighted factor in the multi-faceted Edmondson analysis (an assumption that is not necessarily mandated by H.J. Inc.), it may be trumped by other factors of the Edmondson analysis. Although H.J. Inc. stresses that RICO is directed towards "long- term criminal conduct," id., it also makes plain that a pattern can be defined with "reference to a range of different ordering principles or relationships between predicates, within the expansive bounds set." Id. at 239, 109 S.Ct. 2893.

Finally, not to be overlooked is the character of the alleged racketeering activity. The amended complaint describes a business dispute about cost and income projections, and the priority of allocations, rather than a wide-ranging series of extensive criminal schemes. Market's conduct can basically be characterized as beginning with fraudulent budget underestimates, with the subsequent predicate acts serving as attempts to cover up or shift the debt burden caused by cost overruns. Additionally, many of the predicate acts consist of mailings of annual financial reporting statements that Market was ostensibly obligated to provide to Western. ...

Neither the instant case nor Edmondson establishes a per se rule for RICO pattern analysis. Instead, the court continues to endorse a case-by-case, fact-specific approach. The six factors prescribed in Edmondson should be applied in a manner that is fluid, flexible, and commonsensical, rather than rigid or formulaic. Holding that the district court did not err in ruling that Western failed to allege a pattern of racketeering activity is consistent with this method of analysis._ Accordingly, we affirm the order dismissing the complaint.

Page 495. **Add to note 4, in the mid-paragraph after "magnitude of the criminal operation?":**

See, e.g., United States v. Yeager, 210 F. 3d 1315 (11th Cir. 2000) (holding that a sentencing enhancement for a criminal's leadership role can be based on defendant's role in the over-all RICO conspiracy, and it is not necessary to find that defendant played a leadership role in the underlying drug conspiracy).

Page 499.   In note 2, first paragraph. Substitute 1962(d) for the references to 1964(d).

Page 500.   Delete existing note 3 and add as notes 3, 4 and 5.

3. In *Smith v. Berg*, 247 F.3d 532 (3d Cir. 2001), the Third Circuit changed its mind and adopted the majority position:

> *Reves* is not a conspiracy decision; its holding focuses solely on what is required to violate § 1962(c) as a principle in the first degree. *Reves* says nothing about the scope of § 1962(d).
>
> In *Salinas*, the defendant was charged with criminal violations of both section 1962(c) and section 1962(d) but convicted on the conspiracy charge alone. The Supreme Court resolved a conflict among the Courts of Appeals, finding--as had the majority of our sister Courts of Appeals--that a RICO conspiracy defendant need not himself commit or agree to commit predicate acts. In upholding the result in the *Salinas* case, the Supreme Court found that a violation of section 1962(c) was not a prerequisite to a violation of section 1962(d). Rather, the Court found that for purposes of conspiracy it "suffices that [defendant] adopt the goal of furthering or facilitating the criminal endeavor." Moreover, the Supreme Court provided an extensive discussion indicating that RICO's conspiracy section--section 1962(d)--is to be interpreted in light of the common law of criminal conspiracy and that all that is necessary for such a conspiracy is that the conspirators share a common purpose.
>
> Thus, as the District Court observed, *Salinas* makes "clear that § 1962(c) liability is not a prerequisite to § 1962(d) liability." The plain implication of the standard set forth in *Salinas* is that one who opts into or participates in a conspiracy is liable for the acts of his co-conspirators which violate section 1962(c) even if the defendant did not personally agree to do, or to conspire with respect to, *any* particular element. ...

In accord with the general principles of criminal conspiracy law, a defendant may be held liable for conspiracy to violate section 1962(c) if he knowingly agrees to facilitate a scheme which includes the operation or management of a RICO enterprise.

4. What led the Third Circuit to change its mind in *Berg,* supra? Did the court take account of the concern about rendering *Reves* "nugatory" raised in note 2 *supra*? Should it at least have discussed the issue?

5. The courts have permitted convictions and cumulative sentences when the same conduct is charged as both a RICO conspiracy and a violation of the general conspiracy statute, 18 U.S.C. § 371. *See, e.g., United States v. Barton,* 647 F.2d 224 (2d Cir. 1981). Cumulative sentences have also been allowed where other conspiracy charges are combined with a RICO conspiracy charge. *See, e.g., United States v. Kragness,* 830 F.2d 842 (8th Cir. 1987) (RICO conspiracy and various drug conspiracies); *United States v. Kimble,* 719 F.2d 1253 (5th Cir. 1983) (RICO conspiracy and civil rights conspiracy under 18 U.S.C. § 241). Regarding cumulative sentencing in RICO conspiracy cases, see Nancy L. Ickler, Note, *Conspiracy to Violate RICO: Expanding Traditional Conspiracy Law,* 58 NOTRE DAME L. REV. 587 (1983).

Can RICO conspiracies and general conspiracies have different statute of limitations dates? If so, it may then be possible to be prosecuted for RICO conspiracy after the statute of limitations for general conspiracy has passed. Is this a sound result? *See* Ellen Jancko-Baken, Note, *When Will the Idling Statute of Limitations Start Running in RICO Conspiracy Cases?*, 10 CARDOZO L. REV. 2167 (1989).

Page 510.   **Add to note 2.**

Complaints involving unions, either brought by union members against employers or brought by plaintiffs against the unions themselves, have proven particularly conducive to civil RICO claims, especially recently. *See,* e.g., *Tho Dinh Tran v. Alphonse Hotel Corp,* 281 F.3d 23 (2d Cir. 2002); *Wall v. Roman,* 18 Fed. Appx. 41 (2d Cir. 2001) (unpublished opinion); *Forbes v. Eagleson,* 228 F.3d 471 (3d cir. 2000).

Page 510.   **Add to note 5.**

Some courts have also construed civil RICO's statute of limitations to bar many claims by holding that civil RICO accrues at the time a plaintiff knew, or should have known, of his or her injury. *See Lares Group, II v. Tobin,* 221 F.3d 41 (1st Cir. 2000); *Scott v. Boos,* 215 F.3d 940 (9th Cir. 2000).

Page 511.   **Add as note 7 and renumber accordingly notes 8 through 12.**

7. In *Beck v. Prupis*, 529 U.S. 494, 120 S.Ct. 1608 (2000), the Court adopted a limitation on the use of conspiracy to violate the RICO statute as a basis for a civil RICO action:

> Justice <u>THOMAS</u> delivered the opinion of the Court.
> ...
>
> The question before us is whether a person injured by an overt act done in furtherance of a RICO conspiracy has a cause of action under § 1964(c), even if the overt act is not an act of racketeering. We conclude that such a person does not have a cause of action under § 1964(c).
> ...
>
> Petitioner, Robert A. Beck II, is a former president, CEO, director, and shareholder of Southeastern Insurance Group. Respondents...are former senior officers and directors of SIG
>
> Beginning in or around 1987, certain directors and officers of SIG, including respondents, began engaging in acts of racketeering....
>
> During most of the time he was employed at SIG, petitioner was unaware of these activities. In early 1988, however, petitioner discovered respondents' unlawful conduct and contacted regulators concerning the financial statements. Respondents then orchestrated a scheme to remove petitioner from the company. They hired an insurance consultant to write a false report suggesting that petitioner had failed to perform his material duties. The day after this report was presented to the SIG board of directors, the board fired petitioner, relying on a clause in his contract providing for termination in the event of an "inability or substantial failure to perform [his] material duties." Petitioner sued respondents, asserting, among other things, a civil cause of action under § 1964(c). In particular, petitioner claimed that respondents used or invested income derived from a pattern of racketeering activity to establish and operate an enterprise, in violation of § 1962(a); acquired and maintained an interest in and control of their enterprise through a pattern of racketeering activity, in violation of § 1962(b); engaged in the conduct of the enterprise's affairs through a pattern of racketeering activity, in violation of § 1962(c); and, most importantly for present purposes, conspired to commit the aforementioned acts, in violation of § 1962(d). With respect to this last claim, petitioner's theory was that his injury was proximately caused by an overt act--namely, the termination of his employment--done in furtherance of respondents' conspiracy, and that § 1964(c) therefore provided a cause of action.
>
> ...

We granted certiorari, 526 U.S. 1158, 119 S.Ct. 2046, 144 L.Ed.2d 213 (1999), to resolve a conflict among the Courts of Appeals on the question whether a person injured by an overt act in furtherance of a conspiracy may assert a civil RICO conspiracy claim under § 1964(c) for a violation of § 1962(d) even if the overt act does not constitute "racketeering activity." The majority of the Circuits to consider this question have answered it in the negative. Other Circuits have allowed RICO conspiracy claims where the overt act was, as in the instant case, merely the termination of employment, and was not, therefore, racketeering activity.

This case turns on the combined effect of two provisions of RICO that, read in conjunction, provide a civil cause of action for conspiracy. Section 1964(c) states that a cause of action is available to anyone "injured ... by reason of a violation of section 1962." Section 1962(d) makes it unlawful for a person "to conspire to violate any of the provisions of subsection (a), (b), or (c) of this section." To determine what it means to be "injured ... by reason of" a "conspir[acy]," we turn to the well-established common law of civil conspiracy.[6]

...

By the time of RICO's enactment in 1970, it was widely accepted that a plaintiff could bring suit for civil conspiracy only if he had been injured by an act that was itself tortious. ...

The principle that a civil conspiracy plaintiff must claim injury from an act of a tortious character was so widely accepted at the time of RICO's adoption as to be incorporated in the common understanding of "civil conspiracy." ...We presume, therefore, that when Congress established in RICO a civil cause of action for a person "injured ... by reason of" a "conspir[acy]," it meant to adopt these well-established common-law civil conspiracy principles.

...

---

[6] Petitioner suggests that we should look to criminal, rather than civil, common-law principles to interpret the statute. We have turned to the common law of criminal conspiracy to define what constitutes a violation of § 1962(d), see *Salinas v. United States*, 522 U.S. 52, 63-65, 118 S.Ct. 469, 139 L.Ed.2d 352 (1997), a mere violation being all that is necessary for criminal liability. This case, however, does not present simply the question of what constitutes a violation of § 1962(d), but rather the meaning of a civil cause of action for private injury by reason of such a violation. In other words, our task is to interpret §§ 1964(c) and 1962(d) in conjunction, rather than § 1962(d) standing alone. The obvious source in the common law for the combined meaning of these provisions is the law of civil conspiracy.

As at common law, a civil conspiracy plaintiff cannot bring suit under RICO based on injury caused by *any* act in furtherance of a conspiracy that might have caused the plaintiff injury. Rather, consistency with the common law requires that a RICO conspiracy plaintiff allege injury from an act that is analogous to an "ac[t] of a tortious character," see 4 Restatement (Second) of Torts § 876, Comment *b*, meaning an act that is independently wrongful under RICO. The specific type of act that is analogous to an act of a tortious character may depend on the underlying substantive violation the defendant is alleged to have committed. However, respondents' alleged overt act in furtherance of their conspiracy is not independently wrongful under any substantive provision of the statute. Injury caused by such an act is not, therefore, sufficient to give rise to a cause of action under § 1964(c).[10]

…

Petitioner … asserts that under our view of the statute, any person who had a claim for a violation of § 1962(d) would necessarily have a claim for a violation of § 1962(a), (b), or (c). However, contrary to petitioner's assertions, our interpretation of § 1962(d) does not render it mere surplusage. Under our interpretation, a plaintiff could, through a § 1964(c) suit for a violation of § 1962(d), sue co-conspirators who might not themselves have violated one of the substantive provisions of § 1962.

We conclude, therefore, that a person may not bring suit under § 1964(c) predicated on a violation of § 1962(d) for injuries caused by an overt act that is not an act of racketeering or otherwise unlawful under the statute.

[Justice STEVENS, with whom Justice SOUTER joined, dissented]

---

[10] Respondents argue that a § 1962(d) claim must be predicated on an *actionable* violation of §§ 1962(a)-(c). However, the merit of this view is a different (albeit related) issue from the one on which we granted certiorari, namely, whether a plaintiff can bring a § 1962(d) claim for injury flowing from an overt act that is not an act of racketeering. Therefore, … we do not resolve whether a plaintiff suing under § 1964(c) for a RICO conspiracy must allege an actionable violation under §§ 1962(a)-(c), or whether it is sufficient for the plaintiff to allege an agreement to complete a substantive violation and the commission of at least one act of racketeering that caused him injury.

Note

Does *Beck v. Prupis* have any implications for the *Reves*-conspiracy issue discussed in the new note 3 for page 500, *supra* in this Supplement?

Page 513. **In the first sentence following "F. THE RICO PROSECUTORIAL GUIDELINES" replace the date in the parentheses with the following:**

(Aug. 1999)

Chapter 11A

ANTI-TERRORISM ENFORCEMENT

INTRODUCTION

Following the September 11, 2002 attacks on the World Trade Center and the Pentagon and the crash of the third airliner in Pennsylvania, a number of significant steps aimed at increasing the effectiveness of enforcement against terrorist activity were taken by the Congress and the federal government. For example, the USA PATRIOT ("Uniting and Strengthening America by Providing Appropriate Tools Required to Intercept and Obstruct Terrorism") Act was enacted. The Act included provisions dealing with electronic surveillance and grand jury secrecy, broadened authority to deal with money laundering and to address certain types of immigration matters and facilitated information sharing between the intelligence and criminal prosecution arms of the federal government. Also in recognition of the continuing terrorist threat and the need to strengthen the FBI's capacity to interdict terrorist acts, over 500 FBI agents were shifted into anti-terrorism investigative activity, with most of them being taken from drug enforcement, and the remainder shifted from white collar and violent crimes investigations.

The PATRIOT Act effected only minimal changes in the federal criminal laws relating to terrorism. Numerous substantive crime provisions, found in Title 18, U.S.C. §§ 2331 et seq., aimed at terrorist activity had been enacted earlier as part of anti-terrorist statutory packages legislated, in 1986 in the Omnibus Diplomatic Security and Antiterrorism Act, and especially in1996 in the Antiterrorism and Effective Death Penalty Act (AEDPA).

Section A infra contains material that treats the different definitions of terrorism and definitional approaches that one finds in the federal criminal laws and raises issues regarding the function(s) of these definitions. Section B briefly notes the different types of crimes generally relied upon in terrorism prosecutions and then focuses on the crime that in the post 9/11 period seems to have become the federal prosecutor's favorite terrorism offense, 18 U.S.C. §2339B, a type of organizational crime different from any we have seen thus far.

A. DEFINITIONS OF TERRORISM AND THE USE OF THE CONCEPT IN THE CRIMINAL PROCESS

Crimes specially aimed at prosecuting terrorist activity take different forms. Some do not contain a definition of terrorism, but rather are aimed at kinds of criminal acts that most people would probably agree constitutes terrorism.(E.g., 18

U.S.C. § 2332f, bombing of places of public use, government transportation facilities, public transportation systems and infrastructure facilities). Some federal terrorism offenses do contain language defining terrorism or a terrorism purpose, but one finds different definitions used in different offenses. Also how the concept is used and who decides the terrorism issue varies from offense to offense. (Compare 18 U.S.C. § 2332(d) with 2332b(g)(5)).

The following case contains material that presents different variations on how terrorism is defined and definitional approaches to the concept. How many different definitions and definitional approaches can you find in the case? The definitions are used for different purposes or functions in the criminal justice system. How many different purposes or functions can you identify mentioned in the case? Are there other purposes or functions for a terrorism definition, not mentioned in the case, which you can think of?

United States v. Salim

2003 WL 22208640 (S.D.N.Y.)

[The defendant, while a federal prisoner charged with terrorism offenses, stabbed a guard in the eye with a sharpened comb. The stabbing became the basis for additional counts which were severed and as to which the defendant pleaded guilty. The issue before the court was what sentencing enhancements should be imposed under the Sentencing Guidelines in connection with the stabbing-related offenses to which he pleaded guilty. The government argued that the stabbing convictions were subject to a terrorism enhancement.]

Batts, J.

Terrorism Enhancement--U.S.S.G. § 3A1.4

The Government argues that, pursuant to U.S.S.G. § 3A1.4, the Court should increase Defendant's Offense Level by 12 and increase Defendant's Criminal History Category from I to VI, because the attempted murder to which Defendant pleaded guilty "involved, or was intended to promote, a federal crime of terrorism." In its submissions and in argument at the *Fatico* hearing, the Government has consistently argued Defendant pleaded guilty to conduct that was part of a "single course of conduct" to take hostages and coerce the government, and therefore Defendant's conduct falls within the definition of a "federal crime of terrorism," 18 U.S.C. § 2332b(g)(5).

Section 3A1.4 of the U.S. Sentencing Guidelines provides:

§ 3A1.4. *Terrorism*

(a) If the offense is a felony that involved, or was intended to promote, a federal crime of terrorism, increase by 12 levels; but if the resulting offense level is less than level 32, increase to level 32. ...

The Commentary to U.S.S.G. § 3A1.4 directs that "Federal crime of terrorism is defined at 18 U.S.C. § 2332b(g)(5)." A "Federal crime of terrorism" as defined at 18 U.S.C. 2332b(g)(5) is "an offense that –

> (A) is calculated to influence or affect the conduct of government by intimidation or coercion, or to retaliate against government conduct; and
> (B) is a violation of--
> i) ... [numerous sections, including] § 1114 (relating to killing or attempted killing of officers and employees of the United States) ...

Defendant makes a number of legal arguments against the application of the terrorism enhancement to his sentence. Defendant argues: (1) in promulgating U.S.S.G. § 3A1.4, the Sentencing Commission exceeded its authority and contravened the intent of Congress; ... (3) the "motivational" requirement of 18 U.S.C. § 2332b(g)(5)(A) must be proven by the Government by a heightened standard of proof; ... and (5) the Government seeks enhancement under § 3A1.4 solely on the basis of allegations of Defendant's claimed links to terrorism.

Additionally, at the ... hearing, defense counsel argued: ... (2) U.S.S.G. § 3A1.4 should not apply here because Defendant's conduct on November 1, 2000 [the day of the stabbing, ed.] did not amount to "terrorism" or "terrorist activity."

1. Sentencing Commission's Authority to Promulgate U.S.S.G. § 3A1.4

Defendant pleaded guilty to attempted murder of a federal official, 18 U.S.C. § 1114, which is one of the offenses enumerated at 18 U.S.C. § 2332b(g)(5)(B). Pursuant to U.S.S.G. § 3A1.4, the terrorism enhancement applies if the Court is convinced by a preponderance of the evidence that Defendant's conduct, having met the requirements 18 U.S.C. § 2332b(g)(5)(B), "involved or tended to promote a federal crime of terrorism." U.S.S.G. § 3A1.4.

A review of the history of U.S.S.G. § 3A1.4 is helpful to its analysis. In 1994, Congress directed the Commission to provide an appropriate enhancement for any felony that "involved or is intended to promote international terrorism." Violent Crime Control and Law Enforcement Act of 1994, Pub L. No. 103-322, § 120004, 108 Stat. 1796, 2022 (1994). The Sentencing Commission responded by replacing the then existing "Terrorism" upward departure provision, with a new "International Terrorism" enhancement at § 3A1.4.

This first version of U.S.S.G. § 3A1.4 read as follows:
Section 3A1. 4--Terrorism:
(a) If the offense is a felony that *involved, or was intended to promote, international terrorism,*[1] increase by 12 levels; but if the resulting offense

---

[1] For a definition of "International Terrorism," U.S.S.G. § 3A1.4, Application Note 1 referred to 18 U.S.C. § 2331 (1996), which reads in pertinent part:

As used in this chapter -

level is less than level 32, increase to level 32. ...

U.S.S.G. § 3A1.4 (1995).

Section 730 of the Antiterrorism and Effective Death Penalty Act of 1996 ("AEDPA") provided in full:

> The United States Sentencing Commission shall forthwith, in accordance with the procedures set forth in section 21(a) of the Sentencing Act of 1987, ... amend the sentencing guidelines so that the chapter 3 adjustment relating to international terrorism only applies to Federal crimes of terrorism, as defined in section 2332b(g) of title 18, United States Code.

In response to this Congressional directive, the Sentencing Commission promulgated Amendment 539, amending § 3A1.4:

> Section 3A1.4 is amended in the title by deleting "International". Section 3A1.4(a) is amended by deleting "international" and inserting in lieu thereof "a federal crime of". The Commentary to § 3A1.4 captioned "Application Notes" is amended in Note 1 in the first sentence by deleting "international" and inserting in lieu thereof "a federal crime of"; and in the second sentence by deleting "International" and inserting in lieu thereof "Federal crime of", and by deleting "2331" and inserting in lieu thereof "2332b(g)".

This amendment implements section 730 of the Antiterrorism and Effective

---

> (1) the term "international terrorism" means activities that--
>
> (A) involve violent acts or acts dangerous to human life that are a violation of the criminal laws of the United States or of any State, or that would be a criminal violation if committed within the jurisdiction of the United States or of any State;
>
> (B) appear to be intended--
>
>> (i) to intimidate or coerce a civilian population;
>>
>> (ii) to influence the policy of a government by intimidation or coercion; or
>>
>> (iii) to affect the conduct of a government by mass destruction, assassination, or kidnapping; and
>
> (C) occur primarily outside the territorial jurisdiction of the United States, or transcend national boundaries in terms of the means by which they are accomplished, the persons they appear intended to intimidate or coerce, or the locale in which their perpetrators operate or seek asylum ...

18 U.S.C. § 2331 (1996).

Death Penalty Act of 1996, Pub.L. 104-132, 110 Stat. 1303. That section requires the Commission to amend the sentencing guidelines so that the adjustment in § 3A1.4 (relating to international terrorism) applies more broadly to a "Federal crime of terrorism," as defined in 18 U.S.C. § 2332b(g), ...United States Sentencing Guidelines Manual, Appendix C, Amdt. 539 (effective Nov. 1, 1996).

On November 1, 2002, without explanation or direction from Congress, the Sentencing Commission amended U.S.S.G. § 3A1.4, Note 1 to read as follows[2]:

> 1. "Federal Crime of Terrorism Defined." --- For purposes of this guideline, "federal crime of terrorism" has the meaning given that term in 18 U.S.C. § 2332b(g)(5).

---

[2]In Amendment 637, the Commission also added a new Note 2 to the Commentary accompanying U.S.S.G. § 3A1.4:

> *Harboring, Concealing, and Obstruction Offenses.*--For purposes of this guideline, an offense that involved (A) harboring or concealing a terrorist who committed a federal crime of terrorism (such as an offense under 18 U.S.C. § 2339 or § 2339A); or (B) obstructing an investigation of a federal crime of terrorism, shall be considered to have involved, or to have been intended to promote, that federal crime of terrorism.

United States Sentencing Commission, U.S. Sentencing Guidelines Manual, Appendix C, Amdt. 637 (effective Nov. 1, 2002).

Amendment 637 also added a new Note 4 to the Commentary accompanying U.S.S.G. § 3A1.4:

> *Upward Departure Provision.*--By the terms of the directive to the Commission in section 730 of the Antiterrorism and Effective Death Penalty Act of 1996, the adjustment provided by this guideline applies only to federal crimes of terrorism. However, there may be cases in which (A) the offense was calculated to influence or affect the conduct of government by intimidation or coercion, or to retaliate against government conduct but the offense involved, or was intended to promote, an offense other than one of the offenses specifically enumerated in 18 U.S.C. § 2332b(g)(5)(B); or (B) the offense involved, or was intended to promote, one of the offenses specifically enumerated in 18 U.S.C. § 2332b(g)(5)(B), but the terrorist motive was to intimidate or coerce a civilian population, rather than to influence or affect the conduct of government by intimidation or coercion, or to retaliate against government conduct. In such cases an upward departure would be warranted, except that the sentence resulting from such a departure may not exceed the top of the guideline range that would have resulted if the adjustment under this guideline had been applied.

United States Sentencing Commission, U.S. Sentencing Guidelines Manual, Appendix C, Amdt. 637 (effective Nov. 1, 2002).

U.S. Sentencing Guidelines Manual, Supplement to Appendix C, Amendment 637 (effective November 1, 2002).

Comparing the prior versions of U.S.S.G. § 3A1.4 with the version at issue here, it is clear that the Sentencing Commission interpreted the directive of Section 730 of AEDPA as instructing the Commission to substitute the term "federal crime of terrorism" for "international terrorism," while leaving the rest of U.S.S.G. § 3A1.4 untouched. Defendant argues that, because U.S.S.G. § 3A1.4 applies to any offense that "involved, or was intended to promote, a federal crime of terrorism," instead of limiting application to offenses enumerated at 18 U.S.C. § 2332b(g)(5)(B), the Sentencing Commission exceeded its authority and contravened the intent of Congress by promulgating U.S.S.G. § 3A1.4, and therefore the enhancement cannot apply to Defendant.

Defendant argues further that the legislative history of Section 730 of AEDPA, in response to which the United States Sentencing Commission promulgated U.S.S.G. § 3A1.4, indicates that Congress clearly intended for the terrorism enhancement to apply *only* to offenses enumerated at § 2332b(g)(5)(B). This question is a matter of first impression in this Circuit.

Defendant relies heavily upon arguments articulated in Judge Cohn's dissenting opinion in *United States v. Graham,* a Sixth Circuit decision. *See generally United States v. Graham,* 275 F.3d 490, 529-37 (Cohn, J., dissenting), *cert. denied,* 535 U.S. 1026 (2002). In *Graham,* the Sixth Circuit held that application of U.S.S.G. § 3A1.4 to crimes not enumerated at 18 U.S.C. § 2332b(g)(5)(B) was consistent with the text of U.S.S.G. § 3A1.4, so long as in sentencing the defendant the district court "identif[ies] which enumerated 'Federal crime of terrorism' the defendant intended to promote, satisf[ies] the elements of 18 U.S.C. § 2332b(g)(5)(A), and support[s] its conclusions by a preponderance of the evidence with facts from the record." *Graham,* 273 F.3d at 517 (6th Cir.2001). The *Graham* majority addressed neither the question of the Sentencing Commission's authority nor the proper scope of U.S.S.G. § 3A1.4 in light thereof. However, in a lengthy dissent, Judge Avern Cohn concluded that application of U.S.S.G. § 3A1.4 to offenses of conviction that are not enumerated at 18 U.S.C. § 2332b(g)(5)(B) exceeds the authority of the United States Sentencing Commission. *See Graham,* 273 F.3d at 537.

Even if this Court were to follow the reasoning in Judge Cohn's dissenting opinion, his argument would not control the facts of this case. Defendant here pleaded guilty to an offense that is specifically enumerated at 18 U.S.C. § 2332b(g)(5)(B)--specifically, attempted murder of officers and employees of the United States in violation of 18 U.S.C. § 1114. Because Defendant was convicted of an offense enumerated at 18 U.S.C. § 2332b(g)(5)(B), this Court need not reach the question whether the Sentencing Commission exceeded its authority by expanding the application of U.S.S.G. § 3A1.4 to offenses of conviction that are not enumerated at 18 U.S.C. § 2332b(g)(5)(B).

. . .

7. Definition of "Terrorism"

Defendant argues that U.S.S.G. § 3A1.4 is not applicable on the instant facts because Defendant's conduct on November 1, 2000 did not amount to "terrorism" or "terrorist activity." Specifically, Defendant cites a House Judiciary Committee report, which accompanied a draft of legislation that directed the Sentencing Commission to promulgate the applicable version of U.S.S.G. § 3A1.4, and which states that the purpose of the sentencing enhancement was to "establish significant and meaningful penalties for those who undertake criminal activities in the name of political change." Also citing definitions of terrorism contained in other statutory and regulatory provisions, 28 CFR § 0.85 (FBI definition), 22 U.S.C. § 2656(f) (State Department), Defendant argues that "political change" is the "touchstone" of terrorism, and that since Defendant had no intention to effect "political" change in attacking Officer Pepe, his sentence should not be increased under the "terrorism" enhancement at U.S.S.G. § 3A1.4.

The authorities upon which Defendant relies do not support his argument. The House Judiciary Committee's stated purpose in drafting the sentencing provisions in H.R. 1710 is at best a weak guide in interpreting the meaning of "Federal crime of terrorism." To begin, H.R. 1710 was never passed; instead, on the same day the House Judiciary Committee reported its amendments to H.R. 1710, Representative Henry Hyde introduced in the House of Representatives H.R. 2703, a new version of the Anti-Terrorism and Effective Death Penalty Act. Furthermore, while H.R. 1710 contained a definition of terrorism that specifically referred to conduct with social and political "ends," and may have reflected a desire by its

---

[3] Section 315 of H.R. 1710 provided:

Section 2331 of title 18, United States Code, is amended--

(1) so that paragraph (1) reads as follows:

'(1) the term 'terrorism' means the use of force or violence in violation of the criminal laws of the United States or of any State, or that would be in violation of the criminal laws of the United States or of any State if committed within the jurisdiction of the United States or that State that appears to be intended to achieve political or social ends by--

'(A) intimidating or coercing a segment of the population;

'(B) influencing or coercing a government official or officials; or

'(C) affecting the conduct of a government through assassination or kidnapping;';

(2) by inserting after paragraph (1) the following:

(2) the term 'international terrorism' means terrorism that occurs primarily outside the territorial jurisdiction of the United States, or transcends national boundaries in terms of the means by which it is accomplished, the persons it appears intended to intimidate or coerce, or

drafters to reach defendants who "undertake criminal activities in the name of political change," the enacted version of the Anti-Terrorism and Effective Death Penalty Act ("AEDPA") contained no such reference. Instead, as enacted, AEDPA provided a definition of "federal crime of terrorism" within a newly-created 18 U.S.C. § 2332b.

More to the point, while the legislative history, statutes and code sections to which Defendant refers might inform a general discussion about "terrorism," U.S.S.G. § 3A1.4 specifically provides that "Federal crime of terrorism" is defined at 18 U.S.C. § 2332b(g)(5). Thus, whether or not Defendant's conduct falls outside the definitions of terrorism provided at 22 U.S.C. § 2656(f) or 28 C.F.R. § 0.85 is irrelevant to a determination of whether or not Defendant's conduct constitutes a "Federal crime of terrorism." Since the Sentencing Commission has directed the Court to refer to 18 U.S.C. § 2332b(g)(5) for a definition of "Federal crime of terrorism," speculation about what is or is not a "touchstone" of terrorism is immaterial. Accordingly, the Court declines to construe a "Federal crime of terrorism" to require political or social ends.

IV. APPLICATION OF U.S.S.G. § 3A1.4 TO SOLELY DOMESTIC CONDUCT

Section 3A1.4 of the U.S. Sentencing Guidelines provides:

(a) If the offense is a felony that involved, or was intended to promote, a federal crime of terrorism, increase by 12 levels; but if the resulting offense level is less than level 32, increase to level 32.

...The Commentary to § 3A1.4 explains that "[s]ubsection (a) increases the offense level if the offense involved or was intended to promote a Federal crime of terrorism as defined at 18 U.S.C. § 2332b(g)(5)." U.S.S.G. § 3A1.4,

...

Section 2332b is entitled "Acts of terrorism transcending national boundaries," and consists of seven subsections. Subsection "(a)" enumerates "Prohibited acts;" subsection "(b)" details "Jurisdictional bases;" subsection "(c)" lists "Penalties" for violations of the section; subsection "(d)" states the "Proof requirements" for prosecutions under the section; subsection "(e)" states offenses over which there is "Extraterritorial jurisdiction;" subsection "(f)" provides the

---

the locale in which its perpetrators operate or seek asylum;'; and

(3) by redesignating existing paragraphs (2) through (4) as paragraphs (3) through (5), respectively.

H.R. 1710, 104th Cong., § 315 (1995).

Attorney General with "Investigative authority" with respect to "all Federal crimes of terrorism;" subsection "(g)" provides "Definitions" for terms, "As used in [Section 2332b]."

Apart from the definition contained at 18 U.S.C. 2332b(g)(5), the term "Federal crime of terrorism" appears only at 18 U.S.C. § 2332b(f). ... Whether Defendant's conduct, involving solely domestic activities, falls within the scope of the term "Federal crime of terrorism" is a question this Court considers according to standard principles of statutory interpretation. To aid in its analysis of this question, by Order of December 19, 2002 the Court directed the parties to brief the question whether Defendant's conduct, a solely domestic crime, fell within the definition of the term "Federal crime of terrorism," as defined in 18 U.S.C. § 2332b(g).

The Government argues that the definition of a "Federal crime of terrorism" found at 18 U.S.C. 2332b(g)(5) applies to offenses enumerated in Section 2332b(g)(5)(B) without regard to the location where the offense was committed, "so long as the factual predicate contained in Section 2332b(g)(5)(A) is met." Specifically, the Government argues that the plain language of Section 2332b(g)(5) does not distinguish between domestic and international conduct, and that the list of predicate offenses at 2332b(g)(5)(B) includes laws prohibiting criminal acts that are "primarily domestic, primarily international, and both domestic and international in their likely place of commission." The Government argues that because the plain language of the statute is clear, the title of 18 U.S.C. § 2332b, "Acts of terrorism transcending national boundaries," has "no bearing on, and does not affect, the plain language of" the statute. The Government further argues that 18 U.S.C. § 2332b(g)(5) is, like § 2332b(f), "completely unrelated to" the title of the section, "Acts of terrorism transcending national boundaries," because if Congress had intended to require conduct transcending national boundaries for these sections, it would have specifically set this forth, by referring explicitly in the text of 2332b(g) and 2332b(f) to § 2332b(g)(1), which provides a definition of "conduct transcending national boundaries."

The Government further argues that the legislative history of 18 U.S.C. § 2332b indicates that Congress removed the limitation on the sweep of § 2332b to solely international conduct, and the final draft included no such limitation.

The Government also notes that AEDPA was passed in 1996 in response to a bombing of the federal building in Oklahoma City, "a purely domestic crime of terrorism," and that upon signing the legislation, President Clinton acknowledged that AEDPA resulted from his requests to Federal law enforcement officials to assess tools needed to help them meet the challenge of domestic terrorism. The Government further argues that references to later bills and amendments to § 2332b show that the intent of Congress was not to limit the definition of "Federal crime of terrorism" to conduct with an "international dimension."

---

[4] Indeed, 18 U.S.C. § 2332b(f) is the only place the term is used in the entire United States Code.

Additionally, the Government argues that the history of U.S.S.G. § 3A1.4 and application of the enhancement in cases show that a "Federal crime of terrorism" can be an offense involving solely domestic conduct. Specifically, the Government argues that Congress intended that the current U.S.S.G. § 3A1.4 to apply to crimes of terrorism without regard to whether they were international or domestic, as evident from Congress' direction to the Sentencing Commission to amend the existing U.S.S.G. § 3A1.4, which applied to "International terrorism," so that it would apply "more broadly" to a Federal crime of terrorism,. (*Id.* at 18-20 .) Finally, the Government argues that other courts have applied § 3A1.4 to purely domestic offenses.

Defendant argues the Government's plain-meaning interpretation of 18 U.S.C. § 2332b is flawed because it fails to read the definition of "Federal crime of terrorism" as set forth at 18 U.S.C. § 2332b(g)(5) in context….Defendant argues further that, because the title of § 2332b is "Acts of Terrorism Transcending National Boundaries," and the phrase "conduct transcending national boundaries" is defined at 18 U.S.C. § 2332b(g)(1), it is "obvious that the prohibited conduct under the entire Statute" must be transnational.
Defendant also argues that the Government's review of the legislative history is inadequate, as it does not take account of the Conference Committee to the final version of AEDPA or the House Judiciary Committee Report that accompanied an earlier version of AEDPA. Defendant notes that the House Judiciary Report, H.R. 104-383, which accompanied an early version of AEDPA, stated that the version of 18 U.S.C. § 2332b contained therein was limited to crimes "committed in a manner transcending national boundaries." Defendant also notes that the Conference Committee Report that accompanied the final version of AEDPA, H.R. 104-518, contains language that limits the jurisdiction of courts over cases brought under § 2332b, and also notes that Section 2332b "creates a new federal criminal prohibition on acts of terrorism transcending national boundaries." Defendant argues that these reports "unequivocally demonstrate[ ] that Congress intended to limit a 'Federal crime of terrorism' to *trans-national* conduct."

Defendant argues that the Government has provided no evidence to support its argument that § 2332b(g)(5) is intended to be read "in isolation" from the rest of section 2332b, and further argues that debates on other bills and the statements of former President Clinton on signing AEDPA are not authority upon which the Court can rest its determination of whether the statute was intended to apply to solely domestic conduct. (*Id.* at 14.) Defendant argues further that neither the history of U.S.S.G. § 3A1.4 nor case law on § 3A1.4 demonstrates that a "Federal crime of terrorism" as defined at § 2332b(g) applies to a solely domestic crime. Defendant notes that a prior version of U.S.S.G. § 3A1.4 applied to international terrorism, and that Congress directed the Sentencing Commission to amend the enhancement to apply "only to Federal crimes of terrorism," and that this amendment reflected "the realization that the sentencing enhancement provision needed to be equally applicable to trans-national as to international terrorism," as well as the belief that Section 3A1.4 should "not sweep too broadly." Defendant also notes that in passing the USA PATRIOT Act, Pub.L.No. 107-56, 107th Cong., 1st Sess., 115 Stat. 376 (2001), Congress created a definition for "domestic terrorism" at 18 U.S.C. § 2331(5)(C) that prohibits terrorist activities that "occur primarily within the territorial jurisdiction of the United States," but did not amend U.S.S.G. § 3A1.4 to apply to "domestic terrorism."

In its reply, the Government argues Defendant's statutory interpretation fails because reference to headings, titles, and the "Whole Act" rule are only of use where the statute is ambiguous, and here the statute is unambiguous. ...The Government further argues that reading §§ 2332b(f) and 2332b(g) to reach more broadly than the rest of § 2332b to international and domestic conduct is "sensible," since § 2332b(f) provides the Attorney General with investigative authority, which "would not contain a geographical limitation of any kind."

This definition of a "Federal crime of terrorism" reconciles the textual directives of the different subsections of 18 U.S.C. § 2332b, as well as the specific and broad context in which the term "Federal crime of terrorism" occurs. First, by defining the term by reference to its usage in § 2332b, the Court adheres to the textual direction at 18 U.S.C. § 2332b(g) that "Federal crime of terrorism" is defined by reference to its usage "in this section," and to the principal of statutory construction that provisions are construed by reference to the specific and broad context in which they occur. Second, construing "Federal crime of terrorism" to require "conduct transcending national boundaries" provides the Attorney General with authority to investigate offenses involving conduct occurring outside the United States as well as within the United States, 18 U.S.C. 2332b(g)(1), authority which is indeed "in addition to" other investigative authority provided under Title 18, as required by 18 U.S.C. 2332b(f). Third, construing the definition of "Federal crime of terrorism" at 2332b(g)(5) to require conduct transcending national boundaries, allows the term to have a single meaning in 18 U.S.C. § 2332b. Finally, defining a "Federal crime of terrorism" to involve conduct transcending national boundaries harmonizes the definition, and the resulting scope of investigative authority of the Attorney General, with the focus of 18 U.S.C. 2332b as a whole-- which is "Acts of terrorism transcending national boundaries."

Accordingly, the Court finds the plain meaning of the statutory language to require that a "Federal crime of terrorism," as defined at 18 U.S.C. 2332b(g), is one that involves conduct transcending national boundaries.

...

e. USA PATRIOT Act

On October 26, 2001, Congress passed the Uniting and Strengthening America by Providing Appropriate Tools Required to Intercept and Obstruct Terrorism (USA PATRIOT) Act of 2001. Pub.L. No. 107-56, 115 Stat. 272 (2001). Section 802(a)(2) to (4) of the USA PATRIOT Act added a new subsection (5) to 18 U.S.C. § 2331, the Definitional section for "Chapter 113B--Terrorism" of Title 18:

(5) the term "domestic terrorism" means activities that--

(A) involve acts dangerous to human life that are a violation of the criminal laws of the United States or of any State;

(B) appear to be intended--

    (i) to intimidate or coerce a civilian population;

    (ii) to influence the policy of a government by intimidation or coercion; or

    (iii) to affect the conduct of a government by mass destruction, assassination, or kidnapping; and

(C) occur primarily within the territorial jurisdiction of the United States. 18 U.S.C. § 2331(5)....

The views of the Congress that enacted the USA PATRIOT Act "cannot control the interpretation of an earlier enacted statute." However, the fact that a subsequent Congress interpreted its existing provisions within Chapter 113B, including the definition of "Federal crime of terrorism" at 2332b(g), as not providing a satisfactory means of reaching "domestic terrorism" is further evidence that the term "Federal crime of terrorism" cannot be construed to include "domestic terrorism...

This Court has found that Defendant's attack on Officer Pepe was calculated to influence or affect the conduct of government by intimidation or coercion, and was also calculated to retaliate against government conduct. However, because there is no evidence that Defendant's attack on Officer Pepe involved conduct transcending national boundaries, the Court finds that the Government has not established by a preponderance that Defendant's relevant conduct included a "Federal crime of terrorism." As defined at 18 U.S.C. 2332b(g)(5), a "Federal crime of terrorism" is one that meets the two prongs set forth at 18 U.S.C. §§ 2332b(g)(5)(A) and (B), and that involves conduct that transcends national boundaries. There is no evidence in the record that Defendant's relevant conduct involved *any* conduct transcending national boundaries. The attack on Officer Pepe occurred at the MCC, in New York, New York. Defendant testified, and the Government does not dispute, that while Defendant was incarcerated at the MCC prior to November 1, 2000, he wrote the notes and lists discovered after the attack. There has been no allegation, nor any evidence offered, that shows Defendant was acting in concert with persons outside of the United States.

In view of this deficiency, the Court finds insufficient evidence to conclude Defendant's conduct amounted to a "Federal crime of terrorism," as defined at 18 U.S.C. § 2332b(g)(5). Accordingly, the Court declines to apply the sentence enhancement at U.S.S.G. § 3A1.4 to Defendant's sentence.

Notes

1. Despite the fact that a number of different definitions of terrorism or a terrorism purpose can be found in the federal criminal laws, it is difficult to find a federal criminal statute that makes terrorism or a terrorism purpose an element of a federal crime. See, e.g.18 U.S.C. § 2332, which provides that before a prosecution

under this section can be initiated, the Attorney General must certify that the crime (killing or assaulting a U.S. national abroad) was committed with a terrorist purpose (i.e., intent to coerce or retaliate against a government or civilian population), but this feature of the offense that the Attorney General certifies is not treated as an element of the offense.

Also *see, e.g.*, 18 U.S.C. § 2339B, where, as mentioned in the principal case, the phrase "federal crime of terrorism" is defined and used in the section to delimit the Attorney General's investigative authority, but the definition is not an element of the offense(s) described in the section.

Is a counter-example, 18 U.S.C. § 2339C. which defines an offense prohibiting the financing of terrorism and includes a definition of terrorism as one of the provisions of the Act?

Would you expect there to be on the statute books a number of offenses that contain as one of their elements a terrorism purpose, whether defined in general or specific terms?

2. Is it common or uncommon to include within a criminal statute the motive with which the act was done? Is that kind of element appropriate to consider in determining the penalty established for the offense? Can you think of any offenses where the motive is included as an element of the offense? Is it preferable to take such a factor into account at the sentencing stage rather than the guilt phase of the criminal process? Note, of course, that the main provision at issue in the *Salim* case relates to the consideration of motive at the sentencing stage.

3. Are there specific pragmatic reasons why making a terrorist purpose (no matter how defined) an element of an offense is generally not a desirable approach?

4. As suggested in the Introduction to this section (and as *Salim* indicates), there are a number of different definitions and definitional approaches to the subject of terrorism and a terrorist purpose that are reflected in the federal criminal laws. The differences relate both to the international and domestic feature and to differences in how the terrorist purpose is specifically defined as well as whether specific offenses are listed in the definition or whether the kind of crimes is left open-ended. Is it desirable to decide upon a single, commonly and consistently used definition? If so, how would you define the concept?

B. ENFORCEMENT AGAINST TERRORIST ORGANIZATIONAL ACTIVITY

1. Introduction[*]

"Over the course of recent decades, while there have been a number of major

---

[*]This introduction is excerpted from NORMAN ABRAMS, ANTI-TERRORISM AND CRIMINAL ENFORCEMENT 82-83 (Thomson/West 2003).

terrorism events in, or directly involving the United States, there have not been a large number of prosecutions arising out of such events nor a very large body of accumulated criminal case law related to such matters. Among the most well-known of the recent major instances of terrorism prior to September 11, 2001, and some of the prosecutions instituted in their wake were the 1995 Oklahoma City bombing [*See United States v. McVeigh*, 153 F.3d 1166 (10th Cir. 1998)]; the first World Trade Center bombing in 1993 [*see, e.g., United States v. Salameh, et al.*, 261 F.3d 271 (2d Cir. 2001 (August 6, 2001)) and see the earlier opinion in the same case, 152 F.3d 88 (1998)]; the 1998 bombings of U.S. embassies in Nairobi, Kenya and Dar Es Salaam, Tanzania [*see United States v. Bin Laden et al.*, 92 F.Supp. 2d 225 (S.D. N.Y. 2000)],

"Post 9/11 prosecutions include: the prosecution of Zacarias Moussaoui, in the Eastern District of Virginia, 2001, who is alleged to have been intended to be the so-called 20th terrorist in the 9/11 bombing of the World Trade Center, the prosecution of Richard Reid, the so-called shoe bomber; the prosecution of John Walker Lindh, the so-called American Taliban, and the prosecution of the so-called Lackawanna six in upstate New York and of James Earnest Ujaaama in the state of Washington. The Reid and Walker Lindh cases ended in pleas of guilty. The Moussaoui trial is on-going ....

"These cases generally illustrate the fact that both terrorism crimes as well as more traditional federal crimes are often charged in such cases. They also illustrate a recurring phenomenon in federal criminal prosecutions—the charging in a single case of a multiplicity of different offenses, made possible by the overlapping nature of many crimes in the federal criminal code.

"McVeigh, for example, was convicted of charges involving use of a weapon of mass destruction, 18 U.S.C. §2332a, destruction by explosives, 18 U.S.C. § 844, and homicide offenses, 18 U.S.C. § 1111 and 1114. The convictions in the Salameh case similarly were based in 18 U.S.C. § 844 as well as using explosives to bomb automobiles used in interstate commerce, with reckless disregard for human life, 18 U.S.C. § 33, assaulting federal officers, § 111, using a destructive device in a crime of violence, 18 U.S.C. § 924, and traveling in interstate commerce with intent to commit certain crimes, 18 U.S.C. § 1952. In the Bin Laden prosecution, the charged offenses involved conspiring to kill U.S. nationals under 18 U.S.C. § 2332 and destruction of national defense facilities, 18 U.S.C. § 2155 as well as offenses that had been used in the earlier cases, namely, Title 18, U.S.C.§§ 844, 2332a and 1111, 1114.

"Moussaoui was charged with conspiring to commit acts of terrorism transcending national boundaries, 18 U.S.C. § 2332b, to commit air piracy, 49 U.S.C. § 46502, to destroy aircraft, 18 U.S.C. 32, to use weapons of mass destruction, 18 U.S.C. §2332a, to murder U.S. employees, 18 U.S.C. § 1114 and 1117, and to destroy property, 18 U.S.C. § 844."

2.   18 U.S.C. § 2339B

18 U.S.C. § 2339B makes it a federal crime to knowingly provide material

support or resources to a foreign terrorist organization. 2339B incorporates by reference a definition of material support or resources that is found in 18 U.S.C. § 2339A. (This definition is reproduced in the *Sattar* case, below.) 2339B also provides that the designation of an organization as a "foreign terrorist organization" (i.e. one of elements of the 2339B offense) is made under the provisions of 8 U.S.C. § 1189.

Section 2339B has been used as the basis for criminal charges in a wide range of different kinds of factual contexts. For example, it has been used in the prosecution of an individual who volunteered to fight in a foreign army and ended up fighting against U.S. forces in Afghanistan, the Walker Lindh case, *United States v. Lindh, 212 F.Supp. 2d 541 (E.D. Va. 2002)*. It has also been to prosecute individuals who traveled to Afghanistan to participate in an alleged terrorist group training camp. See *United States v. Goba, 220 F.Supp 2d 182 (W.D.N.Y. 2002)* (the Lackawanna six case) and against an individual who allegedly was trying to set up a terrorist training facility in the state of Washington (the prosecution of Earnest James Ujaama). It has been used to prosecute individuals who allegedly transferred funds to a designated foreign terrorist organization (see *United States v. Rahmani, 209 F.Supp. 2d 1045 (C.D. Cal. 2002)*. And it has been used as the basis for charges against an attorney representing a federal prisoner charged with terrorism offenses where the government alleges that the attorney became a conduit for passing information to the prisoner's confederates. See the *Sattar* case, below.

What is there about 2339B that makes it such a ubiquitous prosecutorial weapon usable in so many different kinds of factual contexts to prosecute so many different kinds of conduct?

Note that most of the cases in which a prosecution under 2339B has been initiated have not gone to trial, let alone been reviewed at the appellate level. The result is that we have only a limited number of judicial interpretations of the specific terms of 2339B.

United States v. Sattar
272 F.Supp.2d 348 (S.D. N.Y. 2003)

OPINION AND ORDER

<u>KOELTL</u>, District Judge.

The defendants in this case--Ahmed Abdel Sattar, a/k/a "Abu Omar," a/k/a "Dr. Ahmed" ("Sattar"), Yassir Al-Sirri, a/k/a "Abu Ammar" ("Al-Sirri"), Lynne Stewart ("Stewart") and Mohammed Yousry ("Yousry")--were charged in a five-count indictment on April 8, 2002 ("Indictment"). The First Count of the Indictment charges Sattar, Al-Sirri, Stewart and Yousry, together with others known and unknown with conspiring to provide material support and resources to a foreign terrorist organization ("FTO") in violation of <u>18 U.S.C. § 2339B</u>. Count Two charges each of the defendants with providing and attempting to provide material support and resources to an FTO in violation of <u>18 U.S.C. §§ 2339B</u> and <u>2</u>. Count

Three charges Sattar and Al-Sirri with soliciting persons to engage in crimes of violence in violation of 18 U.S.C. § 373. Count Four charges Sattar, Stewart and Yousry with conspiring to defraud the United States in violation of 18 U.S.C. § 371. Finally, Count Five charges Stewart with making false statements in violation of 18 U.S.C. §§ 1001 and 2. Defendants Sattar, Stewart and Yousry now move to dismiss the Indictment on various grounds.

I.

The Indictment alleges the following facts. At all relevant times, the Islamic Group, a/k/a "Gama'a al-Islamiyya," a/k/a/ "IG," a/k/a "al-Gama'at," a/k/a "Islamic Gama'at," a/k/a/ "Egyptian al-Gama'at al Islamiyya," ("IG"), existed as an international terrorist group dedicated to opposing nations, governments, institutions, and individuals that did not share IG's radical interpretation of Islamic law. (…IG also opposed the United States because the United States had taken action to thwart IG, including by the arrest, conviction, and continued confinement of its spiritual leader Omar Ahmad Ali Abdel Rahman, a/k/a "Omar Ahmed Ali," a/k/a "Omar Abdel Al-Rahman," a/k/a "The Sheikh," a/k/a "Sheikh Omar" ("Sheikh Abdel Rahman").

IG has allegedly operated in the United States from the early 1990s until the date of the filing of the Indictment, particularly in the New York metropolitan area. According to the Indictment, IG's objectives in the United States include (1) the establishment of the United States as a staging ground for violent acts against targets in the United States and abroad; (2) the recruitment and training of members; and (3) fundraising for jihad actions in the United States and overseas. Since Sheikh Abdel Rahman's imprisonment, the Indictment alleges that IG members in the United States have also functioned as a worldwide communications hub for the group, in part by facilitating communications between IG leaders and Sheik Abdel Rahman. IG was designated as a foreign terrorist organization by the Secretary of State on October 8, 1997 pursuant to Title 8, United States Code, Section 1189 and was redesignated as such on October 8, 1999 and again on October 5, 2001.

The Indictment alleges that Sheikh Abdel Rahman has been one of IG's principal leaders and a high-ranking member of jihad organizations based in Egypt and elsewhere since the early 1990s. …The Indictment charges that Sheik Abdel Rahman, among other things, provided guidance about what actions, including acts of terrorism, were permissible or forbidden under his interpretation of Islamic law; gave strategic advice on how to achieve IG's goals; recruited persons and solicited them to commit violent jihad acts; and sought to protect IG from infiltration by law enforcement.

Sheikh Abdel Rahman was convicted in October 1995 of engaging in a seditious conspiracy to wage a war of urban terrorism against the United States, including the 1993 World Trade Center bombing and a plot to bomb New York City landmarks. He was also found guilty of soliciting crimes of violence against the United States military and Egyptian President Hosni Mubarak. In January 1996 Sheik Abdel Rahman was sentenced to life imprisonment plus 65 years. …

Sheikh Abdel Rahman has been incarcerated at the Federal Medical Center in Rochester, Minnesota since in or about 1997. ...

The Bureau of Prisons... imposed Special Administrative Measures ("SAMs") upon Sheikh Abdel Rahman.... The SAMs limited certain privileges in order to "persons against the risk of death or serious bodily injury that might otherwise result." The limitations include restrictions ... prohibited him from speaking to the media. All Counsel for Sheikh Abdel Rahman were obligated to sign an affirmation acknowledging that they and their staff would abide fully by the SAMs.... Since at least...May 1998, counsel agreed not to use "meetings, correspondence, or phone calls with Abdel Rahman to pass messages between their parties (including, but not limited to, the media) and Abdel Rahman.

Defendant Stewart was Sheikh Abdel Rahman's counsel during his 1995 criminal trial and has continued to represent him since his conviction. The Indictment alleges that over the past several years, Stewart has facilitated and concealed messages between her client and IG leaders around the world in violation of the SAMs limiting Sheik Abdel Rahman's communications from prison. During a May 2000 visit to Sheikh Abdel Rahman in prison, Stewart allegedly allowed defendant Yousry, who acted as the Arabic interpreter between Sheikh Abdel Rahman and his attorneys, to read letters from defendant Sattar and others regarding IG matters and to discuss with her client whether IG should continue to comply with a cease-fire that had been supported by factions within IG since in or about 1998. According to the Indictment, Yousry provided material support and resources to IG by covertly passing messages between IG representatives and Sheik Abdel Rahman regarding IG's activities. The Indictment alleges that Stewart took affirmative steps to conceal the May 2000 discussions from prison guards and subsequently, in violation of the SAMs, announced to the media that Sheikh Abdel Rahman had withdrawn his support for the cease-fire. The Indictment charges that in or about May 2000 Stewart submitted an affirmation to the United States Attorney's Office for the Southern District of New York (the "May Affirmation") that falsely stated, among other things, that she agreed to abide by the terms of the SAMs applicable to Sheikh Abdel Rahman and that she would not use her meetings, correspondence or phone calls with Sheikh Abdel Rahman to pass messages between Sheikh Abdel Rahman and third parties including but not limited to the media.

The Indictment also charges that Sattar is an active IG leader who serves as a vital link between Sheik Abdel Rahman and the worldwide IG membership. The Indictment contends that Sattar operates as a communications center for IG from New York City through frequent telephonic contact with IG leaders around the world. More specifically, the Indictment alleges that Sattar provides material support and resources to IG by relaying messages between IG leaders abroad and Sheik Abdel Rahman through visits and phone calls by Sheikh Abdel Rahman's interpreter and attorneys; arranging and participating in three-way phone calls connecting IG leaders around the world to facilitate discussion and coordination of IG activities; passing messages and information from one IG leader and to other group leaders and members; and by providing financial support.

Defendant Al-Sirri was arrested in the United Kingdom in October 2001 until which time, the Indictment alleges, he was the head of the London-based

Islamic Observation Center. The Indictment charges that Al-Sirri, like Sattar, facilitated IG communications worldwide and provided material support and resources, including financial support, to the FTO. Al-Sirri was allegedly in frequent telephone contact with Sattar and other IG leaders regarding the dissemination of IG statements on various issues.

The defendants make the following motions. Sattar and Stewart move to dismiss Counts One and Two on the ground that 18 U.S.C. § 2339B is unconstitutionally vague and overbroad. ... Title 18, United States Code, Section 2339B provides, in relevant part:

> Whoever, within the United States or subject to the jurisdiction of the United States, knowingly provides material support or resources to a foreign terrorist organization, or attempts or conspires to do so, shall be [guilty of a crime].
> 18 U.S.C. § 2339B(a)(1).

At all relevant times, "material support or resources" was defined as:

> currency or other financial securities, financial services, lodging, training, safehouses, false documentation or identification, communications equipment, facilities, weapons, lethal substances, explosives, personnel, transportation, and other physical assets, except medicine or religious materials.
> 18 U.S.C. §§ 2339A(b) & 2339B(g)(4).

A foreign "terrorist organization" is defined as "an organization designated" under 8 U.S.C. § 1189 as a foreign "terrorist organization." 18 U.S.C. § 2339B(g)(6).

Section 2339B, which is alleged to have been violated in this case, requires only that a person "knowingly" "provides" "material support or resources" to a "foreign terrorist organization." Section 2339A criminalizes the provision of "material support or resources" "knowing or intending that they are used in preparation for, or in carrying out," a violation of various criminal statutes. No such specific criminal intent provision is included in § 2339B. Section 2339A defines "material support or resources" as indicated above. That definition includes no amount or other measure of magnitude and is carried over into § 2339B.

The Indictment alleges that the defendants conspired to provide and

---

[1] Pub.L. No. 107-56, § 805(a)(2), Oct. 26, 2001, 115 Stat. 377, 380, 381, modified the definition of "material support or resources" to include monetary instruments and expert advice or assistance. The parties agree that the modified definition of "material support or resources" does not apply retroactively to the conduct charged in the Indictment.

provided communications equipment, personnel, currency, financial securities and financial services (currency, financial securities, and financial services hereinafter "currency"), and transportation to IG.

A.

The defendants argue that 18 U.S.C. § 2339B is unconstitutionally vague specifically with regard to the statute's prohibition on "providing" material support or resources in the form of "communications equipment" and "personnel." With respect to communications equipment, the Indictment alleges, among other things, that "the defendants and the unindicted co-conspirators provided communications equipment and other physical assets, including telephones, computers and telefax machines, owned, operated and possessed by themselves and others, to IG, in order to transmit, pass and disseminate messages, communications and information between and among IG leaders and members in the United States and elsewhere around the world...." The Government has argued that the defendants provided a communications pipeline by which they transmitted messages from Sheikh Abdel Rahman in prison to IG leaders and members throughout the world. Among the specific instances of the use of communications equipment, the Indictment points to the fact that Sattar had telephone conversations with IG leaders in which he related Sheikh Abdel Rahman's instructions to IG leaders and Stewart released Sheikh Abdel Rahman's statement to the press in which Sheikh Abdel Rahman withdrew his support from the then-existing cease-fire. With respect to the provision of personnel, the Indictment alleges that "the defendants and the unindicted co-conspirators provided personnel, including themselves, to IG, in order to assist IG leaders and members in the United States and elsewhere around the world, in communicating with each other...." The defendants argue that the statute fails to provide fair notice of what acts are prohibited by the prohibition against the provision of "communications equipment" and "personnel."

A criminal statute implicating First Amendment rights "must 'define the criminal offense with sufficient definiteness that ordinary people can understand what conduct is prohibited and in a manner that does not encourage arbitrary and discriminatory enforcement.' " _United States v. Rahman,_ 189 F.3d 88, 116 (2d Cir.1999) (quoting _Kolender v. Lawson,_ 461 U.S. 352, 357, 103 S.Ct. 1855, 75 L.Ed.2d 903 (1983)). ..._see also Handakas,_ 286 F.3d at 111 ("The principle that a statute must provide both 'notice' and 'explicit standards' to survive an 'as- applied' constitutional challenge based on vagueness is well established."). A "void for vagueness" challenge does not necessarily mean that the statute could not be applied in some cases but rather that, as applied to the conduct at issue in the criminal case, a reasonable person would not have notice that the conduct was unlawful and there are no explicit standards to determine that the specific conduct was unlawful.

First, with regard to the "provision" of "communications equipment," Sattar and Stewart argue that the Indictment charges them with merely talking and that the acts alleged in the Indictment constitute nothing more than using communications equipment rather than providing such equipment to IG. For example, the Indictment charges Sattar with participating in and arranging numerous telephone calls between IG leaders in which IG business was discussed, ... The Indictment describes numerous other telephone calls in which Sattar participated. Stewart is charged with, among other things, providing communications equipment to IG by announcing

Sheikh Abdel Rahman's withdrawal of support for the cease-fire in Egypt and thereby making the statements of the otherwise isolated leader available to the media.

The defendants look to the legislative history of the statute as evidence that Congress did not intend § 2339B to criminalize the mere use of communications equipment, rather than the actual giving of such equipment to IG. The legislative history states:

The ban does not restrict an organization's or an individual's ability to freely express a particular ideology or political philosophy. Those inside the United States will continue to be free to advocate, think and profess the attitudes and philosophies of the foreign organizations. *They are simply not allowed to send material support or resources to those groups, or their subsidiary groups, overseas.* H.R. Rep. 104-383 at 45 (emphasis added). Thus, the defendants argue, simply making a phone call or similarly communicating one's thoughts does not fall within the ambit of § 2339B.

The defendants are correct and by criminalizing the mere use of phones and other means of communication the statute provides neither notice nor standards for its application such that it is unconstitutionally vague as applied. The Government argued in its brief that the defendants are charged not merely with using their own phones or other communications equipment but with actively making such equipment available to IG and thus "providing" IG with communications resources that would otherwise be unavailable to the FTO. That argument, however, simply ignores the reality of the facts charged in the Indictment in which various defendants are accused of having participated in the use of communications equipment. The Government subsequently changed course and stated at oral argument that the mere use of one's telephone constitutes criminal behavior under the statute and that, in fact, "use equals provision." The Government also argued that using the conference call feature on a person's phone in furtherance of an FTO was prohibited.

Such changes in the Government's interpretation of § 2339B demonstrate why the provision of communications equipment as charged in the Indictment is unconstitutionally vague: a criminal defendant simply could not be expected to know that the conduct alleged was prohibited by the statute. ...

The defendants were not put on notice that merely using communications equipment in furtherance of an FTO's goals constituted criminal conduct. Moreover, the Government's evolving definition of what it means to provide communications equipment to an FTO in violation of § 2339B reveals a lack of prosecutorial standards that would "permit 'a standardless sweep [that] allows policemen, prosecutors, and juries to pursue their personal predilections.' " For these reasons, § 2339B is void for vagueness as applied to the allegations in the Indictment.

Second, the defendants argue, § 2339B is unconstitutionally vague as applied to the allegations in the Indictment relating to the "provision" of "personnel." The defendants urge the Court to follow the Ninth Circuit Court of Appeals' decision in *Humanitarian Law Project v. Reno*, 205 F.3d 1130, 1137 (9th

Cir.2000), which found that "[i]t is easy to see how someone could be unsure about what [§ 2339B] prohibits with the use of the term 'personnel,' as it blurs the line between protected expression and unprotected conduct." The Court of Appeals thus affirmed the district court's finding that the use of the term "personnel" in § 2339B was unconstitutionally vague.

The Government relies on *United States v. Lindh,* 212 F.Supp.2d 541, 574 (E.D.Va.2002), which rejected *Humanitarian Law Project* and found that the alleged plain meaning of personnel--"an employment or employment-like relationship between the persons in question and the terrorist organization"-- gave fair notice of what conduct is prohibited under the statute and thus was not unconstitutionally vague. In that case, the court rejected a vagueness challenge in the context of a person who joined certain foreign terrorist organizations in combat against American forces. In defining the reach of the term personnel, the court found that it was not vague because it applied to "employees" or "employee-like operatives" or "quasi-employees" who work under the "direction and control" of the FTO. Whatever the merits of *Lindh* as applied to a person who provides himself or herself as a soldier in the army of an FTO, the standards set out there are not found in the statute, do not respond to the concerns of the Court of Appeals in *Humanitarian Law Project,* and do not provide standards to save the "provision" of "personnel" from being unconstitutionally vague as applied to the facts alleged in the Indictment. The fact that the "hard core" conduct in *Lindh* fell within the plain meaning of providing personnel yields no standards that can be applied to the conduct by alleged "quasi-employees" in this case. ...

It is not clear from § 2339B what behavior constitutes an impermissible provision of personnel to an FTO. Indeed, as the Ninth Circuit Court of Appeals stated in *Humanitarian Law Project,* "Someone who advocates the cause of the [FTO] could be seen as supplying them with personnel." *Humanitarian Law Project,* 205 F.3d at 1137. The Government accuses Stewart of providing personnel, including herself, to IG. In so doing, however, the Government fails to explain how a lawyer, acting as an agent of her client, an alleged leader of an FTO, could avoid being subject to criminal prosecution as a "quasi-employee" allegedly covered by the statute. At the argument on the motions, the Government expressed some uncertainty as to whether a lawyer for an FTO would be providing personnel to the FTO before the Government suggested that the answer may depend on whether the lawyer was "house counsel" or an independent counsel--distinctions not found in the statute.

The Government concedes that the statute does not prohibit mere membership in an FTO, and indeed mere membership could not constitutionally be prohibited without a requirement that the Government prove the defendants' specific intent to further the FTO's unlawful ends. *See NAACP v. Claiborne Hardware Co.,* 458 U.S. 886, 920, 102 S.Ct. 3409, 73 L.Ed.2d 1215 (1982) ("For liability to be imposed by reason of association alone, it is necessary to establish that the group itself possessed unlawful goals and that the individual held a specific intent to further those illegal aims."); *see also Boim v. Quranic Literacy Inst. and Holy Land Fnd. for Relief and Dev.,* 291 F.3d 1000, 1021-24 (7th Cir.2002). The Government attempts to distinguish the provision of "personnel" by arguing that it applies only to providing "employees" or "quasi-employees" and those acting under the "direction and control" of the FTO. But the terms "quasi-employee" or "employee-like operative" or "acting at the direction and control of the organization" are terms that are nowhere found in the statute or reasonably inferable from it.

Moreover, these terms and concepts applied to the prohibited provision of personnel provide no notice to persons of ordinary intelligence and leave the standards for enforcement to be developed by the Government. When asked at oral argument how to distinguish being a member of an organization from being a quasi-employee, the Government initially responded "You know it when you see it." While such a standard was once an acceptable way for a Supreme Court Justice to identify obscenity, see *Jacobellis v. Ohio,* 378 U.S. 184, 197, 84 S.Ct. 1676, 12 L.Ed.2d 793 (1964) (Stewart, J. concurring), it is an insufficient guide by which a person can predict the legality of that person's conduct. …

Moreover, the Government continued to provide an evolving definition of "personnel" to the Court following oral argument on this motion. Added now are "those acting as full-time or part-time employees or otherwise taking orders from the entity" who are therefore under the FTO's "direction or control." (Gov. Letter dated June 27, 2003 at 2 n. 1.)

The Government argues, moreover, that the Court should construe the statute to avoid constitutional questions. However, the Court "is not authorized to rewrite the law so it will pass constitutional muster." *Humanitarian Law Project,* 205 F.3d at 1137-38 (rejecting Government's suggestion to construe "personnel" as used in § 2339B as "under the direction or control" of an FTO). The Government also suggested at oral argument that perhaps a heightened scienter standard should be read into the statute, in some circumstances, in defining the provision of personnel. But that specific intent is not contained in the statute and thus could not give notice to persons about their allegedly prohibited conduct. Moreover, the Government subsequently withdrew its suggestion after oral argument. The statute's vagueness as applied to the allegations in the Indictment concerning the provision of personnel is a fatal flaw that the Court cannot cure by reading into the statute a stricter definition of the material support provision than the statute itself provides. …

CONCLUSION

The motions to dismiss Counts One and Two as void for vagueness are granted. The motions to dismiss those Counts on all other grounds are denied. …

[The Government has filed a notice of appeal from the order of the court in the above case dismissing the first two counts of the indictment. *See United States v. Sattar,* 2003 WL 22137012 (S.D.NY.) ed.]

Notes

1. Was the determination by the court that the relevant provision was unconstitutionally vague as applied correct? Or should the court have ruled instead that the conduct engaged in by the defendants did not fall within the ambit of the statute? Why do you think that the court followed the route that it took?

2. Section 2339B can be viewed as a kind of organizational crime. Compare it, for example, with the RICO statute. Whereas RICO, viewed in general terms, makes criminal conducting the affairs of an organization through criminal activity, 2339B criminalizes providing various kinds of assistance to a criminal organization. In effect, it can be viewed as a specialized form of an aider and abettor statute.

3. Is there something wrong with criminalizing the aiding and abetting of a criminal organization rather than the aiding and abetting of specific criminal conduct? Does that permit imposing serious criminal penalties when the aider and abettor is quite remote from the feared criminal conduct? Is this possibly why so many different kinds of conduct are subject to being prosecuted under 2339B?

4. What role should the mens rea play in the context of this type of offense? What is the required mens rea under the statute, that is, what exactly does knowingly modify? Note that because 2339B prosecutions have not generally gone to trial, we as yet know little about how the mens rea of the offense will be interpreted.

5. As mentioned earlier, the designation of an organization as a foreign terrorist organization is handled under the terms of another statute, 8 U.S.C. § 1189. Legal issues relating to the designation procedure have been addressed in a number of cases. See, e.g., *National Council of Resistance v. Department of State, 251 F.3d 192 (D.C. Cir. 2001); United States v. Rahmani, 209 F.Supp.2d 1045 (C.D.. Cal. 2002); People's Mojahedin Organization v. Department of State, 327 F.3d 1238 (D.C. Cir. 2003).* Section 2339B provides that such a designation cannot be challenged in a criminal prosecution under 2339B. The legality of that preclusion was also addressed in the *Sattar* case, in a portion of the opinion omitted here.

6. Two days after the opinion in *Sattar* was rendered, a legislative bill was introduced dealing with interpretative issues under 2339B and 2339A. Excerpts from the legislative bill are reproduced below. How do the provisions of the legislative bill relate to the decision in *Sattar*?

108th CONGRESS, 1st Session

HR 2858

Introduced in House

July 24, 2003

H. R. 2858
To prohibit material support for terrorism, and for other purposes.

IN THE HOUSE OF REPRESENTATIVES

July 24, 2003

Mr. GREEN of Wisconsin introduced the following bill; which was referred to the Committee on the Judiciary

A BILL

To prohibit material support for terrorism, and for other purposes.Be it enacted by the Senate and House of Representatives of the United States of America in Congress assembled,

SECTION 1. SHORT TITLE.

This Act may be cited as the 'Material Support to Terrorism Prohibition Enhancement Act of 2003'.

....

(d) Section 2339B of title 18, United States Code, is amended by adding at the end the following new subsection:

'(h) PROVISION OF PERSONNEL- No person may be prosecuted under this section in connection with the term 'personnel' unless that person has knowingly provided, attempted to provide, or conspired to provide a terrorist organization with one or more individuals (who may be or include himself) to work in concert with the organization or under its direction or control.'.

CHAPTER 13

THE CRIMINAL CIVIL RIGHTS STATUTES

Page 542.   **Insert at the end of note 1.**

In ruling on the civil provisions of the Violence Against Women Act, the Supreme Court rejected the claim that the Act could be sustained under Congress's power under § 5 of the Fourteenth Amendment. The Court's opinion (which also considered the scope of Congress's authority under the Commerce Clause, is reprinted *supra* at 4-18.

Page 569.   **Insert at the end of note 1.**

1(a). White supremacists who forced black and Hispanic victims out of a public park by force were convicted of violating 18 U.S.C. §§ 242 and 245(b)(2)(B). In *United States v. Allen*, 341 F.3d 870 (9th Cir. 2003), the court upheld their convictions, concluding that the park was a place of "public accommodation" under § 241, and upholding the constitutionality of § 245 as an appropriate exercise of Congressional power under both the Commerce Clause and the Thirteenth Amendment. Under *Lopez* and *Morrison* the question for Commerce Clause purposes is whether § 245 regulates conduct that substantially affects interstate commerce. The court emphasized that the statute in question (unlike the statutes in *Lopez* and *Morrison*) is part of a comprehensive body of civil rights legislation aimed at ending discrimination previously found to have an adverse impact on interstate commerce. Section 245 is the criminal counterpart of legislation previously upheld by the Court in *Katzenbach v. McClung*, 379 U.S. 294 (1964), and *Heart of Atlanta Motel, Inc. v. United States*, 379 U.S. 241 (1964). If Congress had the authority to enact the civil provisions, it had the authority to enact the criminal provisions as well. The court also ruled that the statute could be upheld under the Thirteenth Amendment, which gives Congress the power to abolish the badges and incidents of slavery. Reasoning that the Thirteenth Amendment permits Congress to reach private conduct, the court concluded that interfering with a person's use of a public park because he is black was a badge of slavery.

CHAPTER 14

FALSE STATEMENTS

TO LAW ENFORCEMENT AGENTS

18 U.S.C. § 1001

Page 579   **Insert at the end of the page.**

Other statutes prohibit false statements in particular contexts, or those made to particular government officials or agencies. The Sarbanes Oxley Act of 2002 added a new provision, 18 U.S.C. § 1350, in response to corporate accounting scandals; it requires the CEO and CFO of corporations regulated under the Securities and Exchange Act of 1934 to certify the accuracy of the periodic financial statements that must be filed with the SEC, and provides criminal penalties for knowing or wilful violations.

§ 1350. Failure of corporate officers to certify financial reports

(a) Certification of periodic financial reports.--Each periodic report containing financial statements filed by an issuer with the Securities Exchange Commission pursuant to section 13(a) or 15(d) of the Securities Exchange Act of 1934 (15 U.S.C. 78m(a) or 78o(d)) shall be accompanied by a written statement by the chief executive officer and chief financial officer (or equivalent thereof) of the issuer.

(b) Content.--The statement required under subsection (a) shall certify that the periodic report containing the financial statements fully complies with the requirements of section 13(a) or 15(d) of the Securities Exchange Act of 1934 (15 U.S.C. 78m or 78o(d)) and that information contained in the periodic report fairly presents, in all material respects, the financial condition and results of operations of the issuer.

(c) Criminal penalties.--Whoever–

(1) certifies any statement as set forth in subsections (a) and (b) of this section knowing that the periodic report accompanying the statement does not comport with all the requirements set forth in this section shall be fined not more than $1,000,000 or imprisoned not more than 10 years, or both; or

(2) willfully certifies any statement as set forth in subsections (a) and (b) of this section knowing that the periodic report accompanying the statement does not comport with all the requirements set forth in this section shall be fined not more than $5,000,000, or imprisoned not more than 20 years, or both.

CHAPTER 15

OBSTRUCTION OF JUSTICE:

INTERFERENCE WITH WITNESSES

Page 614.   **Insert at end of the introduction.**

Recent cases have highlighted the usefulness of the obstruction of justice statutes in the investigation and prosecution of complex financial transactions. In 2001, Enron, which was one of the world's largest electricity and natural gas traders, first announced a $618 million third quarter loss, and then announced that it had overstated its earnings by $567 million since 1997. Shortly thereafter it filed for bankruptcy and announced 4,000 layoffs. These events triggered an SEC investigation (and ultimately a criminal investigation) into the labyrinth of complex accounting procedures Enron had used to obscure its financial situation.

The first prosecutions did not focus on the underlying transactions. Instead, prosecutors targeted Enron's accounting firm, Arthur Anderson, and focused on its conduct in seeking to block the earliest stages of the investigation. Anderson was charged with violating 18 U.S.C. § 1512(e), which makes it a crime to "alter, destroy, mutilate or conceal an object with intent to impair the object's integrity or availability for use in an official proceeding."

For an interesting description of the government's theory and the deputy attorney general's comments at a press conference announcing the charges against Arthur Anderson, see http://www.usdoj.gov/dag/speech/2002/031402newsconferncearthurandersen.htm

On the eve of Arthur Anderson's trial, the government announced the guilty plea and cooperation agreement of senior Anderson accountant David Duncan, who supervised the Enron account. Duncan testified as a government witness, and acknowledged giving his subordinates a document policy "reminder" that was interpreted as an order to shred Enron-related documents. In response, Anderson employees shredded nearly 4,000 pounds of documents in three days (including more than 2,300 pounds in a single day). Although the government's case focused on Duncan, the jury (which originally deadlocked) eventually convicted and reported that it had found most damning the conduct of attorney Nancy Temple, who edited an e-mail by Duncan to remove references to misrepresentations in Enron's earnings statement.

For an in depth look at the Anderson case, see Stephan Landsman, *Death of an Accountant: The Jury Convicts Arthur Anderson of Obstruction of Justice*, 78 CHI. KENT L. REV. 1203 (2003), *available online* at http://lawreview.kentlaw.edu/articles/78-3/landsman.pdf .

The Anderson conviction led to the collapse of a big eight accounting firm, and set the stage for the prosecution of numerous Enron insiders as well as key figures in outside entities that assisted Enron in its financial machinations. Subsequently the government indicted other Enron executives and individuals outside Enron who participated in various transactions.

Various materials relating to these cases are available online:

● the Arthur Anderson indictment:

http://news.findlaw.com/hdocs/docs/enron/usandersen030702ind.pdf

● the cooperation agreement with David Duncan, who oversaw Enron's audits from the Houston office of Arthur Andersen

http://news.findlaw.com/hdocs/docs/enron/usduncan040602agr.pdf

● links to sites concerning Enron investigations (including links to material from the Department of Justice, Congress, the SEC, etc.):

http://www.bu.edu/lawlibrary/research/hottopic/enroninvest.htm#doj

More recently, the government pursued a similar strategy in the case of former Credit Suisse First Boston (CSFB) banker Frank Quattrone, who was a central figure in the government's investigation into widespread abuses of the initial public offering (IPO) market. After CSFB paid the government $100 million in civil fines, Quattrone was indicted on obstruction of justice charges accusing him of directing CSFB employees to destroy documents that had been subpoenaed by the SEC. After six days of deliberation, the jury was unable to reach agreement, and a mistrial was declared on October 26, 2003. Some commentators suggested that the result would give comfort to other high profile defendants awaiting trial, such as Martha Stewart, who faces charges of both obstruction of justice and securities fraud.

Page 617.   18 U.S.C. § 1512 has been amended by the 21st Century Department of Justice Appropriations Act and the Sarbanes Oxley Act. The new and amended language is indicated in italics.

Note that in addition to new subsction (a)(2), which deals with witness tampering using physical force, subsection (c) now deals explicitly with the destruction or alteration of documents or records in "any official proceeding," and makes that conduct punishable by up to twenty years imprisonment. Subsection (c) thus can be seen as a response to the document destruction in cases like Arthur Anderson.

§ 1512. Tampering with a witness, victim, or an informant

(a)(1) Whoever kills or attempts to kill another person, with intent to--

    (A) prevent the attendance or testimony of any person in an official proceeding;

    (B) prevent the production of a record, document, or other object, in an official proceeding; or

    (C) prevent the communication by any person to a law enforcement officer or judge of the United States of information relating to the commission or possible commission of a Federal offense or a violation of conditions of probation, parole, or release pending judicial proceedings;

shall be punished as provided in *paragraph (3)*.

(2) Whoever uses physical force or the threat of physical force against any person, or attempts to do so, with intent to--

    (A) influence, delay, or prevent the testimony of any person in an official proceeding;

    (B) cause or induce any person to--

    (i) withhold testimony, or withhold a record, document, or other object, from an official proceeding;

    (ii) alter, destroy, mutilate, or conceal an object with intent to impair the integrity or availability of the object for use in an official proceeding;

    (iii) evade legal process summoning that person to appear as a witness, or to produce a record, document, or other object, in an official proceeding; or

    (iv) be absent from an official proceeding to which that person has been summoned by legal process; or

    (C) hinder, delay, or prevent the communication to a law enforcement officer or judge of the United States of information relating to the commission or possible commission of a Federal offense or a violation of conditions of probation, supervised release, parole, or release pending judicial proceedings;

shall be punished as provided in paragraph (3).

(3) The punishment for an offense under this subsection is--

    (A) in the case of murder (as defined in section 1111), the death penalty or imprisonment for life, and in the case of any other killing, the punishment provided in section 1112;

>*(B)* in the case of--

>>*(i)* an attempt to murder; or

>>*(ii)* the use or attempted use of physical force against any person; imprisonment for not more than 20 years; and

>*(C)* in the case of the threat of use of physical force against any person, imprisonment for not more than 10 years.

(b) *Whoever knowingly uses intimidation*, threatens, or corruptly persuades another person, or attempts to do so, or engages in misleading conduct toward another person, with intent to--

(1) influence, delay, or prevent the testimony of any person in an official proceeding;

(2) cause or induce any person to--

>**(A)** withhold testimony, or withhold a record, document, or other object, from an official proceeding;

>**(B)** alter, destroy, mutilate, or conceal an object with intent to impair the object's integrity or availability for use in an official proceeding;

>**(C)** evade legal process summoning that person to appear as a witness, or to produce a record, document, or other object, in an official proceeding; or

>**(D)** be absent from an official proceeding to which such person has been summoned by legal process; or

(3) hinder, delay, or prevent the communication to a law enforcement officer or judge of the United States of information relating to the commission or possible commission of a Federal offense or a violation of conditions of probation *supervised release*, parole, or release pending judicial proceedings;

shall be fined under this title or imprisoned not more than ten years, or both.

(c) Whoever corruptly--

>*(1) alters, destroys, mutilates, or conceals a record, document, or other object, or attempts to do so, with the intent to impair the object's integrity or availability for use in an official proceeding; or*

>*(2) otherwise obstructs, influences, or impedes any official proceeding, or attempts to do so,*

shall be fined under this title or imprisoned not more than 20 years, or both.

(d) Whoever intentionally harasses another person and thereby hinders, delays, prevents, or dissuades any person from--

or attempts to do so, shall be fined under this title or imprisoned not more than one year, or both.

(e) In a prosecution for an offense under this section, it is an affirmative defense, as to which the defendant has the burden of proof by a preponderance of the evidence, that the conduct consisted solely of lawful conduct and that the defendant's sole intention was to encourage, induce, or cause the other person to testify truthfully.

(f) For the purposes of this section--

> **(1)** an official proceeding need not be pending or about to be instituted at the time of the offense; and
>
> **(2)** the testimony, or the record, document, or other object need not be admissible in evidence or free of a claim of privilege.

(g) In a prosecution for an offense under this section, no state of mind need be proved with respect to the circumstance--

> **(1)** that the official proceeding before a judge, court, magistrate judge, grand jury, or government agency is before a judge or court of the United States, a United States magistrate judge, a bankruptcy judge, a Federal grand jury, or a Federal Government agency; or
>
> **(2)** that the judge is a judge of the United States or that the law enforcement officer is an officer or employee of the Federal Government or a person authorized to act for or on behalf of the Federal Government or serving the Federal Government as an adviser or consultant.

(h) There is extraterritorial Federal jurisdiction over an offense under this section.

(i) A prosecution under this section or section 1503 may be brought in the district in which the official proceeding (whether or not pending or about to be instituted) was intended to be affected or in the district in which the conduct constituting the alleged offense occurred.

(j) If the offense under this section occurs in connection with a trial of a criminal case, the maximum term of imprisonment which may be imposed for the offense shall be the higher of that otherwise provided by law or the maximum term that could have been imposed for any offense charged in such case.

(k) Whoever conspires to commit any offense under this section shall be subject to the same penalties as those prescribed for the offense the commission of which was the object of the conspiracy.

Page 619. 18 U.S.C. § 1513 was also amended by both the 21st Century Department of Justice Appropriations Act and the Sarbanes Oxley Act.

In subsections (a)(1)(B) and (b)(2) the term "supervised release" was inserted following "probation."

In addition, apparently through inattention Congress added two new subsections to § 1513, each designated as (e). They provide:

> (e) Whoever knowingly, with the intent to retaliate, takes any action harmful to any person, including interference with the lawful employment or livelihood of any person, for providing to a law enforcement officer any truthful information relating to the commission or possible commission of any Federal offense, shall be fined under this title or imprisoned not more than 10 years, or both.

> (e) Whoever conspires to commit any offense under this section shall be subject to the same penalties as those prescribed for the offense the commission of which was the object of the conspiracy.

Finally, Sarbanes Oxley also added two new criminal statutes, 18 U.S.C. §§ 1519 and 1520, which are reprinted below. Section 1519 (like § 1512(c)) criminalizes the destruction of documents, though the scope of the two provisions varies slightly. Section 1520, in contrast, establishes a positive duty to retain certian materials. Both sections are a response to cases like Arthur Anderson.

§ 1519. Destruction, alteration, or falsification of records in Federal investigations and bankruptcy

Whoever knowingly alters, destroys, mutilates, conceals, covers up, falsifies, or makes a false entry in any record, document, or tangible object with the intent to impede, obstruct, or influence the investigation or proper administration of any matter within the jurisdiction of any department or agency of the United States or any case filed under title 11, or in relation to or contemplation of any such matter or case, shall be fined under this title, imprisoned not more than 20 years, or both.

§ 1520. Destruction of corporate audit records

(a)(1) Any accountant who conducts an audit of an issuer of securities to which section 10A(a) of the Securities Exchange Act of 1934 (15 U.S.C. 78j-1(a)) applies, shall maintain all audit or review workpapers for a period of 5 years from the end of the fiscal period in which the audit or review was concluded.

(2) The Securities and Exchange Commission shall promulgate, within 180 days, after adequate notice and an opportunity for comment, such rules and

regulations, as are reasonably necessary, relating to the retention of relevant records such as workpapers, documents that form the basis of an audit or review, memoranda, correspondence, communications, other documents, and records (including electronic records) which are created, sent, or received in connection with an audit or review and contain conclusions, opinions, analyses, or financial data relating to such an audit or review, which is conducted by any accountant who conducts an audit of an issuer of securities to which section 10A(a) of the Securities Exchange Act of 1934 (15 U.S.C. 78j- 1(a)) applies. The Commission may, from time to time, amend or supplement the rules and regulations that it is required to promulgate under this section, after adequate notice and an opportunity for comment, in order to ensure that such rules and regulations adequately comport with the purposes of this section.

(b) Whoever knowingly and willfully violates subsection (a)(1), or any rule or regulation promulgated by the Securities and Exchange Commission under subsection (a)(2), shall be fined under this title, imprisoned not more than 10 years, or both.

(c) Nothing in this section shall be deemed to diminish or relieve any person of any other duty or obligation imposed by Federal or State law or regulation to maintain, or refrain from destroying, any document.

CHAPTER 16

THE CHOICE BETWEEN FEDERAL

OR STATE PROSECUTION

AND THE POSSIBILITY

OF DUPLICATIVE PROSECUTIONS

Pages 643-48.   Read in conjunction with sections A and B.

Many of the factors discussed in these sections played a role in determining the jurisdiction that would first prosecute John Muhammad and Lee Malvo, whose sniper attacks terrorized the Washington D.C. area in 2002. Attacks occurred in both Virginia and Maryland, and a regional task force was formed to investigate the cases. Although they were arrested on federal warrants, the FBI, the Maryland State Police, and the Montgomery County police were all involved in their capture.

As the press accounts reveal, each of the prosecutors involved badly wanted to prosecute Muhammad and Malvo. Six of the ten sniper slayings were committed in Maryland, and a seventh victim who was killed in Virginia was a Maryland resident. Moreover, the arrests occurred in Maryland, and the men were initially held in custody in a county jail. But ultimately the United States controlled the decision, and it chose Virginia.

The defendants were arrested pursuant to federal warrants, and thus arraigned in federal court after a brief period of detention in a county facility. That physical custody pursuant to the original charges put the United States in the driver's seat to prosecute or decide which state should do so. Of course murder is not a federal offense, but by this point in the course you should realize that a determined federal prosecutor can usually find some way to reach criminal conduct. In this case, the mechanism was the Hobbs Act. There had been a demand for $10 million dollars to stop the killings, and this was the basis for the Hobbs Act extortion charges. Although the charges included the commission of murder in the course of extortion, and some of the charges carried the potential for the death penalty, there were problems with keeping the case in the federal system. In the first place, the evidence connecting the defendants to the murders was much stronger than the evidence connecting the defendants to the extortion note. Moreover, the heart of the federal case had to be extortion, rather than murder, and federal law did not allow the execution of juveniles. In fact, it appears that the final decision turned on where it was most likely that both defendants could be executed. Maryland's governor had imposed a moratorium on carrying out death sentences, and its law too barred the execution of juveniles. Virginia law, in contrast, permitted the execution of juveniles, and Virginia has been one of the leading states in terms of the number of executions carried out. So Attorney General John Ashcroft made the decision to allow Virginia to take the cases. How was this accomplished? The defendants were in federal custody, and they were moved from a federal facility in Maryland to one in Virginia, from which they were released into the custody of Virginia state officials. The Maryland prosecutors (and the victims they represented) were left out in the cold.

For an interesting account of the jurisdictional battle, see Sari Horwitz & Michael E. Fuane, *Jurisdictions Vied to Prosecute Pair*, WASH. POST, Oct. 9, 2003, at A1, *available online* at 2003 WL 62221661.

Page 661.   Insert at the beginning of the Notes.

Another example of the some of the issues raised in *Heath* is the state prosecution of Terry Nichols, who was convicted in federal court of (1) conspiracy (with Timothy McVeigh) to use weapon of mass destruction, and (2) eight counts of involuntary manslaughter relating to federal personnel killed in the Oklahoma City bombing. Although Nichols is now serving a life term with no possibility of release, the state has charged him with 168 counts of murder, and is seeking the death penalty.

The state charges have been controversial. Critics say a state prosecution is redundant and would cost Oklahoma millions of dollars while not necessarily yielding a death penalty. Legal experts also question whether a conviction would hold up. In 1996, a judge ordered the federal trials moved to Denver, saying Nichols and McVeigh could not be tried fairly in Oklahoma.

By 1992 Nichols's lead local attorney had already spent $1.7 million on his defense, and at that point he had not been paid for a year. The lawyer -- who said he was forced to lay off his investigative and support staff a year ago -- has also filed a request to withdraw from the case if additional funding is denied.

Page 663.   Insert at the end of note 3.

For a comprehensive analysis of dual sovereignty, see ADAM HARRIS KURLAND, SUCCESSIVE CRIMINAL PROSECUTIONS : THE DUAL SOVEREIGNTY EXCEPTION TO DOUBLE JEOPARDY IN STATE AND FEDERAL COURTS (2001).

Page 665.   Insert before Note 5.

4(a). What if federal law incorporates state law? Can it still be said that each prosecution is that of a separate sovereign? In *United States v. Angleton*, 314 F.3d 767 (5th Cir. 2002), a defendant who had been acquitted in state court of his wife's murder was charged in federal court with murder for hire. The statute, 18 U.S.C. § 1958(a) makes it a federal crime to travel (or cause another to travel) in interstate commerce or use the mails or a facility of interstate commerce with the intent that murder be committed *in violation of the laws of any state* in return for anything of pecuniary value. The defendant argued that when one sovereign is derivatively enforcing the law of another sovereign by incorporating it as a central element of its own statute, successive prosecutions should be barred. The court of appeals rejected this claim, noting that Congress can define crimes as it deems proper, and may make derivative use of borrowed terms, without undermining the principle of dual sovereignty. Given the number of federal crimes that incorporate state law definitions (including the RICO and money laundering statutes), a contrary ruling would have had far reaching consequences.

4(b). An interesting wrinkle on the basic dual sovereignty problem arose in *United States v. Lara*, 324 F.3d 635 (8th Cir. 2003) (en banc), a case involving a federal prosecution for an assault on a federal officer following a tribal prosecution for the same offense. The case split the en banc court, and the Supreme Court has granted certiorari.

As noted on page 661 of the main text, the Supreme Court held in *United States v. Wheeler*, 435 U.S. 313 (1978), that a Navajo tribal prosecution under the tribal code was the action of a separate sovereign, and hence the Double Jeopardy Clause did not bar a later federal prosecution based upon the same offense. In *Lara* the defendant, although an Indian, was not a member of the tribe in question. A majority of the en banc court concluded that his prosecution occurred pursuant to power delegated to the tribal court by the Indian Civil Rights Act, and accordingly that a subsequent federal prosecution brought under 18 U.S.C. § 111(a)(1) (assault on a federal officer) would violate Double Jeopardy. The dissenting judges argued that in enacting the Indian Civil Rights Act Congress had exercised its plenary legislative power over federal common law and Indian affairs to delineate the scope of inherent Indian sovereignty. Thus the tribal court's jurisdiction exercised pursuant to the Act was still the jurisdiction of the sovereign tribe, not federal authority delegated by Congress. As such, the dissent concluded, dual sovereignty was the proper analysis. The Supreme Court granted certiorari to resolve the issue. *United States v. Lara, cert. granted*, 72 U.S.L.W. 3106, 3202, 3234 (U.S., Sept. 30, 2003) (No. 03-107).

CHAPTER 17

THE SENTENCING GUIDELINES

Page 722   **Insert after note 1.**

In two important cases the Supreme Court returned to some of the issues raised when the sentencer considers conduct not encompassed in the elements of the offense. The first case, reprinted below, arose under a state statute, but its constitutional ruling governs federal proceedings as well. As you read the decision, think about what it means for the Guidelines system and for the various federal statutes prescribing mandatory minimum sentences.

Apprendi v. New Jersey, 530 U.S. 466 (2000)

Justice STEVENS delivered the opinion of the Court.

A New Jersey statute classifies the possession of a firearm for an unlawful purpose as a "second-degree" offense. N.J. Stat. Ann. § 2C:39- 4(a) (West 1995). Such an offense is punishable by imprisonment for "between five years and 10 years." § 2C:43-6(a)(2). A separate statute, described by that State's Supreme Court as a "hate crime" law, provides for an "extended term" of imprisonment if the trial judge finds, by a preponderance of the evidence, that "[t]he defendant in committing the crime acted with a purpose to intimidate an individual or group of individuals because of race, color, gender, handicap, religion, sexual orientation or ethnicity." N.J. Stat. Ann. § 2C:44-3(e) (West Supp. 1999-2000). The extended term authorized by the hate crime law for second-degree offenses is imprisonment for "between 10 and 20 years."

The question presented is whether the Due Process Clause of the Fourteenth Amendment requires that a factual determination authorizing an increase in the maximum prison sentence for an offense from 10 to 20 years be made by a jury on the basis of proof beyond a reasonable doubt.

I

At 2:04 a.m. on December 22, 1994, petitioner Charles C. Apprendi, Jr., fired several .22-caliber bullets into the home of an African-American family that had recently moved into a previously all-white neighborhood in Vineland, New Jersey. Apprendi was promptly arrested and, at 3:05 a.m., admitted that he was the shooter. After further questioning, at 6:04 a.m., he made a statement--which he later retracted--that even though he did not know the occupants of the house personally, "because they are black in color he does not want them in the neighborhood."

* * * * *

The parties entered into a plea agreement, pursuant to which Apprendi pleaded guilty to two counts (3 and 18) of second-degree possession of a firearm for an unlawful purpose,, and one count (22) of the third-degree offense of unlawful possession of an antipersonnel bomb; the prosecutor dismissed the other 20 counts. Under state law, a second-degree offense carries a penalty range of 5 to 10 years; a third-degree offense carries a penalty range of between 3 and 5 years. As part of the plea agreement, however, the State reserved the right to request the court to impose a higher "enhanced" sentence on count 18 (which was based on the December 22 shooting) on the ground that that offense was committed with a biased purpose. Apprendi, correspondingly, reserved the right to challenge the hate crime sentence enhancement on the ground that it violates the United States Constitution.

* * * * *

After the trial judge accepted the three guilty pleas, the prosecutor filed a formal motion for an extended term. The trial judge thereafter held an evidentiary hearing on the issue of Apprendi's "purpose" for the shooting on December 22. Apprendi adduced evidence from a psychologist and from seven character witnesses who testified that he did not have a reputation for racial bias. He also took the stand himself, explaining that the incident was an unintended consequence of overindulgence in alcohol, denying that he was in any way biased against African-Americans, and denying that his statement to the police had been accurately described. The judge, however, found the police officer's testimony credible, and concluded that the evidence supported a finding "that the crime was motivated by racial bias." Having found "by a preponderance of the evidence" that Apprendi's actions were taken "with a purpose to intimidate" as provided by the statute, the trial judge held that the hate crime enhancement applied. Rejecting Apprendi's constitutional challenge to the statute, the judge sentenced him to a 12-year term of imprisonment on count 18, and to shorter concurrent sentences on the other two counts.

Apprendi appealed, arguing, inter alia, that the Due Process Clause of the United States Constitution requires that the finding of bias upon which his hate crime sentence was based must be proved to a jury beyond a reasonable doubt.

* * * * *

Our answer to that question was foreshadowed by our opinion in Jones v. United States, 526 U.S. 227 (1999), construing a federal statute. We there noted that "under the Due Process Clause of the Fifth Amendment and the notice and jury trial guarantees of the Sixth Amendment, any fact (other than prior conviction) that increases the maximum penalty for a crime must be charged in an indictment, submitted to a jury, and proven beyond a reasonable doubt." The Fourteenth Amendment commands the same answer in this case involving a state statute.

III.

In his 1881 lecture on the criminal law, Oliver Wendell Holmes, Jr., observed: "The law threatens certain pains if you do certain things, intending thereby to give you a new motive for not doing them. If you persist in doing them, it has to inflict the pains in order that its threats may continue to be believed." New Jersey threatened Apprendi with certain pains if he unlawfully possessed a weapon and with additional pains if he selected his victims with a purpose to intimidate them because of their race. As a matter of simple justice, it seems obvious that the procedural safeguards designed to protect Apprendi from unwarranted pains should apply equally to the two acts that New Jersey has singled out for punishment. Merely using the label "sentence enhancement" to describe the latter surely does not provide a principled basis for treating them differently.

At stake in this case are constitutional protections of surpassing importance: the proscription of any deprivation of liberty without "due process of law," and the guarantee that "[i]n all criminal prosecutions, the accused shall enjoy the right to a speedy and public trial, by an impartial jury." Taken together, these rights indisputably entitle a criminal defendant to a jury determination that he is guilty of every element of the crime with which he is charged, beyond a reasonable doubt.

* * * * *

Any possible distinction between an "element" of a felony offense and a ""sentencing factor" was unknown to the practice of criminal indictment, trial by jury, and judgment by court as it existed during the years surrounding our Nation's founding. As a general rule, criminal proceedings were submitted to a jury after being initiated by an indictment containing "all the facts and circumstances which constitute the offence, stated with such certainty and precision, that the defendant may be enabled to determine the species of offence they constitute, in order that he may prepare his defence accordingly . . . and *that there may be no doubt as to the judgment which should be given, if the defendant be convicted.*"

Thus, with respect to the criminal law of felonious conduct, "the English trial judge of the later eighteenth century had very little explicit discretion in sentencing. The substantive criminal law tended to be sanction-specific: it prescribed a particular sentence for each offense."

This practice at common law held true when indictments were issued pursuant to statute. Just as the circumstances of the crime and the intent of the defendant at the time of commission were often essential elements to be alleged in the indictment, so too were the circumstances mandating a particular punishment. ""Where a statute annexes a higher degree of punishment to a common-law felony, if committed under particular circumstances, an indictment for the offence, in order to bring the defendant within that higher degree of punishment, must expressly charge it to have been committed under those circumstances, and must state the circumstances with certainty and precision. * * * *

We should be clear that nothing in this history suggests that it is impermissible for judges to exercise discretion - taking into consideration various factors relating both to offense and offender - in imposing a judgment within the range prescribed by statute. We have often noted that judges in this country have long exercised discretion of this nature in imposing sentence *within statutory limits* in the individual case. * * * [O]ur periodic recognition of judges' broad discretion in sentencing -- since the 19th-century shift in this country from statutes providing fixed-term sentences to those providing judges discretion within a permissible range -- has been regularly accompanied by the qualification that that discretion was bound by the range of sentencing options prescribed by the legislature.

The historic link between verdict and judgment and the consistent limitation on judges' discretion to operate within the limits of the legal penalties provided highlight the novelty of a legislative scheme that removes the jury from the determination of a fact that, if found, exposes the criminal defendant to a penalty exceeding the maximum he would receive if punished according to the facts reflected in the jury verdict alone. [10]

We do not suggest that trial practices cannot change in the course of centuries and still remain true to the principles that emerged from the Framers' fears "that the jury right could be lost not only by gross denial, but by erosion." Jones [v. United States,] 526 U. S. 227, 247-48. But practice must at least adhere to the basic principles undergirding the requirements of trying to a jury all facts necessary to constitute a statutory offense, and proving those facts beyond reasonable doubt. As we made clear in *Winship*, the "reasonable doubt" requirement "has a vital role in our criminal procedure for cogent reasons." 397 U. S. at 363. Prosecution subjects the criminal defendant both to the possibility that he may lose his liberty upon conviction and the certainty that he would be stigmatized by the conviction. We thus require this, among other, procedural protections in order to "provide concrete substance for the presumption of innocence," and to reduce the risk of imposing such deprivations erroneously. If a defendant faces punishment beyond that provided by statute when an offense is committed under certain circumstances but not others, it is obvious that both the loss of liberty and the stigma attaching to the offense are heightened; it necessarily follows that the defendant should not - at the moment the State is put to proof of those circumstances - be deprived of protections that have, until that point, unquestionably attached.

---

[10] * * * The evidence we describe that punishment was, by law, tied to the offense (enabling the defendant to discern, barring pardon or clergy, his punishment from the face of the indictment), and the evidence that American judges have exercised sentencing discretion within a legally prescribed range (enabling the defendant to discern from the statute of indictment what maximum punishment conviction under that statute could bring), point to a single, consistent conclusion: The judge's role in sentencing is constrained at its outer limits by the facts alleged in the indictment and found by the jury. Put simply, facts that expose a defendant to a punishment greater than that otherwise legally prescribed were by definition "elements" of a separate legal offense.

Since *Winship*, we have made clear beyond peradventure that Winship's due process and associated jury protections extend, to some degree, to determinations that go not to a defendant's guilt or innocence, but simply to the length of his sentence. This was a primary lesson of *Mullaney v. Wilbur*, 421 U. S. 684 (1975), in which we invalidated a Maine statute that presumed that a defendant who acted with an intent to kill possessed the "malice aforethought" necessary to constitute the State's murder offense (and therefore, was subject to that crime's associated punishment of life imprisonment). The statute placed the burden on the defendant of proving, in rebutting the statutory presumption, that he acted with a lesser degree of culpability, such as in the heat of passion, to win a reduction in the offense from murder to manslaughter (and thus a reduction of the maximum punishment of 20 years).

The State had posited in *Mullaney* that requiring a defendant to prove heat-of-passion intent to overcome a presumption of murderous intent did not implicate *Winship* protections because, upon conviction of either offense, the defendant would lose his liberty and face societal stigma just the same. Rejecting this argument, we acknowledged that criminal law "is concerned not only with guilt or innocence in the abstract, but also with the degree of criminal culpability" assessed. Because the "consequences" of a guilty verdict for murder and for manslaughter differed substantially, we dismissed the possibility that a State could circumvent the protections of *Winship* merely by redefining the elements that constitute different crimes, characterizing them as factors that bear solely on the extent of punishment.

IV.

It was in *McMillan v. Pennsylvania*, 477 U. S. 79 (1986), that this Court, for the first time, coined the term "sentencing factor" to refer to a fact that was not found by a jury but that could affect the sentence imposed by the judge. That case involved a challenge to the State's Mandatory Minimum Sentencing Act. According to its provisions, anyone convicted of certain felonies would be subject to a mandatory minimum penalty of five years imprisonment if the judge found, by a preponderance of the evidence, that the person "visibly possessed a firearm" in the course of committing one of the specified felonies. Articulating for the first time, and then applying, a multifactor set of criteria for determining whether the *Winship* protections applied to bar such a system, we concluded that the Pennsylvania statute did not run afoul of our previous admonitions against relieving the State of its burden of proving guilt, or tailoring the mere form of a criminal statute solely to avoid *Winship's* strictures.

We did not, however, there budge from the position that (1) constitutional limits exist to States' authority to define away facts necessary to constitute a criminal offense, and (2) that a state scheme that keeps from the jury facts that expose defendants to greater or additional punishment may raise serious constitutional concern. * * *

* * * * *

In sum, our reexamination of our cases in this area, and of the history upon which they rely, confirms the opinion that we expressed in *Jones*. Other than the fact of a prior conviction, any fact that increases the penalty for a crime beyond the prescribed statutory maximum must be submitted to a jury, and proved beyond a reasonable doubt. With that exception, we endorse the statement of the rule set forth in the concurring opinions in that case: "[I]t is unconstitutional for a legislature to remove from the jury the assessment of facts that increase the prescribed range of penalties to which a criminal defendant is exposed. It is equally clear that such facts must be established by proof beyond a reasonable doubt." 526 U. S., at 252-253 (opinion of Stevens, J.); see also *id.*, at 253 (opinion of Scalia, J.).[16]

V.

---

[16]The principal dissent would reject the Court's rule as a ""meaningless formalism," because it can conceive of hypothetical statutes that would comply with the rule and achieve the same result as the New Jersey statute. While a State could, hypothetically, undertake to revise its entire criminal code in the manner the dissent suggests--extending all statutory maximum sentences to, for example, 50 years and giving judges guided discretion as to a few specially selected factors within that range--this possibility seems remote. Among other reasons, structural democratic constraints exist to discourage legislatures from enacting penal statutes that expose every defendant convicted of, for example, weapons possession, to a maximum sentence exceeding that which is, in the legislature's judgment, generally proportional to the crime. This is as it should be. Our rule ensures that a State is obliged "to make its choices concerning the substantive content of its criminal laws with full awareness of the consequence, unable to mask substantive policy choices" of exposing all who are convicted to the maximum sentence it provides. So exposed, ""[t]he political check on potentially harsh legislative action is then more likely to operate."

In all events, if such an extensive revision of the State's entire criminal code were enacted for the purpose the dissent suggests, or if New Jersey simply reversed the burden of the hate crime finding (effectively assuming a crime was performed with a purpose to intimidate and then requiring a defendant to prove that it was not), we would be required to question whether the revision was constitutional under this Court's prior decisions.

Finally, the principal dissent ignores the distinction the Court has often recognized, *see, e.g., Martin v. Ohio*, 480 U. S. 228 (1987), between facts in aggravation of punishment and facts in mitigation. If facts found by a jury support a guilty verdict of murder, the judge is authorized by that jury verdict to sentence the defendant to the maximum sentence provided by the murder statute. If the defendant can escape the statutory maximum by showing, for example, that he is a war veteran, then a judge that finds the fact of veteran status is neither exposing the defendant to a deprivation of liberty greater than that authorized by the verdict according to statute, nor is the Judge imposing upon the defendant a greater stigma than that accompanying the jury verdict alone. Core concerns animating the jury and burden-of-proof requirements are thus absent from such a scheme.

The New Jersey statutory scheme that Apprendi asks us to invalidate allows a jury to convict a defendant of a second-degree offense based on its finding beyond a reasonable doubt that he unlawfully possessed a prohibited weapon; after a subsequent and separate proceeding, it then allows a judge to impose punishment identical to that New Jersey provides for crimes of the first degree, based upon the judge's finding, by a preponderance of the evidence, that the defendant's "purpose" for unlawfully possessing the weapon was to intimidate his victim on the basis of a particular characteristic the victim possessed. In light of the constitutional rule explained above, and all of the cases supporting it, this practice cannot stand.

* * * * *

[New Jersey argues that] the required finding of biased purpose is not an ""element" of a distinct hate crime offense, but rather the traditional ""sentencing factor" of motive.* * * The text of the statute requires the factfinder to determine whether the defendant possessed, at the time he committed the subject act, a "purpose to intimidate" on account of, inter alia, race. By its very terms, this statute mandates an examination of the defendant's state of mind - a concept known well to the criminal law as the defendant's mens rea.

* * * [T]he New Jersey Supreme Court correctly recognized that it does not matter whether the required finding is characterized as one of intent or of motive, because labels do not afford an acceptable answer. That point applies as well to the constitutionally novel and elusive distinction between "elements" and "sentencing factors." Despite what appears to us the clear "elemental" nature of the factor here, the relevant inquiry is one not of form, but of effect -- does the required finding expose the defendant to a greater punishment than that authorized by the jury's guilty verdict?

As the New Jersey Supreme Court itself understood in rejecting the argument that the required "motive" finding was simply a "traditional" sentencing factor, proof of motive did not ordinarily "increase the penal consequences to an actor." Indeed, the effect of New Jersey's sentencing "enhancement" here is unquestionably to turn a second-degree offense into a first-degree offense, under the State's own criminal code. The law thus runs directly into our warning in *Mullaney* that *Winship* is concerned as much with the category of substantive offense as "with the degree of criminal culpability" assessed. This concern flows not only from the historical pedigree of the jury and burden rights, but also from the powerful interests those rights serve. The degree of criminal culpability the legislature chooses to associate with particular, factually distinct conduct has significant implications both for a defendant's very liberty, and for the heightened stigma associated with an offense the legislature has selected as worthy of greater punishment.

The preceding discussion should make clear why the State's reliance on *McMillan* is likewise misplaced. The differential in sentence between what Apprendi would have received without the finding of biased purpose and what he could receive with it is not, it is true, as extreme as the difference between a small fine and mandatory life imprisonment. *Mullaney*, 421 U.S., at 700. But it can hardly be said that the potential doubling of one's sentence--from 10 years to 20--has no more than a nominal effect. Both in terms of absolute years behind bars, and because of the more severe stigma attached, the differential here is unquestionably of constitutional significance. When a judge's finding based on a mere preponderance of the evidence authorizes an increase in the maximum punishment, it is appropriately characterized as "a tail which wags the dog of the substantive offense."

New Jersey would also point to the fact that the State did not, in placing the required biased purpose finding in a sentencing enhancement provision, create a "separate offense calling for a separate penalty." As for this, we agree wholeheartedly with the New Jersey Supreme Court that merely because the state legislature placed its hate crime sentence "enhancer" "within the sentencing provisions" of the criminal code "does not mean that the finding of a biased purpose to intimidate is not an essential element of the offense." Indeed, the fact that New Jersey, along with numerous other States, has also made precisely the same conduct the subject of an independent substantive offense makes it clear that the mere presence of this "enhancement" in a sentencing statute does not define its character.

The New Jersey procedure challenged in this case is an unacceptable departure from the jury tradition that is an indispensable part of our criminal justice system. Accordingly, the judgment of the Supreme Court of New Jersey is reversed, and the case is remanded for further proceedings not inconsistent with this opinion.

SCALIA, J., concurring.

I feel the need to say a few words in response to Justice Breyer's dissent. It sketches an admirably fair and efficient scheme of criminal justice designed for a society that is prepared to leave criminal justice to the State. (Judges, it is sometimes necessary to remind ourselves, are part of the State - and an increasingly bureaucratic part of it, at that.) The founders of the American Republic were not prepared to leave it to the State, which is why the jury- trial guarantee was one of the least controversial provisions of the Bill of Rights. It has never been efficient; but it has always been free.

As for fairness, which Justice Breyer believes "[i]n modern times" the jury cannot provide: I think it not unfair to tell a prospective felon that if he commits his contemplated crime he is exposing himself to a jail sentence of 30 years - and that if, upon conviction, he gets anything less than that he may thank the mercy of a tenderhearted judge (just as he may thank the mercy of a tenderhearted parole commission if he is let out inordinately early, or the mercy of a tenderhearted governor if his sentence is commuted). Will there be disparities? Of course. But the criminal will never get more punishment than he bargained for when he did the crime, and his guilt of the crime (and hence the length of the sentence to which he is exposed) will be determined beyond a reasonable doubt by the unanimous vote of 12 of his fellow citizens.

In Justice Breyer's bureaucratic realm of perfect equity, by contrast, the facts that determine the length of sentence to which the defendant is exposed will be determined to exist (on a more-likely-than-not basis) by a single employee of the State. It is certainly arguable (Justice Breyer argues it) that this sacrifice of prior protections is worth it. But it is not arguable that, just because one thinks it is a better system, it must be, or is even more likely to be, the system envisioned by a Constitution that guarantees trial by jury. What ultimately demolishes the case for the dissenters is that they are unable to say what the right to trial by jury does guarantee if, as they assert, it does not guarantee - what it has been assumed to guarantee throughout our history - the right to have a jury determine those facts that determine the maximum sentence the law allows. They provide no coherent alternative.

Justice Breyer proceeds on the erroneous and all-too-common assumption that the Constitution means what we think it ought to mean. It does not; it means what it says. And the guarantee that "[i]n all criminal prosecutions, the accused shall enjoy the right to...trial, by an impartial jury" has no intelligible content unless it means that all the facts which must exist in order to subject the defendant to a legally prescribed punishment must be found by the jury.

THOMAS, J., with whom Justice Scalia joins as to Parts I and II, concurring.

I join the opinion of the Court in full. I write separately to explain my view that the Constitution requires a broader rule than the Court adopts.

I.

This case turns on the seemingly simple question of what constitutes a ""crime." Under the Federal Constitution, "the accused" has the right (1) "to be informed of the nature and cause of the accusation" (that is, the basis on which he is accused of a crime), (2) to be "held to answer for a capital, or otherwise infamous crime" only on an indictment or presentment of a grand jury, and (3) to be tried by "an impartial jury of the State and district wherein the crime shall have been committed." With the exception of the Grand Jury Clause, the Court has held that these protections apply in state prosecutions. Further, the Court has held that due process requires that the jury find beyond a reasonable doubt every fact necessary to constitute the crime. *In re Winship*, 397 U. S. 358, 364 (1970).

All of these constitutional protections turn on determining which facts constitute the "crime" - that is, which facts are the "elements" or ""ingredients" of a crime. In order for an accusation of a crime (whether by indictment or some other form) to be proper under the common law, and thus proper under the codification of the common-law rights in the Fifth and Sixth Amendments, it must allege all elements of that crime; likewise, in order for a jury trial of a crime to be proper, all elements of the crime must be proved to the jury (and, under *Winship*, proved beyond a reasonable doubt).

. Thus, it is critical to know which facts are elements. This question became more complicated following the Court's decision in *McMillan v. Pennsylvania*, 477

U. S. 79 (1986), which spawned a special sort of fact known as a sentencing enhancement. Such a fact increases a defendant's punishment but is not subject to the constitutional protections to which elements are subject. Justice O'Connor's dissent, in agreement with *McMillan* and *Almendarez-Torres v. United States*, 523 U. S. 224 (1998), takes the view that a legislature is free (within unspecified outer limits) to decree which facts are elements and which are sentencing enhancements.

Sentencing enhancements may be new creatures, but the question that they create for courts is not. Courts have long had to consider which facts are elements in order to determine the sufficiency of an accusation (usually an indictment). The answer that courts have provided regarding the accusation tells us what an element is, and it is then a simple matter to apply that answer to whatever constitutional right may be at issue in a case - here, *Winship* and the right to trial by jury. A long line of essentially uniform authority addressing accusations, and stretching from the earliest reported cases after the founding until well into the 20th century, establishes that the original understanding of which facts are elements was even broader than the rule that the Court adopts today.

This authority establishes that a "crime" includes every fact that is by law a basis for imposing or increasing punishment (in contrast with a fact that mitigates punishment). Thus, if the legislature defines some core crime and then provides for increasing the punishment of that crime upon a finding of some aggravating fact - of whatever sort, including the fact of a prior conviction - the core crime and the aggravating fact together constitute an aggravated crime, just as much as grand larceny is an aggravated form of petit larceny. The aggravating fact is an element of the aggravated crime. Similarly, if the legislature, rather than creating grades of crimes, has provided for setting the punishment of a crime based on some fact - such as a fine that is proportional to the value of stolen goods - that fact is also an element. No multi-factor parsing of statutes, of the sort that we have attempted since *McMillan*, is necessary. One need only look to the kind, degree, or range of punishment to which the prosecution is by law entitled for a given set of facts. Each fact necessary for that entitlement is an element.

II.

Cases from the founding to roughly the end of the Civil War establish the rule that I have described, applying it to all sorts of facts, including recidivism. As legislatures varied common-law crimes and created new crimes, American courts, particularly from the 1840's on, readily applied to these new laws the common-law understanding that a fact that is by law the basis for imposing or increasing punishment is an element.

[This section of the opinion contains a lengthy discussion of cases and treatises.]

Without belaboring the point any further, I simply note that this traditional understanding--that a "crime" includes every fact that is by law a basis for imposing or increasing punishment--continued well into the 20th-century, at least until the middle of the century. In fact, it is fair to say that *McMillan* began a revolution in the law regarding the definition of "crime." Today's decision, far from being a sharp break with the past, marks nothing more than a return to the status quo ante -- the status quo that reflected the original meaning of the Fifth and Sixth Amendments.

* * *

O'CONNOR, J., with whom The Chief Justice, Justice Kennedy, and Justice Breyer join, dissenting.

Last Term, in *Jones v. United States*, 526 U. S. 227 (1999), this Court found that our prior cases suggested the following principle: "[U]nder the Due Process Clause of the Fifth Amendment and the notice and jury trial guarantees of the Sixth Amendment, any fact (other than prior conviction) that increases the maximum penalty for a crime must be charged in an indictment, submitted to a jury, and proven beyond a reasonable doubt." At the time, Justice Kennedy rightly criticized the Court for its failure to explain the origins, contours, or consequences of its purported constitutional principle; for the inconsistency of that principle with our prior cases; and for the serious doubt that the holding cast on sentencing systems employed by the Federal Government and States alike. Today, in what will surely be remembered as a watershed change in constitutional law, the Court imposes as a constitutional rule the principle it first identified in *Jones*.

I.

Our Court has long recognized that not every fact that bears on a defendant's punishment need be charged in an indictment, submitted to a jury, and proved by the government beyond a reasonable doubt. Rather, we have held that the legislature's definition of the elements of the offense is usually dispositive. Although we have recognized that there are obviously constitutional limits beyond which the States may not go in this regard, and that in certain limited circumstances *Winship's* reasonable-doubt requirement applies to facts not formally identified as elements of the offense charged, we have proceeded with caution before deciding that a certain fact must be treated as an offense element despite the legislature's choice not to characterize it as such. We have therefore declined to establish any bright-line rule for making such judgments and have instead approached each case individually, sifting through the considerations most relevant to determining whether the legislature has acted properly within its broad power to define crimes and their punishments or instead has sought to evade the constitutional requirements associated with the characterization of a fact as an offense element.

In one bold stroke the Court today casts aside our traditional cautious approach and instead embraces a universal and seemingly bright-line rule limiting the power of Congress and state legislatures to define criminal offenses and the sentences that follow from convictions thereunder. The Court states: "Other than the fact of a prior conviction, any fact that increases the penalty for a crime beyond the prescribed statutory maximum must be submitted to a jury, and proved beyond a reasonable doubt." In its opinion, the Court marshals virtually no authority to support its extraordinary rule. Indeed, it is remarkable that the Court cannot identify a single instance, in the over 200 years since the ratification of the Bill of Rights, that our Court has applied, as a constitutional requirement, the rule it announces today.

* * * * *

II

That the Court's rule is unsupported by the history and case law it cites is reason enough to reject such a substantial departure from our settled jurisprudence. Significantly, the Court also fails to explain adequately why the Due Process Clauses of the Fifth and Fourteenth Amendments and the jury trial guarantee of the Sixth Amendment require application of its rule. Upon closer examination, it is possible that the Court's "increase in the maximum penalty" rule rests on a meaningless formalism that accords, at best, marginal protection for the constitutional rights that it seeks to effectuate.

Any discussion of either the constitutional necessity or the likely effect of the Court's rule must begin, of course, with an understanding of what exactly that rule is. As was the case in *Jones*, however, that discussion is complicated here by the Court's failure to clarify the contours of the constitutional principle underlying its decision. In fact, there appear to be several plausible interpretations of the constitutional principle on which the Court's decision rests.

For example, under one reading, the Court appears to hold that the Constitution requires that a fact be submitted to a jury and proved beyond a reasonable doubt only if that fact, as a formal matter, extends the range of punishment beyond the prescribed statutory maximum. A State could, however, remove from the jury (and subject to a standard of proof below "beyond a reasonable doubt") the assessment of those facts that define narrower ranges of punishment, within the overall statutory range, to which the defendant may be sentenced. Thus, apparently New Jersey could cure its sentencing scheme, and achieve virtually the same results, by drafting its weapons possession statute in the following manner: First, New Jersey could prescribe, in the weapons possession statute itself, a range of 5 to 20 years' imprisonment for one who commits that criminal offense. Second, New Jersey could provide that only those defendants convicted under the statute who are found by a judge, by a preponderance of the evidence, to have acted with a purpose to intimidate an individual on the basis of race may receive a sentence greater than 10 years' imprisonment.

* * * * * *

Under another reading of the Court's decision, it may mean only that the Constitution requires that a fact be submitted to a jury and proved beyond a reasonable doubt if it, as a formal matter, increases the range of punishment beyond that which could legally be imposed absent that fact. A State could, however, remove from the jury (and subject to a standard of proof below "beyond a reasonable doubt") the assessment of those facts that, as a formal matter, decrease the range of punishment below that which could legally be imposed absent that fact. Thus, consistent with our decision in *Patterson*, New Jersey could cure its sentencing scheme, and achieve virtually the same results, by drafting its weapons possession statute in the following manner: First, New Jersey could prescribe, in the weapons possession statute itself, a range of 5 to 20 years' imprisonment for one who commits that criminal offense. Second, New Jersey could provide that a defendant convicted under the statute whom a judge finds, by a preponderance of the evidence, not to have acted with a purpose to intimidate an individual on the basis of race may receive a sentence no greater than 10 years' imprisonment.

* * * If New Jersey can, consistent with the Constitution, make precisely the same differences in punishment turn on precisely the same facts, and can remove the assessment of those facts from the jury and subject them to a standard of proof below beyond a reasonable doubt, it is impossible to say that the Fifth, Sixth, and Fourteenth Amendments require the Court's rule. For the same reason, the ""structural democratic constraints" that might discourage a legislature from enacting either of the above hypothetical statutes would be no more significant than those that would discourage the enactment of New Jersey's present sentence-enhancement statute * * * *.

Given the pure formalism of the above readings of the Court's opinion, one suspects that the constitutional principle underlying its decision is more far reaching. The actual principle underlying the Court's decision may be that any fact (other than prior conviction) that has the effect, in real terms, of increasing the maximum punishment beyond an otherwise applicable range must be submitted to a jury and proved beyond a reasonable doubt. The principle thus would apply not only to schemes like New Jersey's, under which a factual determination exposes the defendant to a sentence beyond the prescribed statutory maximum, but also to all determinate sentencing schemes in which the length of a defendant's sentence within the statutory range turns on specific factual determinations (e.g., the federal Sentencing Guidelines). Justice Thomas essentially concedes that the rule outlined in his concurring opinion would require the invalidation of the Sentencing Guidelines.

I would reject any such principle. As explained above, it is inconsistent with our precedent and would require the Court to overrule, at a minimum, decisions like *Patterson* * * *. More importantly, given our approval of -- and the significant history in this country of -- discretionary sentencing by judges, it is difficult to understand how the Fifth, Sixth, and Fourteenth Amendments could possibly require the Court's or Justice Thomas' rule. Finally, in light of the adoption of determinate-sentencing schemes by many States and the Federal Government, the consequences of the Court's and Justice Thomas' rules in terms of sentencing schemes invalidated by today's decision will likely be severe.

Prior to the most recent wave of sentencing reform, the Federal Government and the States employed indeterminate-sentencing schemes in which judges and executive branch officials (e.g., parole board officials) had substantial discretion to determine the actual length of a defendant's sentence. Although indeterminate sentencing was intended to soften the harsh and uniform sentences formerly imposed under mandatory-sentencing systems, some studies revealed that indeterminate sentencing actually had the opposite effect. In response, Congress and the state legislatures shifted to determinate- sentencing schemes that aimed to limit judges' sentencing discretion and, thereby, afford similarly situated offenders equivalent treatment. In the Act, Congress created the United States Sentencing Commission, which in turn promulgated the Sentencing Guidelines that now govern sentencing by federal judges.

Whether one believes the determinate-sentencing reforms have proved successful or not--and the subject is one of extensive debate among commentators--the apparent effect of the Court's opinion today is to halt the current debate on sentencing reform in its tracks and to invalidate with the stroke of a pen three decades' worth of nationwide reform, all in the name of a principle with a questionable constitutional pedigree. Indeed, it is ironic that the Court, in the name of constitutional rights meant to protect criminal defendants from the potentially arbitrary exercise of power by prosecutors and judges, appears to rest its decision on a principle that would render unconstitutional efforts by Congress and the state legislatures to place constraints on that very power in the sentencing context.

Finally, perhaps the most significant impact of the Court's decision will be a practical one--its unsettling effect on sentencing conducted under current federal and state determinate-sentencing schemes. As I have explained, the Court does not say whether these schemes are constitutional, but its reasoning strongly suggests that they are not. Thus, with respect to past sentences handed down by judges under determinate-sentencing schemes, the Court's decision threatens to unleash a flood of petitions by convicted defendants seeking to invalidate their sentences in whole or in part on the authority of the Court's decision today. Statistics compiled by the United States Sentencing Commission reveal that almost a half-million cases have been sentenced under the Sentencing Guidelines since 1989. See Memorandum from U.S. Sentencing Commission to Supreme Court Library, dated June 8, 2000 (total number of cases sentenced under federal Sentencing Guidelines since 1989) (available in Clerk of Court's case file). Federal cases constitute only the tip of the iceberg. In 1998, for example, federal criminal prosecutions represented only about 0.4% of the total number of criminal prosecutions in federal and state courts. Because many States, like New Jersey, have determinate-sentencing schemes, the number of individual sentences drawn into question by the Court's decision could be colossal.

Because I do not believe that the Court's "increase in the maximum penalty" rule is required by the Constitution, I would evaluate New Jersey's sentence-enhancement statute, by analyzing the factors we have examined in past cases. First, the New Jersey statute does not shift the burden of proof on an essential ingredient of the offense by presuming that ingredient upon proof of other elements of the offense. Second, the magnitude of the New Jersey sentence enhancement, as applied in petitioner's case, is constitutionally permissible. Under New Jersey law, the weapons possession offense to which petitioner pleaded guilty carries a sentence range of 5 to 10 years' imprisonment. The fact that petitioner, in committing that offense, acted with a purpose to intimidate because of race exposed him to a higher sentence range of 10 to 20 years' imprisonment. The 10-year increase in the maximum penalty to which petitioner was exposed falls well within the range we have found permissible. Third, the New Jersey statute gives no impression of having been enacted to evade the constitutional requirements that attach when a State makes a fact an element of the charged offense. For example, New Jersey did not take what had previously been an element of the weapons possession offense and transform it into a sentencing factor.

In sum, New Jersey "simply took one factor that has always been considered by sentencing courts to bear on punishment"--a defendant's motive for committing the criminal offense--"and dictated the precise weight to be given that factor" when the motive is to intimidate a person because of race. * * * * *

BREYER, J., with whom Chief Justice Rehnquist joins, dissenting.

The majority holds that the Constitution contains the following requirement: ""any fact [other than recidivism] that increases the penalty for a crime beyond the prescribed statutory maximum must be submitted to a jury, and proved beyond a reasonable doubt." This rule would seem to promote a procedural ideal - that of juries, not judges, determining the existence of those facts upon which increased punishment turns. But the real world of criminal justice cannot hope to meet any such ideal. It can function only with the help of procedural compromises, particularly in respect to sentencing. And those compromises, which are themselves necessary for the fair functioning of the criminal justice system, preclude implementation of the procedural model that today's decision reflects. At the very least, the impractical nature of the requirement that the majority now recognizes supports the proposition that the Constitution was not intended to embody it.

I.

In modern times the law has left it to the sentencing judge to find those facts which (within broad sentencing limits set by the legislature) determine the sentence of a convicted offender. The judge's factfinding role is not inevitable. One could imagine, for example, a pure "charge offense" sentencing system in which the degree of punishment depended only upon the crime charged (e.g., eight mandatory years for robbery, six for arson, three for assault). But such a system would ignore many harms and risks of harm that the offender caused or created, and it would ignore many relevant offender characteristics. Hence, that imaginary charge offense system would not be a fair system, for it would lack proportionality, i.e., it would treat different offenders similarly despite major differences in the manner in which each committed the same crime.

There are many such manner-related differences in respect to criminal behavior. Empirical data collected by the Sentencing Commission make clear that, before the Guidelines, judges who exercised discretion within broad legislatively determined sentencing limits (say, a range of 0 to 20 years) would impose very different sentences upon offenders engaged in the same basic criminal conduct, depending, for example, upon the amount of drugs distributed (in respect to drug crimes), the amount of money taken (in respect to robbery, theft, or fraud), the presence or use of a weapon, injury to a victim, the vulnerability of a victim, the offender's role in the offense, recidivism, and many other offense-related or offender-related factors. See United States Sentencing Commission, Supplementary Report on the Initial Sentencing Guidelines and Policy Statements 35-39 (1987) (hereinafter Supplementary Report) (table listing data representing more than 20 such factors); see generally Department of Justice, W. Rhodes & C. Conly, Analysis of Federal Sentencing (May 1981). The majority does not deny that judges have exercised, and, constitutionally speaking, *may* exercise sentencing discretion in this way.

Nonetheless, it is important for present purposes to understand why *judges*, rather than *juries*, traditionally have determined the presence or absence of such sentence-affecting facts in any given case. And it is important to realize that the reason is not a theoretical one, but a practical one. It does not reflect (Justice SCALIA's opinion to the contrary notwithstanding) an ideal of procedural "fairness," but rather an administrative need for procedural compromise. There are, to put it simply, far too many potentially relevant sentencing factors to permit submission of all (or even many) of them to a jury. * * * The Guidelines note that "a sentencing system tailored to fit every conceivable wrinkle of each case can become unworkable and seriously compromise the certainty of punishment and its deterrent effect."

At the same time, to require jury consideration of all such factors - say, during trial where the issue is guilt or innocence - could easily place the defendant in the awkward (and conceivably unfair) position of having to deny he committed the crime yet offer proof about how he committed it, e.g., "I did not sell drugs, but I sold no more than 500 grams." And while special postverdict sentencing juries could cure this problem, they have seemed (but for capital cases) not worth their administrative costs. Hence, before the Guidelines, federal sentencing judges typically would obtain relevant factual sentencing information from probation officers' presentence reports, while permitting a convicted offender to challenge the information's accuracy at a hearing before the judge without benefit of trial-type evidentiary rules .

* * * * *

* * *[This analysis] suggests my basic problem with the Court's rule: A sentencing system in which judges have discretion to find sentencing-related factors is a workable system and one that has long been thought consistent with the Constitution; why, then, would the Constitution treat sentencing statutes any differently?

II.

As Justice Thomas suggests, until fairly recent times many legislatures rarely focused upon sentencing factors. Rather, it appears they simply identified typical forms of antisocial conduct, defined basic "crimes," and attached a broad sentencing range to each definition - leaving judges free to decide how to sentence within those ranges in light of such factors as they found relevant. But the Constitution does not freeze 19th-century sentencing practices into permanent law. And dissatisfaction with the traditional sentencing system (reflecting its tendency to treat similar cases differently) has led modern legislatures to write new laws that refer specifically to sentencing factors.

Legislatures have tended to address the problem of too much judicial sentencing discretion in two ways. First, legislatures sometimes have created sentencing commissions armed with delegated authority to make more uniform judicial exercise of that discretion. Congress, for example, has created a Federal Sentencing Commission, giving it the power to create Guidelines that (within the sentencing range set by individual statutes) reflect the host of factors that might be used to determine the actual sentence imposed for each individual crime....

Second, legislatures sometimes have directly limited the use (by judges or by a commission) of particular factors in sentencing, either by specifying statutorily how a particular factor will affect the sentence imposed or by specifying how a commission should use a particular factor when writing a guideline. Such a statute might state explicitly, for example, that a particular factor, say, use of a weapon, recidivism, injury to a victim, or bad motive, "shall" increase, or "may" increase, a particular sentence in a particular way.

The issue the Court decides today involves this second kind of legislation. The Court holds that a legislature cannot enact such legislation (where an increase in the maximum is involved) unless the factor at issue has been charged, tried to a jury, and found to exist beyond a reasonable doubt. My question in respect to this holding is, simply, "why would the Constitution contain such a requirement"?

III.

In light of the sentencing background described in Parts I and II, I do not see how the majority can find in the Constitution a requirement that "any fact" (other than recidivism) that increases the maximum penalty for a crime "must be submitted to a jury." * * * The majority raises no objection to traditional pre-Guidelines sentencing procedures under which judges, not juries, made the factual findings that would lead to an increase in an individual offender's sentence. How does a legislative determination differ in any significant way? For example, if a judge may on his or her own decide that victim injury or bad motive should increase a bank robber's sentence from 5 years to 10, why does it matter that a legislature instead enacts a statute that increases a bank robber's sentence from 5 years to 10 based on this same judicial finding?

With the possible exception of the last line of Justice SCALIA's concurring opinion, the majority also makes no constitutional objection to a legislative delegation to a commission of the authority to create guidelines that determine how a judge is to exercise sentencing discretion. See also ante, at 2380, n. 11 (THOMAS, J., concurring) (reserving the question). But if the Constitution permits Guidelines, why does it not permit Congress similarly to guide the exercise of a judge's sentencing discretion? That is, if the Constitution permits a delegatee (the commission) to exercise sentencing- related rulemaking power, how can it deny the delegator (the legislature) what is, in effect, the same rulemaking power?

* * * * *

 I certainly do not believe that the present sentencing system is one of "perfect equity," and I am willing, consequently, to assume that the majority's rule would provide a degree of increased procedural protection in respect to those particular sentencing factors currently embodied in statutes. I nonetheless believe that any such increased protection provides little practical help and comes at too high a price. For one thing, by leaving mandatory minimum sentences untouched, the majority's rule simply encourages any legislature interested in asserting control over the sentencing process to do so by creating those minimums. That result would mean significantly less procedural fairness, not more.

* * * * *

Notes

1. As you might imagine, the constitutional ruling in *Apprendi* created a wave of litigation, much of it transitional in nature, concerning the application of the decision to cases in various points in the pipeline and in various procedural postures. Of greater long term concern, however, was the question whether the Court would extend this analysis to sentencing guidelines and mandatory minimum sentencing statutes.

The Court returned to this issue in *Harris v. United States*, 536 U.S. 545 (2002), a 5 to 4 decision declining to extend *Apprendi* to statutory factors that trigger a mandatory minimum sentence. The Court held that the defendant was not entitled to a jury finding by proof beyond a reasonable doubt of the fact that he brandished a firearm in the course of committing a drug trafficking felony, although that finding required the court to impose a mandatory minimum sentence of seven years imprisonment. Writing for the majority, Justice Kennedy explained (emphasis added):

> Read together, *McMillan* and *Apprendi* mean that *those facts setting the outer limits of a sentence, and of the judicial power to impose it, are the elements of the crime for the purposes of the constitutional analysis.* Within the range authorized by the jury's verdict, however, the political system may channel judicial discretion--and rely upon judicial expertise--by requiring defendants to serve minimum terms after judges make certain factual findings. It is critical not to abandon that understanding at this late date. Legislatures and their constituents have relied upon *McMillan* to exercise control over sentencing through dozens of statutes like the one the Court approved in that case. Congress and the States have conditioned mandatory minimum

sentences upon judicial findings that, as here, a firearm was possessed, brandished, or discharged; or among other examples, that the victim was over 60 years of age; that the defendant possessed a certain quantity of drugs; that the victim was related to the defendant; and that the defendant was a repeat offender. We see no reason to overturn those statutes or cast uncertainty upon the sentences imposed under them.

Justice Breyer wrote separately, concurring in part and concurring in the judgment. As in *Apprendi* he emphasized the benefits of the Guidelines and rejected a rigid emphasis on theory that could overwhelm the system without bringing any real benefit. The defector from the *Apprendi* majority was Justice Scalia, who did not write separately.

So, for the moment at least, the Guidelines appear to be on a sound constitutional footing, as long as they do not permit an increase in the authorized sentence. But what exactly does that mean? The Supreme Court has granted certiorari in *Blakely v. Washington*, 47 P.3d 149 (Wash. App. 2002), *appeal denied*, 148 Wash. 1010 (2003), *cert. granted*, U.S. No. 02-1632 (October 20, 2003). The issue in *Blakely* is whether *Apprendi* requires a jury determination, beyond a reasonable doubt, of the facts that justify an upward departure to an "exceptional sentence" under the state guideline statute. Based upon the sentencing court's finding that the offense involved domestic violence and deliberate cruelty toward defendant's wife within sight or sound of a minor child, the court roughly doubled the defendant's sentence, to 90 months. If state law authorizes a sentence of 90 months for this offense, but *only* if the court finds certain aggregating facts, do those facts have to be proved to a jury beyond a reasonable doubt? Blakely will argue that they do, citing *Ring v. Arizona*, 122 S.Ct. 2428 (2002). *Ring*, decided the same term as *Harris*, was a 7 to 2 decision holding the Sixth Amendment right to jury trial was denied by a capital sentencing statute under which trial judge, sitting alone, determines the presence or absence of the aggravating factors necessary for the imposition of the death penalty. *Blakely* will test whether this ruling is effectively limited to death penalty cases, and, if not, how broadly it will sweep. Note that even if *Blakely* gives *Ring* a broad interpretation, there are very few (less than 1%) upward *departures* in the federal courts, though of course there are countless cases in which a wide variety of upward *adjustments* are made.

2. *Apprendi* has provoked an outpouring of excellent scholarship. *See, e.g.*, Nancy J. King & Susan R. Klein, *Essential Elements*, 54 VAND. L. REV. 1467 (2001); Alan C. Michaels, *Trial Rights at Sentencing*, 81 N.C. L. REV. 1771 (2003); Susan Herman, *Applying Apprendi to the Federal Sentencing Guidelines: You Say You Want a Revolution?*, 87 IOWA L. REV. 615 (2002); Elizabeth Olson, *Rethinking Mandatory Minimums After Apprendi*, 96 NW. U. L. REV. 811(2002); Benjamin J. Priester, *Constitutional Formalism and the Meaning of Apprendi v. New Jersey*, 38 AMERICAN CRIMINAL LAW REVIEW 281 (2001). For a strong debate about the impact of *Apprendi* on plea bargaining, see Stephanos Bibas, *Judicial Fact-Finding and Sentence Enhancements in a World of Guilty Pleas*, 110 Yale L.J. 1097 (2001); Stephanos Bibas, *Apprendi and the Dynamics of Guilty Pleas*, 54 STAN. L. REV. 311 (2001); and Nancy J. King & Susan R. Klein, *Apprendi and Plea Bargaining*, 54 STAN. L. REV. 295 (2001).

Page 726 The general standard for departure specified in § 5K2.0 was substantially revised by an emergency amendment in October 2003. The purpose and effect of the change can best be appreciated by reading pages 726-43 of the main text before turning to the materials below.

The material in this section deals with departures, a topic that is in flux (if not revolution) at the instigation of Congress. *Galante* and the notes that follow should give you some idea why Congress was concerned about the potential of downward departures to undermine the Guidelines system and promote disparity. It's quite clear that the defendant in *Galante* would not have received a departure in most other circuits (and probably not if he had been sentenced by many other judges in his own district). Yet under *Koon* the court of appeals sustained the departure.

The issue of departures surfaced in Congress rather suddenly during the spring of 2003 when Representative Feeney introduced a floor amendment to popular legislation already passed by the Senate to fund a nationwide "Amber Alert" system. The amendment was, to put it mildly, a bombshell. Among other things, the amendment would have prohibited downward departures for grounds not specified under §5K2.0, and would have barred downward departures on nine grounds (including family ties, employment, and civic, charitable, and public service). Additionally, the amendment effectively removed the downward departure for aberrant behavior. It imposed a moratorium on the creation of new downward (but not upward) departures, and limited downward departures on remand to those identified in the trial court's original order. The amendment also sought to strengthen oversight of departures by requiring the Attorney General to report every downward departure to both Houses of Congress within 15 days of the court's action, and also required additional reporting of departures by the Chief Judge of each circuit and by the Sentencing Commission. It gave prosecutors more control over acceptance of responsibility departures. And, finally, the amendment provided the appellate courts with sweeping review powers in departure cases. Remarkably, the House passed the amendment with little discussion, and without any consultation with the Sentencing Commission.

There was quite an outpouring of opposition. Members of the federal judiciary, including Chief Justice Rehnquist and Associate Justice Kennedy, publicly noted their strong disapproval of the legislation. The ABA and various public interest and trade groups opposed the measure, and more than 70 law professors signed a letter criticizing the substance and process. On the merits, opponents argued that it was unwise and unnecessary to restrict departures. The original conception of the Guidelines included an important role for departures, and no system of rules can anticipate all cases. On process, opponents objected to radically restructuring sentencing law and procedure on such a casual basis (particularly without consulting the Sentencing Commission, the expert body charged with the oversight of sentencing law). Supporters, in contrast, argued that it was unfair to permit judge's individual preferences to determine the sentence for particular defendants. They cited a recent increase in the number of downward departures, and argued that the oversight provisions and elimination of discretionary downward departures were effective steps to reach the goal of consistency in sentencing.

As a consequence of the public outcry, there was considerable pressure on the House-Senate conferees to curtail some of the more objectionable provisions in the Feeney Amendment. Several major modifications were adopted at conference, and after a short but impassioned debate on the Senate floor both houses passed legislation including the modified Feeney amendment, which is now called the PROTECT Act (Prosecutorial Remedies and Tools Against the Exploitation of Children Today Act of 2003).

The PROTECT Act (which is reprinted in a convenient form at 15 FED. SENT. REP. 358 (2003) made a number of important changes in federal sentencing law. One former United States Attorney summarized the PROTECT Act provisions as follows:

> [T]he revised statute (1) eliminated numerous grounds for downward departure in child-victim, sexual abuse and obscenity cases, (2) expanded the grounds for appellate reversal of downward departures, (3) granted appellate courts the authority to review departure decisions under a de novo standard of review, (4) limited district courts' ability to downwardly depart on remand, (5) prohibited the Commission from creating new downward departure guidelines for the next two years, and (6) conditioned the 'early disposition' departure and three-level acceptance of responsibility adjustment on a government motion.

Alan Vinegrad, *The New Federal Sentencing Law*, 15 FED. SENT. REP. 341 (2003). Note that the elimination of specified downward departure grounds (such as departures based on aberrant behavior, family ties and responsibilities, community ties, military, civic, charitable or public service, employment-related contributions or similar good works) was limited to a discrete category of child-victim, sexual abuse and obscenity offenses. Similarly, downward departures under § 5K2.0 were abolished in only this category of cases. In other cases judges are free to impose downward departures as long as they satisfy § 5K2.0's standard for departure.

But Congress also used the legislation to set in motion a process for further limiting departure law as well as monitoring the grant of departures by individual judges. The conference committee inserted a section in the Act that requiring the Sentencing Commission, within 180 days of the statute's enactment, to review all downward departures authorized by the Guidelines and to promulgate guideline amendments "to ensure that the incidence of downward departures are [sic] substantially reduced." The Act retained the requirement that the Attorney General report downward departures to Congress within 15 days, although it also created an exception that may eliminate this reporting requirement altogether. Under the exception, the 15-day reporting requirement does not take effect if the Attorney General submits a detailed report to the House and Senate Judiciary Committees, within 90 days of the statute's enactment, setting forth procedures by which the Justice Department will ensure that prosecutors oppose unsupported downward departures as well as ensure the "vigorous pursuit of appropriate and meritorious appeals." Attorney General John Ashcroft issued a memorandum to all department personnel regarding departures that appears to meet the statutory requirement. The memorandum is reprinted at 15 FED. SENT. REP. 375 (2003).

The PROTECT Act also restructured the Sentencing Commission itself. Although the current members of the commission are not affected, as to the future, the Act provides that there may be no more than three judges on the seven member commission. This appears to reflect deep Congressional dissatisfaction with the judiciary's attitude regarding sentencing reform.

The Commission released emergency guidelines responding to the PROTECT Act's requirement that it restrict departures. § 2K5.0 has been completely rewritten, as have the specific policy statements dealing with offender characteristics such as family ties and responsibilities. The new family ties policy statement now provides:

§5H1.6. Family Ties and Responsibilities (Policy Statement)

Family ties and responsibilities are not ordinarily relevant in determining whethera departure may be warranted.

Family responsibilities that are complied with may be relevant to the determination of the amount of restitution or fine.

Commentary

Application Note:

1. Circumstances to Consider.—

(A) In General.—In determining whether a departure is warranted under this policy statement, the court shall consider the following non-exhaustive list of circumstances:

(i) The seriousness of the offense.

(ii) The involvement in the offense, if any, of members of the defendant's family.

(iii) The danger, if any, to members of the defendant's family as a result of the offense.

(B) Departures Based on Loss of Caretaking or Financial Support.—A departure under this policy statement based on the loss of caretaking or financial support of the defendant's family requires, in addition to the court's consideration of the non-exhaustive list of circumstances in subdivision (A), the presence of the following circumstances:

(i) The defendant's service of a sentence within the applicable guideline range will cause a substantial, direct, and specific loss of essential caretaking, or essential financial support, to the defendant's family.

(ii) The loss of caretaking or financial support substantially exceeds the harm ordinarily incident to incarceration for a similarly situated defendant. For example, the fact that the defendant's family might incur some degree of financial hardship or suffer to some extent from the absence of a parent through incarceration is not in itself sufficient as a basis for departure because such hardship or suffering is of a sort ordinarily incident to incarceration.

(iii) The loss of caretaking or financial support is one for which no effective remedial or ameliorative programs reasonably are available, making the defendant's caretaking or financial support irreplaceable to the defendant's family.

(iv) The departure effectively will address the loss of caretaking or financial support.

The family ties provision – and other Guidelines dealing with offender characteristics – are now subject to revised § 5K2.0, which is reprinted below. As you read this provision and consider the issues raised by the PROTECT Act, think how the new guideline strikes the balance between the need for uniformity and the need for some individualization. How far did the Commission go in restricting departures? Do you think this will be sufficient to satisfy Congress? One way to think about this is to consider whether *Galante* would come out any differently in the district court. If not, remember that the appellate standard is now *de novo* review.

The broader is whether there is a need for greater uniformity. In your view, do cases like *Galante* show there was a problem? Was it was time for Congress to step in? If so, did it make the right kinds of changes? Of course it remains to be seen how much the lower courts will alter their behavior in cases not involving child victims or sex offenses. Some commentators have predicted that the lower courts will get the message and cut back sharply on departures, not wishing to be put in the Congressional spotlight. Others think that at least some judges are made of sterner stuff, and will continue to depart when they think appropriate, within, of course, the boundaries set by the new guidelines. § 5K2.0 now provides:

§5K2.0. Grounds for Departure (Policy Statement)

(a) UPWARD DEPARTURES IN GENERAL AND DOWNWARD DEPARTURES IN CRIMINAL CASES OTHER THAN CHILD CRIMES AND SEXUAL OFFENSES.—

(1) IN GENERAL.—The sentencing court may depart from the applicable guideline range if—

(A) in the case of offenses other than child crimes and sexual offenses, the court finds, pursuant to 18 U.S.C. § 3553(b)(1), that there exists an aggravating or mitigating circumstance;

or (B) in the case of child crimes and sexual offenses, the court finds, pursuant to 18 U.S.C. § 3553(b)(2)(A)(i), that there exists an aggravating circumstance, of a kind, or to a degree, not adequately taken into consideration by the Sentencing Commission in formulating the guidelines that, in order to advance the objectives set forth in 18 U.S.C. § 3553(a)(2), should result in a sentence different from that described.

(2) DEPARTURES BASED ON CIRCUMSTANCES OF A KIND NOT ADEQUATELY TAKEN INTO CONSIDERATION.—

(A) IDENTIFIED CIRCUMSTANCES.—This subpart (Chapter Five, Part K, Subpart 2 (Other Grounds for Departure)) identifies some of the circumstances that the Commission may have not adequately taken into consideration in determining the applicable guideline range (e.g., as a specific offense characteristic or other adjustment). If any such circumstance is present in the case and has not adequately been taken into consideration in determining the applicable guideline range, a departure consistent with 18 U.S.C. § 3553(b) and the provisions of this subpart may be warranted.

(B) UNIDENTIFIED CIRCUMSTANCES.—A departure may be warranted in the exceptional case in which there is present a circumstance that the Commission has not identified in the guidelines but that nevertheless is relevant to determining the appropriate sentence.

(3) DEPARTURES BASED ON CIRCUMSTANCES PRESENT TO A DEGREE NOT ADEQUATELY TAKEN INTO CONSIDERATION.—A departure may be warranted in an exceptional case, even though the circumstance that forms the basis for the departure is taken into consideration in determining the guideline range, if the court determines that such circumstance is present in the offense to a degree substantially in excess of, or substantially below, that which ordinarily is involved in that kind of offense.

(4) DEPARTURES BASED ON NOT ORDINARILY RELEVANT OFFENDER CHARACTERISTICS AND OTHER CIRCUMSTANCES.—An offender characteristic or other circumstance identified in Chapter Five, Part H (Offender Characteristics) or elsewhere in the guidelines as not ordinarily relevant in determining whether a departure is warranted may be relevant to this determination only if such offender characteristic or other circumstance is present to an exceptional degree.

(b) DOWNWARD DEPARTURES IN CHILD CRIMES AND SEXUAL OFFENSES.—Under 18 U.S.C. § 3553(b)(2)(A)(ii), the sentencing court may impose a sentence below the range established by the applicable guidelines only if the court finds that there exists a mitigating circumstance of a kind, or to a degree, that—

(1) has been affirmatively and specifically identified as a permissible ground of downward departure in the sentencing guidelines or policy statements issued under section 994(a) of title 28, United States Code, taking account of any amendments to such sentencing guidelines or policy statements by act of Congress;

(2) has not adequately been taken into consideration by the Sentencing Commission in formulating the guidelines; and (3) should result in a sentence different from that described.

The grounds enumerated in this Part K of Chapter Five are the sole grounds that have been affirmatively and specifically identified as a permissible ground of downward departure in these sentencing guidelines and policy statements. Thus, notwithstanding any other reference to authority to depart downward elsewhere in this Sentencing Manual, a ground of downward departure has not been affirmatively and specifically identified as a permissible ground of downward departure within the meaning of section 3553(b)(2) unless it is expressly enumerated in this Part K as a ground upon which a downward departure may be granted.

(c) LIMITATION ON DEPARTURES BASED ON MULTIPLE CIRCUMSTANCES.—The court may depart from the applicable guideline range based on a combination of two or more offender characteristics or other circumstances, none of which independently is sufficient to provide a basis for departure, only if—

(1) such offender characteristics or other circumstances, taken together, make the case an exceptional one; and

(2) each such offender characteristic or other circumstance is—

(A) present to a substantial degree; and

(B) identified in the guidelines as a permissible ground for departure, even if such offender characteristic or other circumstance is not ordinarily relevant to a determination of whether a departure is warranted.

(d) PROHIBITED DEPARTURES.—Notwithstanding subsections (a) and (b) of this policy statement, or any other provision in the guidelines, the court may not depart from the applicable guideline range based on any of the following circumstances:

(1) Any circumstance specifically prohibited as a ground for departure in §§5H1.10 (Race, Sex, National Origin, Creed, Religion, and Socio-Economic Status), 5H1.12 (Lack of Guidance as a Youth and Similar Circumstances), the third and last sentences of 5H1.4 (Physical Condition, Including Drug or Alcohol Dependence or Abuse; Gambling Addiction), the last sentence of 5K2.12 (Coercion and Duress), and 5K2.19 (Post-Sentencing Rehabilitative Efforts).

(2) The defendant's acceptance of responsibility for the offense, which may be taken into account only under §3E1.1 (Acceptance of Responsibility).

(3) The defendant's aggravating or mitigating role in the offense, which may be taken into account only under §3B1.1 (Aggravating Role) or §3B1.2 (Mitigating Role), respectively.

(4) The defendant's decision, in and of itself, to plead guilty to the offense or to enter a plea agreement with respect to the offense (i.e., a departure may not be based merely on the fact that the defendant decided to plead guilty or to enter into a plea agreement, but a departure may be based on justifiable, non-prohibited reasons as part of a sentence that is recommended, or agreed to, in the plea agreement and accepted by the court. See §6B1.2 (Standards for Acceptance of Plea Agreement).

(5) The defendant's fulfillment of restitution obligations only to the extent required by law including the guidelines (i.e.,a departure may not be based on unexceptional efforts to remedy the harm caused by the offense).

(6) Any other circumstance specifically prohibited as a ground for departure in the guidelines.

(e) REQUIREMENT OF SPECIFIC WRITTEN REASONS FOR DEPARTURE.—If the court departs from the applicable guideline range, it shall state, pursuant to 18 U.S.C. § 3553(c), its specific reasons for departure in open court at the time of sentencing and, with limited exception in the case of statements received in camera, shall state those reasons with specificity in the written judgment and commitment order.

Commentary

Application Notes:

* * * * *

2. Scope of this Policy Statement.—

(A) Departures Covered by this Policy Statement.—This policy statement covers departures from the applicable guideline range based on offense characteristics or offender characteristics of a kind, or to a degree, not adequately taken into consideration in determining that range. See 18 U.S.C. § 3553(b).

Subsection (a) of this policy statement applies to upward departures in all cases covered by the guidelines and to downward departures in all such cases except for downward departures in child crimes and sexual offenses.

Subsection (b) of this policy statement applies only to downward departures in child crimes and sexual offenses.

(B) Departures Covered by Other Guidelines.—This policy statement does not cover the following departures, which are addressed elsewhere in the guidelines: (i) departures based on the defendant's criminal history (see Chapter Four (Criminal History and Criminal Livelihood), particularly §4A1.3 (Departures Based on Inadequacy of Criminal History Category)); (ii) departures based on the defendant's substantial assistance to the authorities (see §5K1.1 (Substantial Assistance to Authorities)); and (iii) departures based on early disposition programs (see §5K3.1 (Early Disposition Programs)).

3. Kinds and Expected Frequency of Departures under Subsection (a).—As set forth in subsection (a), there generally are two kinds of departures from the guidelines based on offense characteristics and/or offender characteristics: (A) departures based on circumstances of a kind not adequately taken into consideration in the guidelines; and (B) departures based on circumstances that are present to a degree not adequately taken into consideration in the guidelines.

(A) Departures Based on Circumstances of a Kind Not Adequately Taken into Account in Guidelines.—Subsection (a)(2) authorizes the court to depart if there exists an aggravating or a mitigating circumstance in a case under 18 U.S.C. § 3553(b)(1), or an aggravating circumstance in a case under 18 U.S.C. § 3553(b)(2)(A)(i), of a kind not adequately taken into consideration in the guidelines.

(i) Identified Circumstances.—This subpart (Chapter Five, Part K, Subpart 2) identifies several circumstances that the Commission may have not adequately taken into consideration in setting the offense level for certain cases. Offense guidelines in Chapter Two (Offense Conduct) and

adjustments in Chapter Three (Adjustments) sometimes identify circumstances the Commission may have not adequately taken into consideration in setting the offense level for offenses covered by those guidelines. If the offense guideline in Chapter Two or an adjustment in Chapter Three does not adequately take that circumstance into consideration in setting the offense level for the offense, and only to the extent not adequately taken into consideration, a departure based on that circumstance may be warranted.

(ii) Unidentified Circumstances.—A case may involve circumstances, in addition to those identified by the guidelines, that have not adequately been taken into consideration by the Commission, and the presence of any such circumstance may warrant departure from the guidelines in that case. However, inasmuch as the Commission has continued to monitor and refine the guidelines since their inception to take into consideration relevant circumstances in sentencing, it is expected that departures based on such unidentified circumstances will occur rarely and only in exceptional cases.

(B) Departures Based on Circumstances Present to a Degree Not Adequately Taken into Consideration in Guidelines.—

(i) In General.—Subsection (a)(3) authorizes the court to depart if there exists an aggravating or a mitigating circumstance in a case under 18 U.S.C. § 3553(b)(1), or an aggravating circumstance in a case under 18 U.S.C. § 3553(b)(2)(A)(i), to a degree not adequately taken into consideration in the guidelines. However, inasmuch as the Commission has continued to monitor and refine the guidelines since their inception to determine the most appropriate weight to be accorded the mitigating and aggravating circumstances specified in the guidelines, it is expected that departures based on the weight accorded to any such circumstance will occur rarely and only in exceptional cases.

(ii) Examples.—As set forth in subsection (a)(3), if the applicable offense guideline and adjustments take into consideration a circumstance identified in this subpart, departure is warranted only if the circumstance is present to a degree substantially in excess of that which ordinarily is involved in the offense. Accordingly, a departure pursuant to §5K2.7 for the disruption of a governmental function would have to be substantial to warrant departure from the guidelines when the applicable offense guideline is bribery or obstruction of justice. When the guideline covering the mailing of injurious articles is applicable, however, and the offense caused disruption of a governmental function, departure from the applicable guideline range more readily would be appropriate. Similarly, physical injury would not warrant departure from the guidelines when the robbery offense guideline is applicable because the robbery guideline includes a specific adjustment based on the extent of any injury. However, because the robbery guideline does not deal with injury to more than one victim, departure may be warranted if several persons were injured.

(C) Departures Based on Circumstances Identified as Not Ordinarily Relevant.—Because certain circumstances are specified in the guidelines as not ordinarily relevant to sentencing (see, e.g., Chapter Five, Part H (Specific Offender Characteristics)), a departure based on any one of such circumstances should occur only in exceptional cases, and only if the circumstance is present in the case to an exceptional degree. If two or more of such circumstances each is present in the case to a substantial degree, however, and taken together make the case an exceptional one, the court may consider whether a departure would be warranted pursuant to subsection (c). Departures based on a combination of not ordinarily relevant circumstances that are present to a substantial degree should occur extremely rarely and only in exceptional cases. In addition, as required by subsection (e), each circumstance forming the basis for a departure described in this subdivision shall be stated with specificity in the written judgment and commitment order.

4. Downward Departures in Child Crimes and Sexual Offenses.—

(A) Definition.—For purposes of this policy statement, the term 'child crimes and sexual offenses' means offenses under any of the following: 18 U.S.C. § 1201 (involving a minor victim), 18 U.S.C. § 1591, or chapter 71, 109A, 110, or 117 of title 18, United States Code.

(B) Standard for Departure.—

(i) Requirement of Affirmative and Specific Identification of Departure Ground.—The standard for a downward departure in child crimes and sexual offenses differs from the standard for other departures under this policy statement in that it includes a requirement, set forth in 18 U.S.C. §3553(b)(2)(A)(ii)(I) and subsection (b)(1) of this guideline, that any mitigating circumstance that forms the basis for such a downward departure be affirmatively and specifically identified as a ground for downward departure in this part (i.e., Chapter Five, Part K).

(ii) Application of Subsection (b)(2).—The commentary in Application Note 3 of this policy statement, except for the commentary in Application Note 3(A)(ii) relating to unidentified circumstances, shall apply to the court's determination of whether a case meets the requirement, set forth in subsection 18 U.S.C. § 3553(b)(2)(A)(ii)(II) and subsection (b)(2) of this policy statement, that the mitigating circumstance forming the basis for a downward departure in child crimes and sexual offenses be of kind, or to a degree, not adequately taken into consideration by the Commission.

5. Departures Based on Plea Agreements.—Subsection (d)(4) prohibits a downward departure based only on the defendant's decision, in and of itself, to plead guilty to the offense or to enter a plea agreement with respect to the offense. Even though a departure may not be based merely on the fact that the defendant agreed to plead guilty or enter a plea agreement, a departure may be based on justifiable, non-prohibited reasons for departure as part of a sentence that is recommended, or agreed to, in the plea agreement and accepted by the court. See §6B1.2 (Standards for Acceptance of Plea Agreements). In cases in which the court departs based on such reasons as set forth in the plea agreement, the court must state the reasons for departure with specificity in the written judgment and commitment order, as required by subsection (e).

Page 749   **Insert at the end of the discussion of Acceptance of Responsibility**

Under the PROTECT Act, the government now has controls the third point for acceptance of responsibility. This change, like the substantial assistance provision, raises the general question of the balance of authority under the Guidelines regime between the court, the prosecution, and the defense.

CHAPTER 18

FORFEITURE

Page 787. **Insert after the quotation from Blumenson and Nilsen.**

Eric Blumenson and Eva Nilsen report that several states have enacted legislation intended to eliminate the distorting incentives of forfeiture by redirecting the assets to purposes such as drug treatment and education, and prohibiting state law enforcement officials from evading these limitations by turning over seized assets for federal forfeiture. They also describe constitutional litigation in the state and federal courts challenging what they call the "forfeiture reward system." In their view, the conflict of interest implicit in this system can rise to the level of a Due Process violation in cases where (1) asset-rich defendants have been selectively prosecuted, (2) drug buyers are selected for reverse stings in order to allow seizure of the buyer's cash, or (3) very wealthy defendants receive disparate plea offers or sentences because of the assets available for forfeiture. They also identify separation of power objections. *See* Eric C. Blumenson & Eva Nilsen, *The Next Stage of Forfeiture Reform*, 14 FED. SENT. R. 76 (2001). For another attack on drug forfeitures as violative of federalism principles, see Michael J. Duffey, *A Drug War Funded With Drug Money: The Federal Civil Forfeiture Statute and Federalism*, 34 SUFFOLK L. REV. 511 (2001).

Page 789. **Insert at the top of the page.**

But perhaps the political tide is turning once again, at least in connection with the war on terrorism. The USA Patriot Act of 2001 added 18 U.S.C. § 981(a)(1)(G), which authorizes the seizure of the assets of all assets of anyone engaged in terrorism, any property affording any person a "source of influence" over a terrorist organization, and any property derived from or used to commit a terrorist act. Note the breadth of this language. It does not require any nexus between the property in question and any terrorism offense. Instead, it provides that the government can seize and forfeit any and all assets of any person, entity, or organization that is engaged in terrorism against the United States or its citizens, residents, or their property. Although § 981 is a civil provision, in tandem with another new provision it also authorizes criminal forfeiture. In 2000 Congress enacted 28 U.S.C. § 2461(c), which provides that whenever a forfeiture of property is authorized by Congress, but no statutory provision has been made for criminal forfeiture, the government may seek forfeiture in any federal criminal indictment and the court shall, upon conviction, order forfeiture in accordance with the procedures established in 18 U.S.C. § 853(d). These provisions are discussed in Stephan D. Cassella, *Forfeiture of Terrorist Assets Under the USA Patriot Act of 2001*, 34 L & POL'Y INT. BUS. 7 (2002). For a general discussion of federal terrorism legislation, see Chapter 11A of this supplement.

New subsection (e)(4), authorizes the district court to enter a pretrial restraining order requiring a defendant to repatriate and deposit with the court any property that may be seized and forfeited. Failure to comply is punishable by civil and criminal contempt. Section (p), relating to substitute property, has been rewritten to incorporate the notion that at the time of sentencing the court may order the defendant to return property that has been placed beyond the jurisdiction of the court in order that it may be forfeited. It now provides:

(p) Forfeiture of substitute property

(1) In general

Paragraph (2) of this subsection shall apply, if any property described in subsection (a), as a result of any act or omission of the defendant—

(A) cannot be located upon exercise of due diligence;

(B) has been transferred or sold to, or deposited with, a third party;

(C) has been placed beyond the jurisdiction of the court;

(D) has been substantially diminished in value; or

(E) has commingled with other property which cannot be divided without difficulty.

(2) Substitute property

In any case described in subparagraphs (A) through (E) of paragraph (1), the court shall order the forfeiture of any other property of the defendant, up to the value of any property described in subparagraphs (A) through (E) of paragraph (1), as applicable.

(3) Return of the property to jurisdiction

In the case of property described in paragraph (1)(C), the court may, in addition to any other action authorized by this subsection, order the defendant to return the property to the jurisdiction of the court so that the property may be seized and forfeited.

Page 796.   Insert at the end of note 4.

4(a). Many of the forfeiture statutes, including § 853, authorize the forfeiture of "property." But what exactly counts as property for this purpose? Is a license property? Does it matter what kind of license it is? Are the considerations the same as when the courts try to determine whether a scheme to defraud deprived the victim of property for purposes of the mail and wire fraud statutes? For an interesting discussion of these issues see Wesley M. Oliver, *A Round Peg in a Square Hole: Federal Forfeiture of State Professional Licenses*, 28 AM. CRIM. L. REV. 179 (2001). Oliver discusses *United States v. Dicter*, 198 F.3d 1284, 1287-88 (11th Cir. 1999), which upheld the forfeiture of the medical license of a physician who had unlawfully dispensed narcotics without a valid medical purpose. Oliver (who represented Dr. Dicter) concedes that the medical license facilitated the offense, but notes that the doctor's medical school degree did so as well. He argues that the forfeiture of professional licenses "is part of a disturbing trend of federal usurpation of matters traditionally left to the states" – in this case, the sort of hearing that a professional is entitled to before he is prohibited from engaging in his profession, and the proper authorities to determine eligibility to practice. Should federal prosecutors and juries determine who is qualified to practice medicine ... or law?

Page 832.   Insert at the end of note 1.

For a discussion of the innocent owner defense under the new legislation, see Stefan D. Cassella, *The Uniform Innocent Owner Defense to Civil Forfeiture: The Civil Asset Forfeiture Reform Act of 2000 Creates a Uniform Innocent Owner Defense to Most Civil Forfeitures Filed by the Federal Government*, 89 KY. L. REV. 653 (2000-01).

Page 844.   Insert at the end of the page.

5. As the Supreme Court recognized in *Caplin & Drysdale*, forfeiture of assets can prevent defendants from retaining their choice of defense counsel. One commentator has argued that the proper response to this situation is to relax the traditional ban on contingent fee representation in criminal cases. *See* Lindsey N. Godfrey, *Rethinking the Ethical Ban on Criminal Contingent Fees: A Commonsense Approach to Asset Forfeiture*, 79 TEX. L. REV. 1699 (2001). The ABA's current rules assume contingent fees are per se unreasonable in criminal cases. Why should that be so, given that they are common in civil cases? The main objection seems to be that a lawyer whose fee depends upon an acquittal will have a strong incentive to discourage a guilty plea, even if it would be in the client's best interest. One might ask whether this is really much different from the pressures felt by defense counsel in many other contexts, particularly those faced by public defenders and lawyers who represent indigent on a contract basis. In each case, the lawyer has only mininal resources to conduct the defense, and will surely have an economic

incentive to plead a defendant guilty, rather than undergo a costly and lengthy trial. Yet there is no ethical ban on such pressures. In any event, Godfrey argues that a relaxation of the absolute ban on contingent fees is justified in response to forfeitures that may leave the defendant in a complex case with an inadequately prepared and funded public defender.

APPENDIX

Page 859-66 There have been several minor amendments to 21 U.S.C. § 853. Language in several subsections referring to the supervised release provisions in 18 U.S.C. § 3583 has been deleted. The language of subsection (d) has been amended to clarify that a fine is not mandatory in every case. Subsections (b)(1)(C) and (b)(1)(D) have been amended to increase sentences for crimes involving gamma hydroxybutyric acid (GHB), which has been used as a "date rape" drug. Subsection (b)(7)(A) has been amended to include controlled substance analogues, and former subsections (d) to (g) have been renumbered as (c) to (f).

V. SENTENCING GUIDELINES

Page 897. Insert § 2B1.1 (below) and note the amendments to the robbery guideline, 2B3.1, which are described *infra* at 157.

§ 2B1.1. LARCENY, EMBEZZLEMENT, AND OTHER FORMS OF THEFT; OFFENSES INVOLVING STOLEN PROPERTY; PROPERTY DAMAGE OR DESTRUCTION; FRAUD AND DECEIT; FORGERY; OFFENSES INVOLVING ALTERED OR COUNTERFEIT INSTRUMENTS OTHER THAN COUNTERFEIT BEARER OBLIGATIONS OF THE UNITED STATES

(a) Base Offense Level:

> (1) 7, if (A) the defendant was convicted of an offense referenced to this guideline; and (B) that offense of conviction has a statutory maximum term of imprisonment of 20 years or more; or

> (2) 6, otherwise

(b) Specific Offense Characteristics

(1) If the loss exceeded $5,000, increase the offense level as follows:

Loss (Apply the Greatest)	Increase in Level
(A) $5,000 or less	no increase
(B) More than $5,000	add 2
(C) More than $10,000	add 4
(D) More than $30,000	add 6
(E) More than $70,000	add 8
(F) More than $120,000	add 10
(G) More than $200,000	add 12
(H) More than $400,000	add 14
(I) More than $1,000,000	add 16
(J) More than $2,500,000	add 18
(K) More than $7,000,000	add 20
(L) More than $20,000,000	add 22
(M) More than $50,000,000	add 24
(N) More than $100,000,000	add 26
(O) More than $200,000,000	add 28
(P) More than $400,000,000	add 30.

(2) (Apply the greatest) If the offense—

(A) (i) involved 10 or more victims; or (ii) was committed through mass-marketing, increase by 2 levels;

(B) involved 50 or more victims, increase by 4 levels; or

(C) involved 250 or more victims, increase by 6 levels.

(3) If the offense involved a theft from the person of another, increase by 2 levels.

(4) If the offense involved receiving stolen property, and the defendant was a person in the business of receiving and selling stolen property, increase by 2 levels.

(5) If the offense involved misappropriation of a trade secret and the defendant knew or intended that the offense would benefit a foreign government, foreign instrumentality, or foreign agent, increase by 2 levels.

(6) If the offense involved theft of, damage to, or destruction of, property from a national cemetery, increase by 2 levels.

(7) If the offense involved (A) a misrepresentation that the defendant was acting on behalf of a charitable, educational, religious, or political organization, or a government agency; (B) a misrepresentation or other fraudulent action during the course of a bankruptcy proceeding; (C) a violation of any prior, specific judicial or administrative order, injunction, decree, or process not addressed elsewhere in the guidelines; or (D) a misrepresentation to a consumer in connection with obtaining, providing, or furnishing financial assistance for an institution of higher education, increase by 2 levels. If the resulting offense level is less than level 10, increase to level 10.

(8) If (A) the defendant relocated, or participated in relocating, a fraudulent scheme to another jurisdiction to evade law enforcement or regulatory officials; (B) a substantial part of a fraudulent scheme was committed from outside the United States; or (C) the offense otherwise involved sophisticated means, increase by 2 levels. If the resulting offense level is less than level 12, increase to level 12.

(9) If the offense involved (A) the possession or use of any device-making equipment; (B) the production or trafficking of any unauthorized access device or counterfeit access device; or (C)(i) the unauthorized transfer or use of any means of identification unlawfully to produce or obtain any other means of identification; or (ii) the possession of 5 or more means of identification that unlawfully were produced from, or obtained by the use of, another means of identification, increase by 2 levels. If the resulting offense level is less than level 12, increase to level 12.

(10) If the offense involved an organized scheme to steal vehicles or vehicle parts, and the offense level is less than level 14, increase to level 14.

(11) If the offense involved (A) the conscious or reckless risk of death or serious bodily injury; or (B) possession of a dangerous weapon (including a firearm) in connection with the offense, increase by 2 levels. If the resulting offense level is less than level 14, increase to level 14.

(12) (Apply the greater) If—

(A) the defendant derived more than $1,000,000 in gross receipts from one or more financial institutions as a result of the offense, increase by 2 levels; or

(B) the offense (i) substantially jeopardized the safety and soundness of a financial institution; (ii) substantially endangered the solvency or financial security of an organization that, at any time during the offense, (I) was a publicly traded company; or (II) had 1,000 or more employees; or (iii) substantially endangered the solvency or financial security of 100 or more victims, increase by 4 levels.

(C) The cumulative adjustments from application of both subsections (b)(2) and (b)(12)(B) shall not exceed 8 levels, except as provided in subdivision (D).

(D) If the resulting offense level determined under subdivision (A) or (B) is less than level 24, increase to level 24.

(14) If the offense involved—

(A) a violation of securities law and, at the time of the offense, the defendant was (i) an officer or a director of a publicly traded company; (ii) a registered broker or dealer, or a person associated with a broker or dealer; or (iii) an investment adviser, or a person associated with an investment adviser; or

(B) a violation of commodities law and, at the time of the offense, the defendant was (i) an officer or a director of a futures commission merchant or an introducing broker; (ii) a commodities trading advisor; or (iii) a commodity pool operator,

increase by 4 levels.

(c) Cross References

(1) If (A) a firearm, destructive device, explosive material, or controlled substance was taken, or the taking of any such item was an object of the offense; or (B) the stolen property received, transported, transferred, transmitted, or possessed was a firearm, destructive device, explosive material, or controlled substance, apply §2D1.1 (Unlawful Manufacturing, Importing, Exporting, or Trafficking (Including Possession with Intent to Commit These Offenses); Attempt or Conspiracy), §2D2.1 (Unlawful Possession; Attempt or Conspiracy), §2K1.3 (Unlawful Receipt, Possession, or Transportation of Explosive Materials; Prohibited Transactions Involving Explosive Materials), or §2K2.1 (Unlawful Receipt, Possession, or Transportation of Firearms or Ammunition; Prohibited Transactions Involving Firearms or Ammunition), as appropriate.

(2) If the offense involved arson, or property damage by use of explosives, apply §2K1.4 (Arson; Property Damage by Use of Explosives), if the resulting offense level is greater than that determined above.

(3) If (A) neither subdivision (1) nor (2) of this subsection applies; (B) the defendant was convicted under a statute proscribing false, fictitious, or fraudulent statements or representations generally (e.g., 18 U.S.C. § 1001, § 1341, § 1342, or § 1343); and (C) the conduct set forth in the count of conviction establishes an offense specifically covered by another guideline in Chapter Two (Offense Conduct), apply that other guideline.

(4) If the offense involved a cultural heritage resource, apply §2B1.5 (Theft of, Damage to, or Destruction of, Cultural Heritage Resources; Unlawful Sale, Purchase, Exchange, Transportation, or Receipt of Cultural Heritage Resources), if the resulting offense level is greater than that determined above.

Commentary

Statutory Provisions: 7 U.S.C. §§ 6, 6b, 6c, 6h, 6o, 13, 23; 15 U.S.C. §§ 50, 77e, 77q, 77x, 78j, 78ff, 80b-6, 1644, 6821; 18 U.S.C. §§ 38, 225, 285-289, 471-473, 500, 510, 553(a)(1), 641, 656, 657, 659, 662, 664, 1001-1008, 1010-1014, 1016-1022, 1025, 1026, 1028, 1029, 1030(a)(4)-(5), 1031, 1341-1344, 1348, 1350, 1361, 1363, 1702, 1703 (if vandalism or malicious mischief, including destruction of mail, is involved), 1708, 1831, 1832, 1992, 1993(a)(1), (a)(4), 2113(b), 2312-2317, 2332b(a)(1); 29 U.S.C. § 501(c); 42 U.S.C. § 1011; 49 U.S.C. §§ 30170, 46317(a), 60123(b). For additional statutory provision(s), see Appendix A (Statutory Index).

Application Notes:

[The application notes are very extensive. Only a few selected provisions are included here.]

* * * * *

3. Loss Under Subsection (b)(1).—This application note applies to the determination of loss under subsection (b)(1).

(A) General Rule.—Subject to the exclusions in subdivision (D), loss is the greater of actual loss or intended loss.

(i) Actual Loss.—"Actual loss" means the reasonably foreseeable pecuniary harm that resulted from the offense.

(ii) Intended Loss.—"Intended loss" (I) means the pecuniary harm that was intended to result from the offense; and (II) includes intended pecuniary harm that would have been impossible or unlikely to occur (e.g., as in a government sting operation, or an insurance fraud in which the claim exceeded the insured value).

(iii) Pecuniary Harm.—"Pecuniary harm" means harm that is monetary or that otherwise is readily measurable in money. Accordingly, pecuniary harm does not include emotional distress, harm to reputation, or other non-economic harm.

(iv) Reasonably Foreseeable Pecuniary Harm.—For purposes of this guideline, "reasonably foreseeable pecuniary harm" means pecuniary harm that the defendant knew or, under the circumstances, reasonably should have known, was a potential result of the offense.

(v) Rules of Construction in Certain Cases.—In the cases described in subdivisions (I) through (III), reasonably foreseeable pecuniary harm shall be considered to include the pecuniary harm specified for those cases as follows:

(I) Product Substitution Cases.—In the case of a product substitution offense, the reasonably foreseeable pecuniary harm includes the reasonably foreseeable costs of making substitute transactions and handling or disposing of the product delivered, or of retrofitting the product so that it can be used for its intended purpose, and the reasonably foreseeable costs of rectifying the actual or potential disruption to the victim's business operations caused by the product substitution.

(II) Procurement Fraud Cases.—In the case of a procurement fraud, such as a fraud affecting a defense contract award, reasonably foreseeable pecuniary harm includes the reasonably foreseeable administrative costs to the government and other participants of repeating or correcting the procurement action affected, plus any increased costs to procure the product or service involved that was reasonably foreseeable.

(III) Protected Computer Cases.—In the case of an offense involving unlawfully accessing, or exceeding authorized access to, a "protected computer" as defined in 18 U.S.C. § 1030(e)(2), actual loss includes the following pecuniary harm, regardless of whether such pecuniary harm was reasonably foreseeable: reasonable costs to the victim of conducting a damage assessment, and restoring the system and data to their condition prior to the offense, and any lost revenue due to interruption of service.

(B) Gain.—The court shall use the gain that resulted from the offense as an alternative measure of loss only if there is a loss but it reasonably cannot be determined.

(C) Estimation of Loss.—The court need only make a reasonable estimate of the loss. The sentencing judge is in a unique position to assess the evidence and estimate the loss based upon that evidence. For this reason, the court's loss determination is entitled to appropriate deference. See 18 U.S.C. § 3742(e) and (f).

The estimate of the loss shall be based on available information, taking into account, as appropriate and practicable under the circumstances, factors such as the following:

(i) The fair market value of the property unlawfully taken or destroyed; or, if the fair market value is impracticable to determine or inadequately measures the harm, the cost to the victim of replacing that property.

(ii) The cost of repairs to damaged property.

(iii) The approximate number of victims multiplied by the average loss to each victim.

(iv) The reduction that resulted from the offense in the value of equity securities or other corporate assets.

(v) More general factors, such as the scope and duration of the offense and revenues generated by similar operations.

(D) Exclusions from Loss.—Loss shall not include the following:

(i) Interest of any kind, finance charges, late fees, penalties, amounts based on an agreed-upon return or rate of return, or other similar costs.

(ii) Costs to the government of, and costs incurred by victims primarily to aid the government in, the prosecution and criminal investigation of an offense.

(E) Credits Against Loss.—Loss shall be reduced by the following:

(i) The money returned, and the fair market value of the property returned and the services rendered, by the defendant or other persons acting jointly with the defendant, to the victim before the offense was detected. The time of detection of the offense is the earlier of (I) the time the offense was discovered by a victim or government agency; or (II) the time the defendant knew or reasonably should have known that the offense was detected or about to be detected by a victim or government agency.

(ii) In a case involving collateral pledged or otherwise provided by the defendant, the amount the victim has recovered at the time of sentencing from disposition of the collateral, or if the collateral has not been disposed of by that time, the fair market value of the collateral at the time of sentencing.

*****

18. Departure Considerations.—

(A) Upward Departure Considerations.—There may be cases in which the offense level determined under this guideline substantially understates the seriousness of the offense. In such cases, an upward departure may be warranted. The following is a non-exhaustive list of factors that the court may consider in determining whether an upward departure is warranted:

(i) A primary objective of the offense was an aggravating, non-monetary objective. For example, a primary objective of the offense was to inflict emotional harm.

(ii) The offense caused or risked substantial non-monetary harm. For example, the offense caused physical harm, psychological harm, or severe emotional trauma, or resulted in a substantial invasion of a privacy interest (through, for example, the theft of personal information such as medical, educational, or financial records).

(iii) The offense involved a substantial amount of interest of any kind, finance charges, late fees, penalties, amounts based on an agreed-upon return or rate of return, or other similar costs, not included in the determination of loss for purposes of subsection (b)(1).

(iv) The offense created a risk of substantial loss beyond the loss determined for purposes of subsection (b)(1).

(v) In a case involving stolen information from a "protected computer", as defined in 18 U.S.C. § 1030(e)(2), the defendant sought the stolen information to further a broader criminal purpose.

(vi) In a case involving access devices or unlawfully produced or unlawfully obtained means of identification:

(I) The offense caused substantial harm to the victim's reputation or credit record, or the victim suffered a substantial inconvenience related to repairing the victim's reputation or a damaged credit record.

(II) An individual whose means of identification the defendant used to obtain unlawful means of identification is erroneously arrested or denied a job because an arrest record has been made in that individual's name.

(III) The defendant produced or obtained numerous means of identification with respect to one individual and essentially assumed that individual's identity.

(B) Downward Departure Consideration.—There may be cases in which the offense level determined under this guideline substantially overstates the seriousness of the offense. In such cases, a downward departure may be warranted.

Background: This guideline covers offenses involving theft, stolen property, property damage or destruction, fraud, forgery, and counterfeiting (other than offenses involving altered or counterfeit bearer obligations of the United States). It also covers offenses involving altering or removing motor vehicle identification numbers, trafficking in automobiles or automobile parts with altered or obliterated identification numbers, odometer laws and regulations, obstructing correspondence, the falsification of documents or records relating to a benefit plan covered by the Employment Retirement Income Security Act, and the failure to maintain, or falsification of, documents required by the Labor Management Reporting and Disclosure Act.

Because federal fraud statutes often are broadly written, a single pattern of offense conduct usually can be prosecuted under several code sections, as a result of which the offense of conviction may be somewhat arbitrary. Furthermore, most fraud statutes cover a broad range of conduct with extreme variation in severity. The specific offense characteristics and cross references contained in this guideline are designed with these considerations in mind.

The Commission has determined that, ordinarily, the sentences of defendants convicted of federal offenses should reflect the nature and magnitude of the loss caused or intended by their crimes. Accordingly, along with other relevant factors under the guidelines, loss serves as a measure of the seriousness of the offense and the defendant's relative culpability and is a principal factor in determining the offense level under this guideline.

Theft from the person of another, such as pickpocketing or non-forcible purse-snatching, receives an enhanced sentence because of the increased risk of physical injury. This guideline does not include an enhancement for thefts from the person by means of force or fear; such crimes are robberies and are covered under §2B3.1 (Robbery).

A minimum offense level of level 14 is provided for offenses involving an organized scheme to steal vehicles or vehicle parts. Typically, the scope of such activity is substantial, but the value of the property may be particularly difficult to ascertain in individual cases because the stolen property is rapidly resold or otherwise disposed of in the course of the offense. Therefore, the specific offense characteristic of "organized scheme" is used as an alternative to "loss" in setting a minimum offense level.

Use of false pretenses involving charitable causes and government agencies enhances the sentences of defendants who take advantage of victims' trust in government or law enforcement agencies or the generosity and charitable motives of victims. Taking advantage of a victim's self-interest does not mitigate the seriousness of fraudulent conduct; rather, defendants who exploit victims' charitable impulses or trust in government create particular social harm. In a similar vein, a defendant who has been subject to civil or administrative proceedings for the same or similar fraudulent conduct demonstrates aggravated criminal intent and is deserving of additional punishment for not conforming with the requirements of judicial process or orders issued by federal, state, or local administrative agencies.

Offenses that involve the use of financial transactions or financial accounts outside the United States in an effort to conceal illicit profits and criminal conduct involve a particularly high level of sophistication and complexity. These offenses are difficult to detect and require costly investigations and prosecutions. Diplomatic processes often must be used to secure testimony and evidence beyond the jurisdiction of United States courts. Consequently, a minimum offense level of level 12 is provided for these offenses.

* * * * *

Page 897. **Subsection 2B3.1(b)(2) of the robbery guideline has been amended to striking the word "brandish" in order to conform to the guideline definition of the term "display." This is intended to increase the punishment in some circumstances for persons who make the presence of the weapon known to another person, in order to intimidate that person, regardless of whether the weapon is visible.**

Page 899. **Subsection 2B3.2(b)(3) of the extortion guideline has been amended to striking the word "brandish" in order to conform to the guideline definition of the term "display." This is intended to increase the punishment in some circumstances for persons who make the presence of the weapon known to another person, in order to intimidate that person, regardless of whether the weapon is visible.**

Page 902. **Delete the present blackmail guideline and substitute the following.**

§ 2B3.3. Blackmail and Similar Forms of Extortion

(a) Base Offense Level: 9

(b) Specific Offense Characteristic
  (1) If the greater of the amount obtained or demanded (A) exceeded $ 2,000 but did not exceed $ 5,000, increase by 1 level; or (B) exceeded $ 5,000, increase by the number of levels from the table in § 2B1.1 (Theft, Property Destruction, and Fraud) corresponding to that amount.

(c) Cross References
  (1) If the offense involved extortion under color of official right, apply § 2C1.1 (Offering, Giving, Soliciting, or Receiving a Bribe; Extortion Under Color of Official Right).
  (2) If the offense involved extortion by force or threat of injury or serious damage, apply § 2B3.2 (Extortion by Force or Threat of Injury or Serious Damage).

Commentary

Statutory Provisions: 18 U.S.C. §§ 873, 875-877, 1951. For additional statutory provision(s), see Appendix A (Statutory Index).

Application Note:

1. This section applies only to blackmail and similar forms of extortion where there clearly is no threat of violence to person or property. "Blackmail" (18 U.S.C. § 873) is defined as a threat to disclose a violation of United States law unless money or some other item of value is given.

Background: Under 18 U.S.C. § 873, the maximum term of imprisonment authorized for blackmail is one year. Extortionate threats to injure a reputation, or other threats that are less serious than those covered by § 2B3.2, may also be prosecuted under 18 U.S.C. §§ 875-877, which carry higher maximum sentences.

Amendment & Reason: 2B3.3(b) is amended because the Commission struck section 2F1.1, and moved its provisions to 2B1.1.

Page 902   Delete 2C1.1 and substitute the following.

§ 2C1.1. Offering, Giving, Soliciting, or Receiving a Bribe; Extortion Under Color of Official Right

(a) Base Offense Level: 10

(b) Specific Offense Characteristics

(1) If the offense involved more than one bribe or extortion, increase by 2 levels.

(2) (If more than one applies, use the greater):

(A) If the value of the payment, the benefit received or to be received in return for the payment, or the loss to the government from the offense, whichever is greatest (i) exceeded $ 2,000 but did not exceed $ 5,000, increase by 1 level; or (ii) exceeded $ 5,000, increase by the number of levels from the table in § 2B1.1 (Theft, Property Destruction, and Fraud) corresponding to that amount.

(B) If the offense involved a payment for the purpose of influencing an elected official or any official holding a high-level decision-making or sensitive position, increase by 8 levels.

(c) Cross References

(1) If the offense was committed for the purpose of facilitating the commission of another criminal offense, apply the offense guideline applicable to a conspiracy to commit that other offense if the resulting offense level is greater than that determined above.

(2) If the offense was committed for the purpose of concealing, or obstructing justice in respect to, another criminal offense, apply § 2X3.1 (Accessory After the Fact) or § 2J1.2 (Obstruction of Justice), as appropriate, in respect to that other offense if the resulting offense level is greater than that determined above.

(3) If the offense involved a threat of physical injury or property destruction, apply § 2B3.2 (Extortion by Force or Threat of Injury or Serious Damage) if the resulting offense level is greater than that determined above.

(d) Special Instruction for Fines--Organizations

(1) In lieu of the pecuniary loss under subsection (a)(3) of § 8C2.4 (Base Fine), use the greatest of: (A) the value of the unlawful payment; (B) the value of the benefit received or to be received in return for the unlawful payment; or (C) the consequential damages resulting from the unlawful payment.

Commentary

Statutory Provisions: 15 U.S.C. §§ 78dd-1, 78dd-2, 78dd-3; 18 U.S.C. §§ 201(b)(1), (2), 872, 1951. For additional statutory provision(s), see Appendix A (Statutory Index).

Application Notes:

1. "Official holding a high-level decision-making or sensitive position" includes, for example, prosecuting attorneys, judges, agency administrators, supervisory law enforcement officers, and other governmental officials with similar levels of responsibility.

2. "Loss", for purposes of subsection (b)(2)(A), shall be determined in accordance with Application Note 2 of the Commentary to § 2B1.1 (Theft, Property Destruction, and Fraud). The value of "the benefit received or to be received" means the net value of such benefit. Examples: (1) A government employee, in return for a $ 500 bribe, reduces the price of a piece of surplus property offered for sale by the government from $ 10,000 to $ 2,000; the value of the benefit received is $ 8,000. (2) A $ 150,000 contract on which $ 20,000 profit was made was awarded in return for a bribe; the value of the benefit received is $ 20,000. Do not deduct the value of the bribe itself in computing the value of the benefit received or to be received. In the above examples, therefore, the value of the benefit received would be the same regardless of the value of the bribe.

3. Do not apply § 3B1.3 (Abuse of Position of Trust or Use of Special Skill) except where the offense level is determined under § 2C1.1(c)(1), (2), or (3). In such cases, an adjustment from § 3B1.3 (Abuse of Position of Trust or Use of Special Skill) may apply.

4. In some cases the monetary value of the unlawful payment may not be known or may not adequately reflect the seriousness of the offense. For example, a small payment may be made in exchange for the falsification of inspection records for a shipment of defective parachutes or the destruction of evidence in a major narcotics case. In part, this issue is addressed by the adjustments in § 2C1.1(b)(2), and § 2C1.1(c)(1), (2), and (3). However, in cases in which the seriousness of the offense is still not adequately reflected, an upward departure is warranted. See Chapter Five, Part K (Departures).

5. Where the court finds that the defendant's conduct was part of a systematic or pervasive corruption of a governmental function, process, or office that may cause loss of public confidence in government, an upward departure may be warranted. See Chapter Five, Part K (Departures).

6. Subsection (b)(1) provides an adjustment for offenses involving more than one incident of either bribery or extortion. Related payments that, in essence, constitute a single incident of bribery or extortion (e.g., a number of installment payments for a single action) are to be treated as a single bribe or extortion, even if charged in separate counts.

7. For the purposes of determining whether to apply the cross references in this section, the "resulting offense level" means the greater final offense level (i.e., the offense level determined by taking into account both the Chapter Two offense level and any applicable adjustments from Chapter Three, Parts A-D).

Background: This section applies to a person who offers or gives a bribe for a corrupt purpose, such as inducing a public official to participate in a fraud or to influence his official actions, or to a public official who solicits or accepts such a bribe. The maximum term of imprisonment authorized by statute for these offenses is fifteen years under 18 U.S.C. § 201(b) and (c), twenty years under 18 U.S.C. § 1951, and three years under 18 U.S.C. § 872.

The object and nature of a bribe may vary widely from case to case. In some cases, the object may be commercial advantage (e.g., preferential treatment in the award of a government contract). In others, the object may be issuance of a license to which the recipient is not entitled. In still others, the object may be the obstruction of justice. Consequently, a guideline for the offense must be designed to cover diverse situations.

In determining the net value of the benefit received or to be received, the value of the bribe is not deducted from the gross value of such benefit; the harm is the same regardless of value of the bribe paid to receive the benefit. Where the value of the bribe exceeds the value of the benefit or the value of the benefit cannot be determined, the value of the bribe is used because it is likely that the payer of such a bribe expected something in return that would be worth more than the value of the bribe. Moreover, for deterrence purposes, the punishment should be commensurate with the gain to the payer or the recipient of the bribe, whichever is higher.

Under § 2C1.1(b)(2)(B), if the payment was for the purpose of influencing an official act by certain officials, the offense level is increased by 8 levels if this increase is greater than that provided under § 2C1.1(b)(2)(A).

Under § 2C1.1(c)(1), if the payment was to facilitate the commission of another criminal offense, the guideline applicable to a conspiracy to commit that other offense will apply if the result is greater than that determined above. For example, if a bribe was given to a law enforcement officer to allow the smuggling of a quantity of cocaine, the guideline for conspiracy to import cocaine would be applied if it resulted in a greater offense level.

Under § 2C1.1(c)(2), if the payment was to conceal another criminal offense or obstruct justice in respect to another criminal offense, the guideline from § 2X3.1 (Accessory After the Fact) or § 2J1.2 (Obstruction of Justice), as appropriate, will apply if the result is greater than that determined above. For example, if a bribe was given for the purpose of concealing the offense of espionage, the guideline for accessory after the fact to espionage would be applied.

Under § 2C1.1(c)(3), if the offense involved forcible extortion, the guideline from § 2B3.2 (Extortion by Force or Threat of Injury or Serious Damage) will apply if the result is greater than that determined above.

When the offense level is determined under § 2C1.1(c)(1), (2), or (3), an adjustment from § 3B1.3 (Abuse of Position of Trust or Use of Special Skill) may apply.

Section 2C1.1 also applies to extortion by officers or employees of the United States in violation of 18 U.S.C. § 872, and Hobbs Act extortion, or attempted extortion, under color of official right in violation of 18 U.S.C. § 1951. The Hobbs Act, 18 U.S.C. § 1951(b)(2), applies in part to any person who acts "under color of official right." This statute applies to extortionate conduct by, among others, officials and employees of state and local governments. The panoply of conduct that may be prosecuted under the Hobbs Act varies from a city building inspector who demands a small amount of money from the owner of an apartment building to ignore code violations to a state court judge who extracts substantial interest-free loans from attorneys who have cases pending in his court.

Section 2C1.1 also applies to offenses under 15 U.S.C. §§ 78dd-1, 78dd-2, and 78dd-3. Such offenses generally involve a payment to a foreign public official, candidate for public office, or agent or intermediary, with the intent to influence an official act or decision of a foreign government or political party. Typically, a case prosecuted under these provisions will involve an intent to influence governmental action.

Offenses involving attempted bribery are frequently not completed because the victim reports the offense to authorities or is acting in an undercover capacity. Failure to complete the offense does not lessen the defendant's culpability in attempting to use public position for personal gain. Therefore, solicitations and attempts are treated as equivalent to the underlying offense.

Amendment & Reason: The old 2C1.1(b)(2)(A) is struck and replaced by the current version because the criminal statutes under which this guideline is typically used (30A of the Securities Exchange Act of 1934 and sections 104 and 104A of the Foreign Corrupt Practices Act of 1977) involve public corruption of foreign officials and are, therefore, more akin to public corruption cases than commercial bribery cases.

§ 2C1.2. Offering, Giving, Soliciting, or Receiving a Gratuity

(a) Base Offense Level: 7

(b) Specific Offense Characteristics

(1) If the offense involved more than one gratuity, increase by 2 levels.

(2) (If more than one applies, use the greater):

(Λ) If the value of the gratuity (i) exceeded $ 2,000 but did not exceed $ 5,000, increase by 1 level; or (ii) exceeded $ 5,000, increase by the number of levels from the table in § 2B1.1 (Theft, Property Destruction, and Fraud) corresponding to that amount.

(B) If the gratuity was given, or to be given, to an elected official or any official holding a high-level decision-making or sensitive position, increase by 8 levels.

(c) Special Instruction for Fines--Organizations

(1) In lieu of the pecuniary loss under subsection (a)(3) of § 8C2.4 (Base Fine), use the value of the unlawful payment.

Commentary

Statutory Provisions: 18 U.S.C. § 201(c)(1). For additional statutory provision(s), see Appendix A (Statutory Index).

Application Notes:

1. "Official holding a high-level decision-making or sensitive position" includes, for example, prosecuting attorneys, judges, agency administrators, supervisory law

enforcement officers, and other governmental officials with similar levels of responsibility.

2. Do not apply the adjustment in § 3B1.3 (Abuse of Position or [of] Trust or Use of Special Skill).

3. In some cases, the public official is the instigator of the offense. In others, a private citizen who is attempting to ingratiate himself or his business with the public official may be the initiator. This factor may appropriately be considered in determining the placement of the sentence within the applicable guideline range.

4. Related payments that, in essence, constitute a single gratuity (e.g., separate payments for airfare and hotel for a single vacation trip) are to be treated as a single gratuity, even if charged in separate counts.

Background: This section applies to the offering, giving, soliciting, or receiving of a gratuity to a public official in respect to an official act. A corrupt purpose is not an element of this offense. An adjustment is provided where the value of the gratuity exceeded $ 2,000, or where the public official was an elected official or held a high-level decision-making or sensitive position.

Amendment & Reason: References to 2F1.1 are removed because of the section being incorporated into 2B1.1.

§ 2C1.7. Fraud Involving Deprivation of the Intangible Right to the Honest Services of Public Officials; Conspiracy to Defraud by Interference with Governmental Functions

(a) Base Offense Level: 10

(b) Specific Offense Characteristic

  (1) (If more than one applies, use the greater):

    (A) If the loss to the government, or the value of anything obtained or to be obtained by a public official or others acting with a public official, whichever is greater (i) exceeded $ 2,000 but did not exceed $ 5,000, increase by 1 level; or (ii) exceeded $ 5,000, increase by the number of levels from the table in § 2B1.1 (Theft, Property Destruction, and Fraud) corresponding to that amount.

    (B) If the offense involved an elected official or any official holding a high-level decision-making or sensitive position, increase by 8 levels.

(c) Cross References

(1) If the offense was committed for the purpose of facilitating the commission of another criminal offense, apply the offense guideline applicable to a conspiracy to commit that other offense if the resulting offense level is greater than that determined above.

(2) If the offense was committed for the purpose of concealing, or obstructing justice in respect to, another criminal offense, apply § 2X3.1 (Accessory After the Fact) or § 2J1.2 (Obstruction of Justice), as appropriate, in respect to that other offense if the resulting offense level is greater than that determined above.

(3) If the offense involved a threat of physical injury or property destruction, apply § 2B3.2 (Extortion by Force or Threat of Injury or Serious Damage) if the resulting offense level is greater than that determined above.

(4) If the offense is covered more specifically under § 2C1.1 (Offering, Giving, Soliciting, or Receiving a Bribe; Extortion Under Color of Official Right), § 2C1.2 (Offering, Giving, Soliciting, or Receiving a Gratuity), or § 2C1.3 (Conflict of Interest), apply the offense guideline that most specifically covers the offense.

Commentary

Statutory Provisions: 18 U.S.C. §§ 371, 1341-1343.

Application Notes:

1. This guideline applies only to offenses committed by public officials or others acting with them that involve (A) depriving others of the intangible right to honest services (such offenses may be prosecuted under 18 U.S.C. §§ 1341-1343), or (B) conspiracy to defraud the United States by interfering with governmental functions (such offenses may be prosecuted under 18 U.S.C. § 371). "Public official," as used in this guideline, includes officers and employees of federal, state, or local government.

2. "Official holding a high-level decision-making or sensitive position" includes, for example, prosecuting attorneys, judges, agency administrators, supervisory law enforcement officers, and other governmental officials with similar levels of responsibility.

3. "Loss", for purposes of subsection (b)(1)(A), shall be determined in accordance with Application Note 2 of the Commentary to § 2B1.1 (Theft, Property Destruction, and Fraud).

4. Do not apply § 3B1.3 (Abuse of Position of Trust or Use of Special Skill) except where the offense level is determined under § 2C1.7(c)(1), (2), or (3). In such cases, an adjustment from § 3B1.3 (Abuse of Position of Trust or Use of Special Skill) may apply.

5. Where the court finds that the defendant's conduct was part of a systematic or pervasive corruption of a governmental function, process, or office that may cause loss of public confidence in government, an upward departure may be warranted. See Chapter Five, Part K (Departures).

6. For the purposes of determining whether to apply the cross references in this section, the "resulting offense level" means the greater final offense level (i.e., the offense level determined by taking into account both the Chapter Two offense level and any applicable adjustments from Chapter Three, Parts A-D).

Background: The maximum term of imprisonment authorized by statute under 18 U.S.C. §§ 371 and 1341-1343 is five years.

Amendment & Reason: See 2C1.2 Amendment and Reason.

§ 2D1.1.   Unlawful Manufacturing, Importing, Exporting, or Trafficking (Including Possession with Intent to Commit These Offenses); Attempt or Conspiracy

(a) Base Offense Level (Apply the greatest):

(1) 43, if the defendant is convicted under 21 U.S.C. § 841(b)(1)(A), (b)(1)(B), or (b)(1)(C), or 21 U.S.C. § 960(b)(1), (b)(2), or (b)(3), and the offense of conviction establishes that death or serious bodily injury resulted from the use of the substance and that the defendant committed the offense after one or more prior convictions for a similar offense; or

(2) 38, if the defendant is convicted under 21 U.S.C. § 841(b)(1)(A), (b)(1)(B), or (b)(1)(C), or 21 U.S.C. § 960(b)(1), (b)(2), or (b)(3), and the offense of conviction establishes that death or serious bodily injury resulted from the use of the substance; or

(3) the offense level specified in the Drug Quantity Table set forth in subsection (c), except that if the defendant receives an adjustment under § 3B1.2 (Mitigating Role), the base offense level under this subsection shall be not more than level 30.

(b) Specific Offense Characteristics

(1) If a dangerous weapon (including a firearm) was possessed, increase by 2 levels.

(2) If the defendant unlawfully imported or exported a controlled substance under circumstances in which (A) an aircraft other than a regularly scheduled commercial air carrier was used to import or export the controlled substance, or (B) the defendant acted as a pilot, copilot, captain, navigator, flight officer, or any other operation officer aboard any craft or vessel carrying a controlled substance, increase

by 2 levels. If the resulting offense level is less than level 26, increase to level 26.

(3) If the object of the offense was the distribution of a controlled substance in a prison, correctional facility, or detention facility, increase by 2 levels.

(4) If (A) the offense involved the importation of amphetamine or methamphetamine or the manufacture of amphetamine or methamphetamine from listed chemicals that the defendant knew were imported unlawfully, and (B) the defendant is not subject to an adjustment under § 3B1.2 (Mitigating Role), increase by 2 levels.

(5) (Apply the greater):

(A) If the offense involved (i) an unlawful discharge, emission, or release into the environment of a hazardous or toxic substance; or (ii) the unlawful transportation, treatment, storage, or disposal of a hazardous waste, increase by 2 levels.

(B) If the offense (i) involved the manufacture of amphetamine or methamphetamine; and (ii) created a substantial risk of harm to (I) human life other than a life described in subdivision (C); or (II) the environment, increase by 3 levels. If the resulting offense level is less than level 27, increase to level 27.

(C) If the offense (i) involved the manufacture of amphetamine or methamphetamine; and (ii) created a substantial risk of harm to the life of a minor or an incompetent, increase by 6 levels. If the resulting offense level is less than level 30, increase to level 30.

(6) If the defendant meets the criteria set forth in subdivisions (1)-(5) of subsection (a) of § 5C1.2 (Limitation on Applicability of Statutory Minimum Sentences in Certain Cases), decrease by 2 levels.

Amendment & Reason: Section 2D1.1(a)(3) is amended by striking "below." and inserting ", except that if the defendant receives an adjustment under §3B1.2 (Mitigating Role), the base offense level under this subsection shall be not more than level 30."

2D1.2. NO CHANGES

2D1.5. NO CHANGES

2E1.1. NO CHANGES

2F1.1. DELETED

2H1.1. NO CHANGES

2H2.1. NO CHANGES

§ 2S1.1. Laundering of Monetary Instruments; Engaging in Monetary Transactions in Property Derived from Unlawful Activity

(a) Base Offense Level:

(1) The offense level for the underlying offense from which the laundered funds were derived, if (A) the defendant committed the underlying offense (or would be accountable for the underlying offense under subsection (a)(1)(A) of § 1B1.3 (Relevant Conduct)); and (B) the offense level for that offense can be determined; or

(2) 8 plus the number of offense levels from the table in § 2B1.1 (Theft, Property Destruction, and Fraud) corresponding to the value of the laundered funds, otherwise.

(b) Specific Offense Characteristics

(1) If (A) subsection (a)(2) applies; and (B) the defendant knew or believed that any of the laundered funds were the proceeds of, or were intended to promote (i) an offense involving the manufacture, importation, or distribution of a controlled substance or a listed chemical; (ii) a crime of violence; or (iii) an offense involving firearms, explosives, national security, terrorism, or the sexual exploitation of a minor, increase by 6 levels.

(2) (Apply the Greatest):

(A) If the defendant was convicted under 18 U.S.C. § 1957, increase by 1 level.
(B) If the defendant was convicted under 18 U.S.C. § 1956, increase by 2 levels.
(C) If (i) subsection (a)(2) applies; and (ii) the defendant was in the business of laundering funds, increase by 4 levels.

(3) If (A) subsection (b)(2)(B) applies; and (B) the offense involved sophisticated laundering, increase by 2 levels.

Commentary

Statutory Provisions: 18 U.S.C. §§ 1956, 1957. For additional statutory provision(s), see Appendix A (Statutory Index).

Application Notes:

1. Definitions. For purposes of this guideline:

"Crime of violence" has the meaning given that term in subsection (a)(1) of § 4B1.2 (Definitions of Terms Used in Section 4B1.1).

"Criminally derived funds" means any funds derived, or represented by a law enforcement officer, or by another person at the direction or approval of an authorized Federal official, to be derived from conduct constituting a criminal offense.

"Laundered funds" means the property, funds, or monetary instrument involved in the transaction, financial transaction, monetary transaction, transportation, transfer, or transmission in violation of 18 U.S.C. § 1956 or § 1957.

"Laundering funds" means making a transaction, financial transaction, monetary transaction, or transmission, or transporting or transferring property, funds, or a monetary instrument in violation of 18 U.S.C. § 1956 or § 1957.

"Sexual exploitation of a minor" means an offense involving (A) promoting prostitution by a minor; (B) sexually exploiting a minor by production of sexually explicit visual or printed material; (C) distribution of material involving the sexual exploitation of a minor, or possession of material involving the sexual exploitation of a minor with intent to distribute; or (D) aggravated sexual abuse, sexual abuse, or abusive sexual contact involving a minor. "Minor" means an individual under the age of 18 years.

2. Application of Subsection (a)(1).
(A) Multiple Underlying Offenses. In cases in which subsection (a)(1) applies and there is more than one underlying offense, the offense level for the underlying offense is to be determined under the procedures set forth in Application Note 3 of the Commentary to § 1B1.5 (Interpretation of References to Other Offense Guidelines).
(B) Defendants Accountable for Underlying Offense. In order for subsection (a)(1) to apply, the defendant must have committed the underlying offense or be accountable for the underlying offense under § 1B1.3(a)(1)(A). The fact that the defendant was involved in laundering criminally derived funds after the commission of the underlying offense, without additional involvement in the underlying offense, does not establish that the defendant committed, aided, abetted, counseled, commanded, induced, procured, or willfully caused the underlying offense.
(C) Application of Chapter Three Adjustments. Notwithstanding § 1B1.5(c), in cases in which subsection (a)(1) applies, application of any Chapter Three adjustment shall be determined based on the offense covered by this guideline (i.e., the laundering of criminally derived funds) and not on the underlying offense from which the laundered funds were derived.

3. Application of Subsection (a)(2).
(A) In General. Subsection (a)(2) applies to any case in which (i) the defendant did not commit the underlying offense; or (ii) the defendant committed the underlying offense (or would be accountable for the underlying offense under § 1B1.3(a)(1)(A)), but the offense level for the underlying offense is impossible or impracticable to determine.

(B) Commingled Funds. In a case in which a transaction, financial transaction, monetary transaction, transportation, transfer, or transmission results in the commingling of legitimately derived funds with criminally derived funds, the value of the laundered funds, for purposes of subsection (a)(2), is the amount of the criminally derived funds, not the total amount of the commingled funds, if the defendant provides sufficient information to determine the amount of criminally derived funds without unduly complicating or prolonging the sentencing process. If the amount of the criminally derived funds is difficult or impracticable to determine, the value of the laundered funds, for purposes of subsection (a)(2), is the total amount of the commingled funds.

(C) Non-Applicability of Enhancement. Subsection (b)(2)(B) shall not apply if the defendant was convicted of a conspiracy under 18 U.S.C. § 1956(h) and the sole object of that conspiracy was to commit an offense set forth in 18 U.S.C. § 1957.

4. Enhancement for Business of Laundering Funds.

(A) In General. The court shall consider the totality of the circumstances to determine whether a defendant who did not commit the underlying offense was in the business of laundering funds, for purposes of subsection (b)(2)(C).

(B) Factors to Consider. The following is a non-exhaustive list of factors that may indicate the defendant was in the business of laundering funds for purposes of subsection (b)(2)(C):

(i) The defendant regularly engaged in laundering funds.

(ii) The defendant engaged in laundering funds during an extended period of time.

(iii) The defendant engaged in laundering funds from multiple sources.

(iv) The defendant generated a substantial amount of revenue in return for laundering funds.

(v) At the time the defendant committed the instant offense, the defendant had one or more prior convictions for an offense under 18 U.S.C. § 1956 or § 1957, or under 31 U.S.C. § 5313, § 5314, § 5316, § 5324 or § 5326, or any similar offense under state law, or an attempt or conspiracy to commit any such federal or state offense. A conviction taken into account under subsection (b)(2)(C) is not excluded from consideration of whether that conviction receives criminal history points pursuant to Chapter Four, Part A (Criminal History).

(vi) During the course of an undercover government investigation, the defendant made statements that the defendant engaged in any of the conduct described in subdivisions (i) through (iv).

5. (A) Sophisticated Laundering under Subsection (b)(3). For purposes of subsection (b)(3), "sophisticated laundering" means complex or intricate offense conduct pertaining to the execution or concealment of the 18 U.S.C. § 1956 offense. Sophisticated laundering typically involves the use of--

(i) fictitious entities;
(ii) shell corporations;
(iii) two or more levels (i.e., layering) of transactions, transportation, transfers, or transmissions, involving criminally derived funds that were intended to appear

legitimate; or

(iv) offshore financial accounts.

(B) Non-Applicability of Enhancement. If subsection (b)(3) applies, and the conduct that forms the basis for an enhancement under the guideline applicable to the underlying offense is the only conduct that forms the basis for application of subsection (b)(3) of this guideline, do not apply subsection (b)(3) of this guideline.

6. Grouping of Multiple Counts. In a case in which the defendant is convicted of a count of laundering funds and a count for the underlying offense from which the laundered funds were derived, the counts shall be grouped pursuant to subsection (c) of § 3D1.2 (Groups of Closely-Related Counts).

2S1.2. DELETED (CONSOLIDATED WITH 2S1.1 on 11/01/2001).

Reason for Amendment: The 2001 amendment consolidates the money laundering guidelines, §§2S1.1 (Laundering of Monetary Instruments) and 2S1.2 (Engaging in Monetary Transactions in Property Derived from Specified Unlawful Activity), into one guideline that applies to convictions under 18 U.S.C. § 1956 or § 1957, or 21 U.S.C. § 854. The amendment responds in several ways to concerns that the penalty structure existing prior to this amendment for such offenses did not reflect adequately the culpability of the defendant or the seriousness of the money laundering conduct because the offense level for money laundering was determined without sufficient consideration of the defendant's involvement in, or the relative seriousness of, the underlying offense. The amendment promotes proportionality by providing increased penalties for defendants who launder funds derived from more serious underlying criminal conduct, such as drug trafficking, crimes of violence, and fraud offenses that generate relatively high loss amounts, and decreased penalties for defendants who launder funds derived from less serious underlying criminal conduct, such as basic fraud offenses that generate relatively low loss amounts.

First, the amendment ties offense levels for money laundering more closely to the underlying conduct that was the source of the criminally derived funds by separating money laundering offenders into two categories for purposes of determining the base offense level. For direct money launderers (offenders who commit or would be accountable under §1B1.3(a)(1)(A) (Relevant Conduct) for the underlying offense which generated the criminal proceeds), subsection (a)(1) sets the base offense level at the offense level in Chapter Two (Offense Conduct) for the underlying offense (i.e., the base offense level, specific offense characteristics, cross references, and special instructions for the underlying offense). For third party money launderers (offenders who launder the proceeds generated from underlying offenses that the defendant did not commit or would not be accountable for under §1B1.3(a)(1)(A)), subsection (a)(2) sets the base offense level at level 8, plus an increase based on the value of the laundered funds from the table in subsection (b)(1) of §2B1.1 (Theft, Fraud, Property Destruction).

Second, in addition to the base offense level calculation, the amendment provides an enhancement designed to reflect the differing seriousness of the underlying conduct that was the source of the criminally derived funds. Subsection (b)(1) provides a six-level enhancement for third party money launderers who knew or believed that any of the laundered funds were the proceeds of, or were intended to promote, certain types of more serious underlying criminal conduct; specifically, drug trafficking, crimes of violence, offenses involving firearms, explosives, national security, terrorism, and the sexual exploitation of a minor. The Commission determined that defendants who knowingly launder the proceeds of these more serious underlying offenses are substantially more culpable than third party launderers of criminally derived proceeds of less serious underlying offenses.

Third, the amendment provides three alternative enhancements, with the greatest applicable enhancement to be applied. These enhancements are designed to (1) ensure that all direct money launderers receive additional punishment for committing both the money laundering offense and the underlying offense, and (2) reflect the differing seriousness of money laundering conduct depending on the nature and sophistication of the offense. Specifically, subsection (b)(2)(A) provides a one-level increase if the defendant was convicted under 18 U.S.C. § 1957, and subsection (b)(2)(B) provides a two-level increase if the defendant was convicted under 18 U.S.C. § 1956. The one-level difference between these two enhancements reflects the fact that 18 U.S.C. § 1956 has a statutory maximum penalty (20 years' imprisonment) that is twice as long as the statutory maximum penalty for violations of 18 U.S.C. § 1957 (10 years' imprisonment). In addition, subsection (b)(3) provides an additional two-level increase if subsection (b)(2)(B) applies and the offense involved sophisticated laundering such as the use of fictitious entities, shell corporations, two or more levels of transactions, or offshore financial accounts. The Commission determined that, similar to fraud and tax offenses that involve sophisticated means, see subsection (b)(8) of §2B1.1 (Theft, Property Destruction, and Fraud), subsection (b)(2) of §2T1.1 (Tax Evasion; Willful Failure to File Return, Supply Information, or Pay Tax; Fraudulent or False Returns, Statements, or Other Documents), violations of 18 U.S.C. § 1956 that involve sophisticated laundering warrant additional punishment because such offenses are more difficult and time consuming for law enforcement to detect than less sophisticated laundering. As a result of the enhancements provided by subsections (b)(2)(A), (b)(2)(B), and (b)(3), all direct money launderers will receive an offense level that is one to four levels greater than the Chapter Two offense level for the underlying offense, depending on the statute of conviction and sophistication of the money laundering offense conduct.

With respect to third party money launderers, subsection (b)(2)(C) provides a fourlevel enhancement if the defendant is "in the business" of laundering funds. The Commission determined that, similar to a professional "fence", see §2B1.1(b)(4)(B), defendants who routinely engage in laundering funds on behalf of others, and who gain financially from engaging in such transactions, warrant substantial additional punishment because they encourage the commission of additional criminal conduct.

Finally, this amendment provides that convictions under 18 U.S.C. § 1960 are referenced to §2S1.3 (Structuring Transactions to Evade Reporting Requirements).

Operation of money transmitting businesses without an appropriate license is proscribed by 18 U.S.C. § 1960, as are failures to comply with certain reporting requirements issued under 31 U.S.C. § 5330. The Commission determined that offenses involving these regulatory requirements serve many of the same purposes as Currency Transaction Reports, Currency and Monetary Instrument Reports, Reports of Foreign Bank and Financial Accounts, and Reports of Cash Payments over $10,000 Received in a Trade or Business, violations regarding which currently are referenced to §2S1.3, and that, therefore, violations of 18 U.S.C. § 1960 also should be referenced to §2S1.3.

§ 2S1.3. Structuring Transactions to Evade Reporting Requirements; Failure to Report Cash or Monetary Transactions; Failure to File Currency and Monetary Instrument Report; Knowingly Filing False Reports; Bulk Cash Smuggling; Establishing or Maintaining Prohibited Accounts

(a) Base Offense Level:
   (1) 8, if the defendant was convicted under 31 U.S.C. § 5318 or § 5318A; or
   (2) 6 plus the number of offense levels from the table in § 2B1.1 (Theft, Property Destruction, and Fraud) corresponding to the value of the funds, if subsection (a)(1) does not apply.

(b) Specific Offense Characteristics
   (1) If (A) the defendant knew or believed that the funds were proceeds of unlawful activity, or were intended to promote unlawful activity; or (B) the offense involved bulk cash smuggling, increase by 2 levels.

   (2) If the defendant (A) was convicted of an offense under subchapter II of chapter 53 of title 31, United States Code; and (B) committed the offense as part of a pattern of unlawful activity involving more than $ 100,000 in a 12-month period, increase by 2 levels.

   (3) If (A) subsection (a)(2) applies and subsections (b)(1) and (b)(2) do not apply; (B) the defendant did not act with reckless disregard of the source of the funds; (C) the funds were the proceeds of lawful activity; and (D) the funds were to be used for a lawful purpose, decrease the offense level to level 6.

(c) Cross Reference
   (1) If the offense was committed for the purposes of violating the Internal

Revenue laws, apply the most appropriate guideline from Chapter Two, Part T (Offenses Involving Taxation) if the resulting offense level is greater than that determined above.

Commentary

Statutory Provisions: 18 U.S.C. § 1960; 26 U.S.C. §§ 7203 (if a violation based upon 26 U.S.C. § 6050I), 7206 (if a violation based upon 26 U.S.C. § 6050I); 31 U.S.C. §§ 5313, 5314, 5316, 5318, 5318A(b), 5322, 5324, 5326, 5331, 5332. For additional statutory provision(s), see Appendix A (Statutory Index).

Application Notes:

1. Definition of "Value of the Funds". For purposes of this guideline, "value of the funds" means the amount of the funds involved in the structuring or reporting conduct. The relevant statutes require monetary reporting without regard to whether the funds were lawfully or unlawfully obtained.

2. Bulk Cash Smuggling. For purposes of subsection (b)(1)(B), "bulk cash smuggling" means (A) knowingly concealing, with the intent to evade a currency reporting requirement under 31 U.S.C. § 5316, more than $ 10,000 in currency or other monetary instruments; and (B) transporting or transferring (or attempting to transport or transfer) such currency or monetary instruments into or outside of the United States. "United States" has the meaning given that term in Application Note 1 of the Commentary to § 2B5.1 (Offenses Involving Counterfeit Bearer Obligations of the United States).

3. Enhancement for Pattern of Unlawful Activity. For purposes of subsection (b)(2), "pattern of unlawful activity" means at least two separate occasions of unlawful activity involving a total amount of more than $ 100,000 in a 12-month period, without regard to whether any such occasion occurred during the course of the offense or resulted in a conviction for the conduct that occurred on that occasion.

Background: Some of the offenses covered by this guideline relate to records and reports of certain transactions involving currency and monetary instruments. These reports include Currency Transaction Reports, Currency and Monetary Instrument Reports, Reports of Foreign Bank and Financial Accounts, and Reports of Cash Payments Over $ 10,000 Received in a Trade or Business.

This guideline also covers offenses under 31 U.S.C. §§ 5318 and 5318A, pertaining to records, reporting and identification requirements, prohibited accounts involving certain foreign jurisdictions, foreign institutions, and foreign banks, and other types of transactions and types of accounts.

Amendment & Reason: §2S1.3 was amended to incorporate new money laundering provisions created by the PATRIOT Act. Specifically, the amendment provides an alternative base offense level of level 8 in §2S1.3(a) in order to incorporate offenses under 31 U.S.C. §§ 5318 and 5318A. The base offense level of level 8 recognizes the heightened due diligence requirements placed on financial institutions with respect to payable-through accounts, correspondent accounts, and shell banks.

The amendment also amends §2S1.3(b)(1), relating to the promotion of unlawful activity, to provide an alternative prong if the offense involved bulk cash smuggling. This amendment addresses 31 U.S.C. § 5332, added by section 371 of the PATRIOT Act, which prohibits concealing, with intent to evade a currency reporting requirement under 31 U.S.C. § 5316, more than $10,000 in currency or other monetary instruments and transporting or transferring such currency or monetary instruments into or outside of the United States.

Findings set forth in that section of the PATRIOT Act indicate that bulk cash smuggling typically involves the promotion of unlawful activity. The amendment also provides an enhancement in §2S1.3(b) to give effect to the enhanced penalty provisions under 31 U.S.C. § 5322(b) for offenses under subchapter II of chapter 53 of title 31, United Stated Code, if such offenses were committed as part of a pattern of unlawful activity involving more than $100,000 in a 12-month period.

§ 2X1.1. Attempt, Solicitation, or Conspiracy (Not Covered by a Specific Offense Guideline)

(a) Base Offense Level: The base offense level from the guideline for the substantive offense, plus any adjustments from such guideline for any intended offense conduct that can be established with reasonable certainty.

(b) Specific Offense Characteristics

(1) If an attempt, decrease by 3 levels, unless the defendant completed all the acts the defendant believed necessary for successful completion of the substantive offense or the circumstances demonstrate that the defendant was about to complete all such acts but for apprehension or interruption by some similar event beyond the defendant's control.

(2) If a conspiracy, decrease by 3 levels, unless the defendant or a co-conspirator completed all the acts the conspirators believed necessary on their part for the successful completion of the substantive offense or the circumstances demonstrate that the conspirators were about to complete all such acts but for apprehension or interruption by some similar event beyond their control.

(3) (A) If a solicitation, decrease by 3 levels unless the person solicited to commit or aid the substantive offense completed all the acts he believed necessary for successful completion of the substantive offense or the circumstances demonstrate that the person was about to complete all such acts but for apprehension or interruption by some similar event beyond such person's control.

(B) If the statute treats solicitation of the substantive offense identically with the substantive offense, do not apply subdivision (A) above; i.e., the offense level for solicitation is the same as that for the substantive offense.

(c) Cross Reference

(1) When an attempt, solicitation, or conspiracy is expressly covered by another offense guideline section, apply that guideline section.

(d) Special Instruction

(1) Subsection (b) shall not apply to any of the following offenses, if such offense involved, or was intended to promote, a federal crime of terrorism as defined in 18 U.S.C. § 2332b(g)(5):

18 U.S.C. § 81;
18 U.S.C. § 930(c);
18 U.S.C. § 1362;
18 U.S.C. § 1363;
18 U.S.C. § 1992;
18 U.S.C. § 2339A;
18 U.S.C. § 2340A;
49 U.S.C. § 46504;
49 U.S.C. § 46505; and
49 U.S.C. § 60123(b).

Commentary

Statutory Provisions: 18 U.S.C. §§ 371, 372, 2271. For additional statutory provision(s), see Appendix A (Statutory Index).

Application Notes:

1. Certain attempts, conspiracies, and solicitations are expressly covered by other offense guidelines.

Offense guidelines that expressly cover attempts include:
§§ 2A2.1, 2A3.1, 2A3.2, 2A3.3, 2A3.4, 2A4.2, 2A5.1;
§§ 2C1.1, 2C1.2;
§§ 2D1.1, 2D1.2, 2D1.5, 2D1.6, 2D1.7, 2D1.8, 2D1.9, 2D1.10, 2D1.11, 2D1.12, 2D1.13, 2D2.1, 2D2.2, 2D3.1, 2D3.2;
§ 2E5.1;
§ 2M6.1
§ 2N1.1;
§ 2Q1.4.

Offense guidelines that expressly cover conspiracies include:
§ 2A1.5;
§§ 2D1.1, 2D1.2, 2D1.5, 2D1.6, 2D1.7, 2D1.8, 2D1.9, 2D1.10, 2D1.11, 2D1.12. 2D1.13, 2D2.1, 2D2.2, 2D3.1, 2D3.2;

§ 2H1.1;
§ 2M6.1
§ 2T1.9.

Offense guidelines that expressly cover solicitations include:
§ 2A1.5;
§ 2C1.1, 2C1.2;
§ 2E5.1.

2. "Substantive offense," as used in this guideline, means the offense that the defendant was convicted of soliciting, attempting, or conspiring to commit. Under § 2X1.1(a), the base offense level will be the same as that for the substantive offense. But the only specific offense characteristics from the guideline for the substantive offense that apply are those that are determined to have been specifically intended or actually occurred. Speculative specific offense characteristics will not be applied. For example, if two defendants are arrested during the conspiratorial stage of planning an armed bank robbery, the offense level ordinarily would not include aggravating factors regarding possible injury to others, hostage taking, discharge of a weapon, or obtaining a large sum of money, because such factors would be speculative. The offense level would simply reflect the level applicable to robbery of a financial institution, with the enhancement for possession of a weapon. If it was established that the defendants actually intended to physically restrain the teller, the specific offense characteristic for physical restraint would be added. In an attempted theft, the value of the items that the defendant attempted to steal would be considered.

3. If the substantive offense is not covered by a specific guideline, see § 2X5.1 (Other Offenses).

4. In certain cases, the participants may have completed (or have been about to complete but for apprehension or interruption) all of the acts necessary for the successful completion of part, but not all, of the intended offense. In such cases, the offense level for the count (or group of closely related multiple counts) is whichever of the following is greater: the offense level for the intended offense minus 3 levels (under § 2X1.1(b)(1), (b)(2), or (b)(3)(A)), or the offense level for the part of the offense for which the necessary acts were completed (or about to be completed but for apprehension or interruption). For example, where the intended offense was the theft of $ 800,000 but the participants completed (or were about to complete) only the acts necessary to steal $ 30,000, the offense level is the offense level for the theft of $ 800,000 minus 3 levels, or the offense level for the theft of $ 30,000, whichever is greater.

In the case of multiple counts that are not closely related counts, whether the 3-level reduction under § 2X1.1(b)(1), (b)(2), or (b)(3)(A) applies is determined separately for each count.

Background: In most prosecutions for conspiracies or attempts, the substantive offense was substantially completed or was interrupted or prevented on the verge of completion by the intercession of law enforcement authorities or the victim. In such cases, no reduction of the offense level is warranted. Sometimes, however, the arrest occurs well before the defendant or any co-conspirator has completed the acts necessary for the substantive offense. Under such circumstances, a reduction of 3 levels is provided under § 2X1.1(b)(1) or (2).

Amendment & Reason: In response to terrorist attacks, the amendment affecting §2X1.1 (Attempt, Solicitation, or Conspiracy) required that the three level reduction in §2X1.1(b) does not apply to these offenses when committed for a terrorist objective.